JOHN KEATS

From a drawing by Joseph Severn, now in the Harvard Keats Memorial Collection, formerly in the collections of Mrs. James T. Fields and Miss Amy Lowell.

FOREVER YOUNG

A Life of John Keats by

Blanche Colton Williams

G. P. Putnam's Sons, New York

Designed by Robert Josephy

MANUFACTURED IN THE UNITED STATES OF AMERICA

To Shirley Virginia Long

Contents

Contents

PREFACE

I

THIS biography of John Keats, a contribution to the sesqui-centennial of his birth (1795-1945), attempts to revivify the poet as he was in everyday life, and grows from his letters—with the aid of notes to or about him—rather than from his poems. No criticism is embodied except that associated with his imagined point of view.

When the idea occurred to me of a book presenting him in his own times, without regard to all the years since 1821, I marveled that nobody had written such a Life. Playwright and novelist but no biographer had chosen the small space bounding his years, placed an invisible chair somewhere near Keats and sat therein to record something of how he spent his days in thought and act. Even if it were possible, to report the whole of that brief life would overflow the limits of one volume; so I begin with him at twenty-one and a half years, immediately after the publication of his first volume of poems and, shuttling backward now and then through his memory or a dialogue with a contemporary, progress to the end, not quite four years later.

The fewer than one hundred letters known to and pub-lished wholly or partly by Richard Monckton Milnes (later Lord Houghton) has increased to nearly two hundred and fifty in Maurice Buxton Forman's *The Letters of John Keats*. Many of these I have read in the original script, but for convenience, since my aim is not a textual consideration of the documents, I have relied mainly upon Mr. Forman's collection. Most of the letters were published by his father,

Preface

the first great Keats scholar, the late Henry Buxton Forman, whose compilation I have also studied, and I wish to record at once my thanks to both father and son. Many letters have come to light in recent years and, as they were discovered, found publication one by one before being gathered into the latest collection.

I should state that although I frequently quote from these letters, I often transfer thought and diction to the third person. This transference is in harmony with the third person throughout, and I have been scrupulous to indicate by nuance or implication that the manner and the matter are Keats's own. Lest, however, this volume anywhere fails to assign to the poet his ideas and words, this general note reminds the scholar and warns the layman of my approach to the subject, an approach by no means new in fact or fiction.

When the man who was to become Lord Houghton, but who always remained Dicky Milnes to the angels, faced his problem he considered, he says in his Preface, what was best to raise the character of Keats in the minds of most capable judges. For that character was supposed to be "erratic, unlearned, exaggerated, despising proportion; morally weak, gluttonous, of bizarre taste," and the man himself dead as the probable result of "a stupid, savage article in a review." When Milnes, then, discovered from evidence that such opinion was far from the truth, he feared a true picture would not seem true; and, after summing up the truth, he wrote, "I thus came to the conclusion that it was better to act simply as editor of the Life, which was, as it were, already written."

He was near in time to Keats and had he felt disposed might have learned from those still living further details now forever lost. Undoubtedly, even so, he gathered more material than he used, subduing with fine taste all not prime to his purpose. My copy of *Life, Letters, and Literary Remains of John Keats* was sent (1848) by Edward Moxon to Fanny

x

Brawne Lindon, and bears besides her autograph, "Mrs. Lindon, with the Publisher's Compliments and best thanks," indicative of her part in that "Life," a part that might have been more had she and the man who remained merely "Editor" so willed. But nothing is more admirable than the first biographer's establishment of Keats's true nature unless it be his delicacy, his proper respect for the feelings of those still living.

Thirty years before Milnes edited the *Life, Letters,* etc. Wordsworth had expressed himself on the subject of biography, and part of that expression is included in the Preface by Milnes. "Silence is a privilege of the grave," he quotes, "a right of the departed; let him, therefore, who infringes that right by speaking publicly of, for, or against those who cannot speak for themselves, take heed that he open not his mouth without a sufficient sanction." And, speaking of authors, "Our business is with their books to understand and enjoy them. Of poets more especially it is true that if their works be good, they contain within themselves all that is necessary to their being comprehended and relished."

Modern days bring modern ways of irradiating and celebrating the enshrined and ensainted. An age cannot but be grateful to her or him who patiently spends a year or twenty years of life in bringing nearer through his well-built, self-built telescope a poet who, a hundred or two hundred years before, went about like other men and had his own sorrows or joys. The poems of the man certainly then reveal new meanings; in fact, they cannot contain all necessary to their clear apprehension until illumined by the story of the man who set them down with a quill on foolscap or tapped them out on a machine.

No one who remembers the publication of Amy Lowell's *John Keats* (1925) can forget such illumination. Here was a Life by one having not only a great admiration for the poet, a sound sense of his faults as of his virtues—both as man and poet—but wealth enough to order all documents obtainable and patience enough to complete the two big volumes, though the act may have cost her life. Consider the rush of pamphlets and articles and full-length books from then to the present. All follow in the wake of Amy Lowell, if but to show she was somewhere wrong; and in a lesser proportion follow Sir Sidney Colvin's *John Keats* of 1917. All light up the poetry of the man who was Keats. Whoever treads softly, talks softly, amid the Keats Collection, which is the heart of the Treasure Room of Harvard College, must feel that here is a God's Plenty about John Keats: more, a potential dynamo, ready to illuminate at the click of a mental switch. Whoever has entered the little room to the right of the "Spanish Stairs" in Rome has had something of this feeling. Whoever has seen the collection at Wentworth Place, Hampstead, has known it. Whoever has sat down in the Pierpont Morgan Library, New York City, before the Woodhouse Book and other treasures has been thankful for this source of a current between himself and the mind of Keats.

These relics witness, further, the fame of Keats. He craved fame, not only that which "lives and spreads aloft by the perfect witness of all-judging Jove," but that which "grows on mortal soil" as well. If toward the end he became indifferent to fame, it was because he was weary of a struggle he felt could have no satisfactory conclusion, could progress only to his own extinction. Unforgettable his wistful words, "I think I shall be among the English poets after my death," and equally unforgettable Matthew Arnold's assurance, "He is; he is with Shakespeare."

II

I should be intimating something of those older friends or acquaintances comparatively unknown to fame. Of Wordsworth, Hunt, Shelley, Lamb, Hazlitt, Coleridge, and a few others nothing need be said here. Of others, such as George Keats, Thomas Keats, and Fanny Keats, and Fanny Brawne, the volume says or implies enough in the text or appended notes.

Charles and James Ollier were the first publishers of Keats. Disappointed in the sales of *Poems* (1817), they dropped business relations with him but met him now and then, as an instance in this book shows. In the year 1817 they also became Shelley's publishers, bringing out his more mature and important works.

Charles Cowden Clarke (1787-1877), remembered and read today on account of his association with Keats and other writers, was the son of Headmaster John Clarke at Enfield, and his father's assistant. To him Keats owed first enjoyment of Spenser and Shakespeare, knowledge of poetic forms, and perhaps his own decision to write poetry. "C.C.C." was evidently a teacher of inspirational force, a man loved or admired by his students and friends, the literary London "set" of the day. He married Mary V. Novello (1809-1898), of the musical family mentioned by Keats, who with her husband wrote *Recollections of Writers,* while he collaborated with her in the *Concordance to Shakespeare.* They spent their closing years on the Continent, where each lived to be ninety years of age though she being his junior by twenty-two years survived him so far. A few vears before her death she wrote *My Long Life.*

Walter Dendy, Henry Stephens, and George Cooper were fellow-students at Guy's Hospital. Stephens, much later, made a fortune by his manufacture of ink. Edward Holmes, a schoolmate at Enfield, became a music critic and author of a *Life of Mozart.*

George Felton Mathew, early friend in Keats's literary life, apparently did not fulfill his promise of writing and is

Preface

best recalled through the "Epistle" in Keats's *Poems* of 1817. The first couplet observes a "brotherhood in song" and the lines throughout suggest a pleasant youthful comradeship. He reviewed *Poems* (see *infra*), but Keats probably outgrew him after the time they sat and rhymed and thought about Chatterton or enjoyed neighborhood dances and concerts together. In any event, Mathew married, becoming the father of twelve children, and may have lost his epistolary friend through his self-defection. In the Woodhouse Book of the Pierpont Morgan Library are "Stanzas" by Mathew in reply to Keats's "Epistle."

Charles Wells, a schoolmate of Thomas Keats, lost John's friendship by hoaxing Tom, dying of tuberculosis, with letters from a fictitious lady signing herself "Amena." Before he did so, however, he and Keats were for at least a time frequent companions at the theater. He was probably a delightful and entertaining person until forced by his "dangerous and insidious" nature to show horns and cloven hoof. He dropped out immediately and forever, when Keats discovered the authorship of the "Amena" letters, except from the unforgiving anger of Keats.

Richard Abbey was guardian of the Keats children, after the death of a coguardian who by dying left him in entire control. Either through overcaution or meanness or ignorance —he once confessed he did not wholly understand the financial status of his wards—he was unsatisfactory to John, George, and Tom, to whom he appeared a petty tyrant. I am not of those who excuse or condone his inadequacy, if he was inadequate, or his buttoned mouth if he knew more than he revealed. Possibly he was merely ignorant, though his success as a tea and coffee merchant would indicate no lack of knowledge of ways of the business world. On the other hand, none of the Keats boys knew much of the value of money or the source of their own, and they expected Abbey to stand and deliver any sum when challenged. Their expectations seem often to have been disappointed. He worried them along until 1820 when George returned from America to demand a complete settlement of the fortune, some of which had been long in chancery, or such part as concerned himself and John (Tom had died in 1818). He was able also to wind up Tom's estate. Fanny Keats profited most by Abbey's guardianship, financially. She lost inestimably by the close strictures that withheld her from the society of her brothers as well as from normal social life and kept her a little girl well into her teens.

Benjamin Robert Haydon (1786-1846) was a painter who should have been a writer. His diaries flow naturally and entertainingly from an easy pen; his pictures testify chiefly to a desperate desire and ambition to raise the standard of Great Art. Desperate because he lacked the spark that kindles talent into genius, desperate because he was too poor to shut the door of his workroom upon besetting cares—mostly debts— of the outer world. He worked hard and, despite the clutch of circumstance, progressed far in the opinion of critics of his day. The painting noticed in these pages, "Christ's Entry into Jerusalem," now hangs in America, the property of Mount St. Mary Seminary, Norwood, Cincinnati, Ohio. In it the head of Keats most resembles portraits by Severn and, taken with them, may be adjudged the best likeness of Keats around the years 1817, '18, and '19. Haydon's life mask of the poet is doubtless his most valuable relic to posterity. Only from it may one see the young Keats "in the round," and that "special hunger," which gave the title to George O'Neil's book.

If Haydon seems unadmirable in not only taking but begging money from a boy ten years his junior, at least he took from anybody and everybody who helped him, to advance the cause to which he devoted his life. At the age of sixty, tired, harassed and beaten, he slit his throat and shot himself.

Joseph Severn, another artist of the brush who never attained the empyrean and is remembered almost wholly for his association with Keats, was born two years earlier and lived fifty-eight years longer (1793-1879). Enough of his life in this book—implied if not stated—obviates need for much information at this point. It is good to know Severn loved Keats well enough to serve as bodyguard in Rome and on the journey thereto, especially when it is clear that among several friends he was not the best loved by Keats; good to know he placed first his attendance upon the dying poet, who expired in his arms late at night: a man of twenty-seven alone with the younger man of twenty-five. It is also just and pleasing that he, and only he, lies beside his friend in the Protestant Cemetery at Rome. Much of my account of Keats's final days derives from Severn's letters, written at the time, and from his scripts accessible to William Sharp, who wrote the *Life and Letters of Joseph Severn* (1892). I have tried to harmonize the letters with what he himself set down later, the difference arising mainly, one would guess, from imperfect memory and from a predilection for gilding the lapses of time. If Brown was, on the whole, Keats's best friend, Severn was the indispensable friend who stood by in crucial and sad necessity.

James Rice ("Jem" or "Jemmie") is recalled as an honorable, upright young man, who outlived John Keats by only a dozen years. He had not a strong constitution, was often sick and searching for health, yet was possessed of a fine sense of humor and one of the "three witty people all distinct in their excellence," known to Keats in January, 1820. The others were Reynolds and Richards. Of all, he thought Rice the wisest, a man who made you laugh and think, and of him Keats never changed his high opinion.

Thomas Richards is sufficiently characterized in these

pages, but it may be added here that he was the grandfather of Grant Richards. An excellent friend, he appreciated talent and genius, according to Charles Cowden Clarke's *Recollections*. His prospering and converting his money into something like real estate suggests that Keats may have been thinking of him when hoping to salvage enough of his own fortune to invest so as to obtain a little competence. Richards outlived Keats by ten years.

John Hamilton Reynolds ("Jack" or "Caius"), a year older than his comrade in letters, lived until 1852. Regarded as a writer worthy of note, he composed verses "remarkable" in the opinion of Milnes. Byron's praise arose no doubt from the dedication to himself of "Safie, an Eastern Tale." Reynolds wrote sometimes under the signature "John Hamilton," used for *The Garden of Florence*, again signing himself "Peter Corcoran" (*The Fancy*). Had he not bidden farewell to the Muses to become a solicitor, he would have given more worthy hostages to fame. Instead, though surrendering fame to Keats, he never wholly abstained from verse. His sister Jane married Thomas Hood, with whom he collaborated in *Odes and Addresses to Great People*. Clearly from their exchange of letters and the contents of those letters, Keats and he were always on best terms. From this volume it is also obvious that the Reynolds sisters—Mariane and Charlotte as well as Jane—stirred the poet's interest; but as time passed he cared less for them, if his own comments may be taken as pointers.

William Haslam, born in Keats's year, knew him from an early age. From letters to Richard Monckton Milnes, in reply to requests for data needed for the *Life, Letters*, etc.—the original scripts of which are in the Harvard Keats Memorial Collection—he was a faithful friend still, a quarter-century after Keats had passed into the shades. Next to Charles Brown, perhaps equally with Brown, he was always ready with practical assistance. But for Haslam, Keats might have gone alone to Italy (1820) and, as Haslam feared, might have dropped out of sight forever. He did not stop until he found an acceptable companion—Severn, whom nobody else at the moment seems to have thought about. Nor, years after, did he disappoint Milnes, though in his busy life he must have taken considerable "time off" to search out details he had never known, but to which he had clues, and to recall those details with which he was familiar. He died, 1851, financially embarrassed. . . . "If I know what it is to love," he wrote Severn, December, 1820, "I truly love John Keats."

Charles Brown—later known, for the sake of distinction, as Charles Armitage Brown—was nine years older than the poet. After some adventure in business, he settled down on a small income just enough for subsistence if he earned a bit by writing and let his house in the summer months. Some little time before he met Keats in 1817, he had built with Charles W. Dilke the house then—and after other names temporarily supplanted the christening title—known as Wentworth Place. Each man had his semidetached residence, though Dilke's family and Brown were on excellent terms so long as they lived there, and the friends of one were more often than not friends of the other.

In 1818, or thereabout, Brown conceived the idea of a son by his servant girl, Abbie, he presumably supplying the brain and Abbie the brawn—the combination to result in a peculiarly able offspring. The child, Carlino, born 1819, lived to be over eighty, even then losing his life from being run over by a train. Soon after his birth—but after the death of Keats—Brown took his son to Italy for acquiring at first hand the language he himself so much admired. That part of his life associated with the poet is set forth in the pages of this volume. In 1841 he was granted a parcel of land in

New Zealand but, after living there a year only, died and was buried at Taranaki. His was the first memoir of Keats but was published a century later (see bibliography).

So far as the record runs, Brown was Keats's best friend in the final three or four years. Wentworth Place was, after Tom's death, John's home. The two shared expenses, half and half to be sure, but Keats was more often behind than forward with his part, and Brown provided for both. He knew, as an older man would or should know, that his young friend needed a prod as well as encouragement, and the obvious interpretation of that phase of his life from 1817 to 1820 is that he so arranged his affairs as to help Keats. If any doubt exists of his wholehearted loyalty, it attaches to his leaving, 1820, for a second walking tour in Scotland. He never saw Keats again. He must have known when he went away how near to death was the younger man, whom he had just nursed for seven weeks, and yet he went.

This apparent defection complicates the opposing views of Brown and C. W. Dilke about George Keats. Dilke accepted absolutely George's statement—of facts and figures as well as protective attitude toward his older but, generally conceded, less business-like brother. Brown felt that George should have left John more money when he returned to America in 1820. Despite their difference on this point, Dilke wrote that Brown was "the most scrupulously honest man" he ever knew, wanting only nobleness to lift his honesty above the commercial level. That Brown rendered a bill for John's indebtedness to him, a bill with interest, has been offered as proof of his meaner spirit; but if it is remembered that according to his lights this sum would be preferably, and should be preferably, paid by the Keats family, who will not sympathize? And eventually there was enough of John's inheritance to defray all expenses Brown had gladly shouldered while his friend was yet alive. (See also Notes, Chapter XIV.)

Charles Wentworth Dilke (born 1789), of the Navy Pay Office, doting father of Charles W., Junior, and the grandfather of Sir Charles Wentworth Dilke, was a member of the Keats group through his interest in the older dramatists. From talking to him and from hearing Hazlitt lecture, Keats extended considerably his knowledge of such plays as appeared in Dodsley's collection, which Dilke continued in supplemental volumes. He had the spirit of the journalist, interested in current affairs, contributing to better-known reviews and magazines, editing for some ten years the *Athenaeum,* and for three years the *Daily News.* Later, through contributions to the *Athenaeum,* he took part in the controversy over the letters of Junius, and wrote with acumen on Pope. From his notes and letters and the letters of George Keats to him—these also are in the Harvard Keats Memorial Collection—much may be gleaned of his relations with John Keats and others of the circle. Many of his articles, incidentally, were collected as *Papers of a Critic,* for which his grandson wrote a biographical sketch.

Georgiana Augusta Wylie, who married George Keats and went with him to America in 1818, was the maternal ancestor of all Keats descendants in America today. John Keats admired and loved her as his sister, and shared with her mother whatever news came from the two Georges across the ocean. After George's death (at the age of forty-four, Christmas Eve, 1841) she married John Jeffrey. Meanwhile she had returned to England with George (but not in 1820) and apparently helped in settling the debts of John. She maintained relations by correspondence with the Dilkes, writing Maria Dilke when her "old man"—so she called him—wrote to Maria's husband.

Benjamin Bailey, born 1791, the divinity student with

whom Keats roomed a few weeks at Oxford (1817), was for a time a chief correspondent. He was of aid when Keats most needed aid socially and spiritually. Later, from the extant records, one of which is in his own statement, he seems to have been the unwitting—and from a present-day point of view, stupid—purveyor of material that was grist to the mill of *Blackwood's Edinburgh Magazine* and particularly to the article mentioned in the pages hereafter. He married the daughter of Bishop Gleig and for a number of years was a vicar in the North, subsequently Colonial Chaplain of Ceylon, living at Colombo. He died in 1853. For this volume I have made use of a long script, in the hand of his daughter, written from Colombo just after the publication of Milnes's work on Keats. Never aware of the unconsciously bad turn done him by Bailey, Keats lost his early admiration for other reasons. (See the text of this volume and also Notes, Chapter IV.)

John Taylor and James Augustus Hessey (Taylor and Hessey) published Keats's second and third volumes: *Endymion* (1818), and *Lamia, Isabella, Etc.* (1820). The poet was particularly fortunate in their interest, receiving unusual consideration at their hands even though they were never in doubt of his genius.

Richard Woodhouse ("Dick"), their literary critic, was also Keats's friend from the day he urged his publishers to put the poet on their list to that day when on the *Maria Crowther* he took a lock of hair from Keats's head and said good-by. Woodhouse's critical sense was extraordinary and his admiration of Keats, therefore, almost boundless. He saw and warned of pitfalls in the path of the poet, who trusted him and was on occasion saved from the imprudence that had caused him earlier to suffer from provoking those who wielded lances. When a young man, Woodhouse learned shorthand; later he became a barrister and so, trained to write both accurately and stenographically, he is a well of resources for the student of his commonplace books. He foresaw the day when the world would crave knowledge of Taylor and Hessey's writer and, a careful as well as loving Boswell, omitted nothing of value from his firsthand records. The Woodhouse Book in the Morgan Library is a treasure chest, and it is not the only container of his relics. When he died (1834) as Keats had died, of tuberculosis, he left his Keatsiana to the man who would most value his collection— John Taylor, the publisher.

III

The pleasure of writing this volume is heightened by a sense of gratitude to depositories of books, scripts, and other treasures, chief among which are: The Pierpont Morgan Library; the Treasure Room of Harvard College Library, and in particular the Harvard Keats Memorial Collection (HKMC); the New York Public Library; the Library of Hunter College of the City of New York; Haverford College Library, and the Dedham Historical Society, Massachusetts.

Most gladly I return thanks for favors from Miss Alice Brown, Mr. Nelson S. Bushnell, Dr. Kenneth Daughrity, Mr. Thomas E. Drake, Miss Belle DaCosta Greene, Miss Josephine Hewins, Miss Anna B. Hewitt, Mr. William A. Jackson, Mrs. Robert M. Kelly (Eleanor Mercein Kelly), Miss Shirley V. Long, Dr. Claire McGlinchee, Mrs. Attwood Martin (George Madden Martin), Miss Pauline V. Orr, Professor Joseph J. Reilly, Miss Renata Remy, Miss Dallas Rumsey, Mr. Philip Tuley, Mr. Julius H. Tuttle, Miss Isabel L. Walker, Ensign Wirt A. Williams, Jr. and, in unbounded measure, to Miss Naomi Joy Kirk. Miss Kirk, who was requisitioned for the Hampstead Edition of Keats's

Preface

Works, offered me her monumental script of the "Life of George Keats" and generously permitted me to use certain data, for which I am her debtor. She read, besides, the script of this volume and suggested certain emendations for the better, though I hasten to absolve her from whatever infelicities may remain.

I trust that I have omitted nobody from the list of friends and acquaintances and, if inadvertently I have done so, that I shall be forgiven.

Finally, this book is happy in the imprimatur of a House descended from that which introduced to American readers the first biographer of Keats, Richard Monckton Milnes, whose *Life, Letters, and Literary Remains of John Keats* was published by George P. Putnam, 1848. Previously, Wiley and Putnam had published *The Poetical Works of John Keats,* 1846.

Blanche Colton Williams

New York City
January, 1943

FOREVER YOUNG

I. Journey to Southampton, Carisbrooke
(Isle of Wight). Endymion

> "We talk of the immense number of books, the volumes ranged
> thousands by thousands—but perhaps more goes through the
> human intelligence in twelve days than ever was written."
>
> —JOHN KEATS TO BENJAMIN BAILEY.

AT the Bull and Crown, Holborn, Monday, April 14, 1817,
John Keats climbed the ladder to the top of the coach for
Lymington and Poole. He waved a final salute to George
and Tom while the four horses moved briskly from the inn
yard. Half past seven, he verified by his big open-faced,
pearl-studded watch. The night lay ahead before he would
get off at Southampton, eighty miles away, for the Isle of
Wight.

Lively staccato of clip-clop on stones dissolved in a steadier
rhythm. Leaning forward, the red-coated driver cracked his
whip over the team straining to the ascent of Holborn Hill.
Outside the city they struck the even pace they would main-
tain to the end of the first stage twelve or fourteen miles
ahead, where they would be drawn from shafts instantly
receiving a relay.

"It costs more inside," from early childhood Keats had
heard stable talk at the coaching post of the Swan and Hoop.
"And we on top," he knew from experience, "have at this
season all the advantage." Yet already the evening air was

3

colder. He drew about his shoulders the new plaid, a gift from his brothers, settling into its soft warmth even as he settled his mind to reminiscence, to the future and the flying scenery.

"I'll miss my brothers," for they were not often separated. "But Haydon is right. I should be alone for self-improvement. And Goldsmith's *Greece*, which he lent me, also advises a man to retire from the world and in leisure find himself." He had discussed this seclusion with Tom, who agreed it was the very thing; and George—George had not objected. For the good results, then, that would follow this venture, the three had given up quarters at 17 Cheapside, where they had been a short time after leaving the Poultry. Now George and Tom had engaged rooms at Number One, Well Walk, Hampstead, with the family of Bentley the postman, and there he would rejoin them.

True cockney, he was not disturbed at recognizing little or nothing of the small outlying towns and villages in this southwest hegira. Hampstead, Highgate, Walthamstow— haunts so familiar—seemed a long way off, on the other side of London. Was this Richmond? Staines? After pale blur of lamp and fire that half-hid, half-revealed gabled houses and church steeples, obscure light from the stars fell on low, dusty hedgerows of box or taller hawthorn in first leaf.

"The early budders are just new," Keats told himself, and savored a phrase, "green-kirtled spring." There, to the right, the still water of a pond mirrored the coach-lamp beam. Now a birchwood, each tree "as white as a lily and as small as a wand," he all but quoted aloud from Lance, servant to one of *Two Gentlemen of Verona*. His new Shakespeare! Seven volumes, each aptly fitting his pocket, well printed, quaintly illustrated. Out there in the luggage basket. He had bought them only a few days back.

How quiet the top tonight! The few outside passengers

4

isolated from one another, each absorbed in his own meditations, or perhaps dozing. March 3, precisely six weeks ago
today, his first book, *Poems,* had been published. He owed
the enthusiasm of Charles and James Ollier to Leigh Hunt
and Shelley. "But their printer, Richards, and his brother
Tom are my friends more than they." The elder Richards,
like Keats's own father, had managed a livery stable business.
The boys had long known one another.

What would the reviewers make of the one hundred and
twenty pages of *Poems?* So far, only Haydon's encomium, in
the *Champion* of March 9, had appeared, and he was already
acquainted with the artist's complimentary views. Haydon
approved all, from "I stood tip-toe upon a little hill," to
"Sleep and Poetry" closing the volume. Nonetheless, like
the memory of claret on his tongue, some of the phrases lingered: "This young man starts suddenly before us with a
genius that is likely to eclipse them all." And by "all" he
meant Byron, Moore, Campbell, and Rogers. "He relies
directly and wholly on nature." There Haydon was right.
Nor was he too magnanimous, Keats hoped, in declaring that
he was "fated to clothe his poetry with a grand intellectual
light, and to lay his name in the lap of immortality." Certainly, he was "familiar with all that is green, light, and
beautiful in nature."

"Assuredly, I know my imagination is 'very powerful.' "
Sometimes it entirely wiped out the present, material world.
He recalled the day, a year or so ago—no longer than that?
—when as surgeon in Guy's Hospital he had been performing a delicate operation on a temporal artery. Suddenly, his
mind was elsewhere, in a land of faery and, though his hand
finished the work to a nicety, he shuddered to envision what
that dominance by fancy might have wrought.

Hunt had prepared the reading world, he believed, for a
favorable reception of this first book. Last December, the

Examiner had published an article entitled "Young Poets," ending with the critic's comment on Keats. "I had given him my manuscripts," his reveries went on unbroken. The occasional commands of the driver, the sounding horn and pleasant rattle of trace-chains were parts of a harmony familiar always. Hunt had been fairly surprised "with the truth of their ambition and ardent grappling with nature." Gratefully, with all his heart and, he thought, justly, he had dedicated the *Poems* to Hunt. While the "set" chatted around him there at Hunt's cottage in the Vale of Health, on Hampstead Heath, he had withdrawn a trifle to one side and written—for the Olliers were waiting for a dedication— "Glory and loveliness have passed away."

He had amazed them all by finishing so quickly. Charles Ollier seized the script and went away with it; he had prophesied success for the slender volume and had written a sonnet extolling Keats's "upward darting soul, His eager grasp at immortality." Now, in this coach gliding smoothly over the well-kept highway, Keats said to himself, "That was discerning. I must have fame or die."

But those Olliers were disappointed. Since the sales were reportedly near zero, they had lost belief, and George would try to get all copies on hand. He would probably tell them they could go to the devil. Trust George! What could a poet—a poet, mind you, not a mere versifier—do about sales? Wasn't it for the poet to write immortal words; wasn't it for the publisher to sell them—if so mightily concerned about selling?

He had been praised by George and Tom, by Jack Reynolds, Joseph Severn, Haydon, and Hunt, to all of whom he had presented copies inscribed with some pride (admittedly!), "From the author." For his brother's sweetheart, Georgiana Augusta Wylie, "Nymph of the downward smile," he had had a special copy bound in green leather with a gilt border, and his script on the title page, "To G. A. Wylie, from her friends the Author and his Brother George." Georgiana, disinterested Georgiana, the only disinterested woman he had ever known. He had not resisted opportunity for punning when he wrote, "The Author consigns this copy to the Severn with all his heart."

He had made new friends: Benjamin Bailey, studying theology at Oxford. Dick Woodhouse, literary adviser, in his admiration of *Poems* had praised him to Taylor and Hessey —"Mistessey," he chuckled, half-aloud. And Wordsworth? Keats had written in a copy for the supreme of living poets, "With the Author's sincere reverence."

The team was slowing down, perhaps for Bagshot. Dozing passengers, roused by the horn, blinked at glimmer of lanterns and opening of inn doors; presently, the panting horses walked slowly behind grooms to stalls back of the yard. Keats stood up, stretched his five feet and three-quarters of an inch, and drew his shawl more snugly close. "Colder," he felt; maybe he should go inside. Not yet, not yet. "Too much to see, though the sky is overcast."

Again, they set off briskly and, as if refreshed by the new team, he was wider awake to sights and sounds of the road. He watched the lamplight creep along, here and there catching glimpses of the undergrowth. How marvelously well Shakespeare had described it, through Gonzalo's "acre of barren ground—long, heath-brown furze." Park palings rose up to meet the light and, over beyond them, discovered by the reflection of the lamps, the windows of a house, a stone nymph in a fountain.

No moon. Had there been, he would have been rhapsodizing, no doubt. What was there in the moon that moved his heart so potently?

7

Forever Young

When yet a child
I oft have dried my tears when thou hast smiled.

There was no moon

lifting her silver rim
Above a cloud, and with a gradual swim
Coming into the blue with all her light,

as he had seen her come swimming a thousand times. No Cynthia, of whom he had written:

Queen of the wide air; thou most lovely queen
Of all the brightness that mine eyes hath seen.

That poem he had ended:

Now, no more
My wand'ring spirit must no further soar.

But the time had come to celebrate ideal Beauty. This new poem must be "no middle flight." He was about to try his skill in a sustained poem of maybe four thousand lines. He would call it "Endymion."

Shifting his position on the hard slats and bracing his boots against the seat in front, he asked himself, "Have I accomplished sufficient so far?" Not a year and a half had joined the "dark backward and abysm of time" (tremendous phrase, so aptly assigned to Prospero!) since he had entered Guy's, further to qualify as surgeon. Astley Cooper was a winning sort of fellow; but even under the spell of that lecturer on anatomy and physiology, he had scribbled a page about a damsel of "merveillouse beautie slepynge upon the herbys and flourys." He had given her a form, he remembered, like the fairest carving of Queen Cythere, only that it blushed with warmth and life. Walter Dendy, sitting beside him, had goggled at the end of the scrap, asked for the page—and got it.

8

Soon afterward, he had written an "Epistle" to George Felton Mathew; not yet a year ago had published in the *Examiner* his first poem to be printed, "O, Solitude!" He had not won his apothecary's certificate until July 25, 1816. But for his guardian, old Richard Abbey, he never would have apprenticed himself to a doctor, as he had done at fifteen. He recalled a scene between Abbey and Grandmother Jennings. "He has no inclination that I can discover," said his guardian, "for any trade or profession. But he tended his mother well— We might make a doctor out of him."

Hammond lived near Granny, and also drove to Enfield, two miles away, to visit sick boys in Clarke's school. He might as well be understudy to Hammond. Now he frowned at the lost years but, remembering he was young—twenty-one last October 31—he would find in reading and study all he had lost. He would be no more a poet of nature than a poet of the intellect.

2

Breaking in upon memories and hopes, out there a man and a woman went gingerly along; there, another man held a lantern for his mistress. Presently, a barber's pole, a doctor's shop. "Thank the Muses, I found sufficient granite in me to give up that surgeon-apothecary profession!" The tinkle of a sheep bell, dark forms of a flock, the bark of a dog. Numb, sleepy, he descended after riding three stages outside and seated himself within the cellar-like coop. By and by he dozed, now and then waking at a lurch of the carriage, fragments of the past poking up through the stream of consciousness like logs in a current, again dropping below the surface.

He awoke and, his eyes on the path of light visible through the glass door, thought of Enfield and Charles Cowden Clarke. Dear Charles, of the "wise, warm" heart! Before Richard Abbey had sent him, John Keats, flunkeying after

9

old Hammond, carrying surgical boxes and holding horses—
"Come to think of it," he interrupted himself, "Shakespeare
once held horses"—before that wasteland of his life, Charles
had inducted him into poetic appreciation. For, truth to tell,
he had been a pugnacious youngster, ready to fight and properly to be cuffed into submission by George, who could lay
him across legs, longer and sturdier than his own, and spank
until he cried, "Enough!" An usher had once threatened
Tom. Keats had rushed to his younger brother's defense and
struck a pugilist's attitude. The usher laughed, but let
Tom go.

Six or seven months ago he had tried to thank Charles in
an "Epistle" dedicated to him "whose palate gladdens in the
flavor of sparkling Helicon."

> . . . *you first taught me all the sweets of song:*
> *The grand, the sweet, the terse, the free, the fine;*
> *What swell'd with pathos, and what right divine:*
> *Spenserian vowels that elope with ease,*
> *And float along like birds o'er summer seas;*
> *Miltonian storms, and more, Miltonian tenderness;*
> *Michael in arms, and more, meek Eve's fair slenderness.*
> *Who read for me the sonnet swelling loudly*
> *Up to its climax and then dying proudly?*
> *Who found for me the grandeur of the ode,*
> *Growing, like Atlas, stronger for its load?*
> *Who let me taste that more than cordial dram,*
> *The sharp, the rapier-pointed epigram?*
> *Shew'd me that epic was of all the king,*
> *Round, vast, and spanning all like Saturn's ring?*

What might he have been if he had never seen or known
Charles's kindness!

Early in Enfield days, the young master had taught him
how to read history, "upholding the veil from Clio's beauty."

The best sonnet in his *Poems* had written itself from a double fullness owed to Charles.

In the dark coach among the drowsing travelers, he burrowed deeper into the time when he was thirteen or fourteen. At that adventurous age he had been enraptured by Robertson's *History of America.* He remembered his wide-eyed stare of delight over the Portuguese expedition that discovered the Congo, of the long fifteen-hundred-mile advance "beyond the line," when the sailors for the first time under a new heaven observed the stars of another hemisphere. Stars of the Southern Hemisphere! An astronomer—he had glimpsed the possibility—might discover stars not to be found from an English observatory. That image of strange stars, Southern Cross and all, had etched more keenly the picture he had got from Bonnycastle's *Introduction to Astronomy.* Is half of all poetry written about the stars? The engraved plate sprang to memory:

Assigned
As a Reward of Merit
To Ma.ʳ John Keats At
Mr. Clarke's
Enfield
Mids. 1811.

Two years or so later he had given the book to George. . . .

A prolonged blast from the horn broke into his recollections. He bent his vision upon the beam from the lamp: they were skirting the woods, running on the level; he suspected a curve in the road or perhaps a gate.

"What a world of countries I had never smoked up to that reading of Robertson!" He saw again Magellan sail the east coast of South America, Guinea, Malabar, Peru, Mexico— "many goodly states and kingdoms." He had named the new ocean Pacific. "Yet never did I taste its pure serene" . . .

11

much better than his first writing, "Yet never did I know what men could mean."

Those early explorers were eager for gold. Columbus wanted gold. Balboa and Cortez and Pizarro wanted gold. Robertson had made that clear. Mexico and Peru were, literally, "realms of gold." Columbus had circled the West Indies, "Round many western islands have I been," but Cortez and Pizarro had conquered certain realms. Cortez, the dashing, the daring, had burned his ships that his men might not turn back—him not Balboa, Keats remembered as discoverer of the Pacific.

Some of the passengers were picking up small parcels; the coach was slowing down. Could this be Winchester? He stepped out, filling his lungs with air fresh from the sea, while once more they rapidly shifted horses. He looked back to the forest of oak and blackthorn, along which they had run for some miles. Whether the fringe of New Forest or Alice Holt or Bere he did not know—but Alice Holt and Bere were beautiful names! And as he stood there near the break of dawn, he thought he heard the final notes of a nightingale's song. A feeling for Caen Wood and home rushed upon him; he pushed it off and chose to reflect that if nightingales sing much, "it is a sign of warm weather." This forest back there, so densely wooded, might have risen on the sides of Latmos. He turned to sniff the ocean, while the breeze ruffled his long hair—he had taken off his cap—and got back inside. They set out, among stirring leaves, now growing more thinly by the wayside.

The rest of the sonnet "On First Looking into Chapman's Homer" was of but recent origin. Six months ago, in October, he and Charles Clarke had sat up all night over Mr. Alsager's copy of the *Iliad* and the *Odyssey*, translated by the Elizabethan. The shipwreck of Ulysses had ended their intoxication of vicarious adventure. "The sea had soaked his

12

heart through" evoked the last exclamation of joy with which they had shouted and whooped over superb passages, and at daybreak Keats had left Charles at Clerkenwell for his own room in the Poultry. While he walked the two miles, full to bursting of the heroic translation (how he regretted he knew no Greek!), easily he evoked the figure ready in his mind to express something of his feeling about epic Homer and Chapman. He had finished the sonnet and delivered it to Charles's desk before ten o'clock. Charles was still asleep and he had tiptoed softly away. Years after the splendor of discovery and fortunes of conquest had fallen upon his boyish mind like light seeds from the feathered grass out there by the roadside—a good figure that, he might use it later—a plant had sprung up, a seemingly magic plant, as at a fakir's "Presto, arise!" No, by heavens, no! That sonnet had been a long time in seed planted by Robertson and it awaited quickening from the translator of the Greek *Odyssey*. "It *is* a good sonnet," and he repeated it line by line, lips and eyes closed, while the swaying coach neared Southampton.

3

He popped his head out—he would write George and Tom—just as it began to glow eastward. "N.B. This Tuesday saw the sun rise." That *would* astonish them. The light that had illumined his destiny, that had undeviatingly pointed to his place beside the poets, he recalled as the sun came up clear, beyond the South Downs and across the channel, to scatter lingering clouds. Not history, not Chaucer, not even Spenser, but Mary Tighe's *Psyche* had kindled a flame within. He was about to think upon this miracle when, descending the Downs, they entered the region of low shrubbery along the coast. "What a rural dash that yellow furze is cutting!" he silently exclaimed, even as a deeper voice was

13

phrasing, "prickly furze buds lavish gold." Surely, yes, he would begin "Endymion" as of this very April.

He descended at the Coach and Horses in Southampton and claimed his luggage. The stage rolled on to Lymington and Poole.

At breakfast, lonely among strangers, he went and unboxed a volume of Shakespeare. " 'Here's my comfort,' as Stephano says in the *Tempest*," and with it in his pocket set out for the half-mile stroll along High Street to the estuary of the Anton, Southampton Water. "At low tide," he remarked to himself on the pier, "this arm of the ocean hardly fulfills my expectations; perhaps it will mend its ways before three o'clock." At that hour, the booking clerk told him, the boat would leave for Cowes, the Isle of Wight. He walked about the town, meantime, observing that men and women did not differ materially from those he saw habitually, and that Southampton had a very respectable old gate, with two lions to guard it.

"The truth is, I am not interested here. George and Tom and Haydon and Reynolds have been pushing each other out of my brain by turns ever since I was quit of the coach, and even before." He wished one or more of them were sharing this stroll; a kindred spirit was better than solitude, even in a town or city.

That giant painting, now, Haydon's latest experiment in High Art, picturing "Christ's Entry into Jerusalem." Haydon had cited Virgil as precedent enough—had the Latin poet not brought together figures three centuries apart?—for including with the throng about Christ on the ass the figures of Wordsworth, Sir Isaac Newton, Voltaire, and John Keats. One of the ladies, if no more, was of this present age. Would Haydon go on with these anachronisms? Would he continue to paint the Christ so obviously to resemble the artist, Haydon? . . . And Reynolds, who had introduced

14

him to James Rice, and Charles W. Dilke. Reynolds was a writer, yet he would possibly be "articled" to a legal firm. Jemmie Rice, gay, lovable, full of quips. Dilke and his editing and son Charles. That brat of a boy, now seven years old, consumed too much of his father's care and energy. Still, Keats admitted, searching for a pinch of snuff and finding none, Dilke knew a great deal about the Elizabethan dramatists. For a space his attention was devoted to the shops along which he passed, alert for a Rappee sign until, finding it, he went in and bought enough to fill his box.

Before eating a chop and going aboard the boat, he would write his brothers, reminding them to give his love to Fanny. She needed them all but rarely saw any of them. Old Abbey restricted their visits. "He was responsible for my becoming a surgeon," Keats lamented, "when I knew naught else to do. He is annoyed, now I am my own master, he cannot stop me from writing poetry."

A spanking breeze sped the craft along the twenty miles to Cowes. They docked before nightfall.

4

He went on to Newport, spent the night there, and next day visited Shanklin. There he stood looking down at the Chine, that impressive cleft between the cliffs, three hundred feet deep, filled with trees and bushes near the land but, except for primroses, bare as it widened to the ocean. Fishermen's huts on one side, a little waterfall, a white headland, and St. Catherine's Hill; "the sheep in the meadow, the cows in the corn," he repeated. All were beautiful. But expensive. He settled, instead, outside of Newport at Mrs. Cook's, Canterbury House, Castle Road, Carisbrooke. Opening up his books, he stacked them neatly in a corner; his pictures he pinned up in a row on the wall—Haydon, Mary Queen of Scots, and Milton with his daughters.

Walking through a passage he discovered a head of Shakespeare. "I've never seen that engraving," he remarked to his landlady. At the joy of discovery in his voice, "Should you like it, sir?" she asked. "If I might exchange it for the French Ambassador," he suggested, "that hangs above my group."

From a hill near the house if he looked across the Solent he could see England—though he should not forget that politically the Isle of Wight was part of Hampshire—and from his window, the ruins of Carisbrooke Castle. In the ivy tower, he was amused to suspect, lived many a descendant of some old cawer who peeped through the bars at Charles the First when there in prison. Reynolds would smile at this genealogical idea and probably try to compute the generations.

The ocean haunted him continually, making him—as the provincials spoke the word—"narvus." Muted, the susurrus drew from him the beginning:

> *It keeps eternal whisperings around*
> *Desolate shores . . .*

and all that follows to the last line:

> *Until ye start as if the sea-nymphs quired!*

Inexpressibly weary and lonely, he lay down to sleep.

Next morning, disturbed that certain cups, books, and baskets promised by Reynolds' sisters and Mrs. Dilke were missing from his other box, he wrote Jack to demand what they could say for themselves. And since Shakespeare's birthday was approaching, "I'll tell you what—if I should receive a letter from you and another from my brothers on that day, 'twould be a parlous good thing. Whenever you write, say a word or two on some passage in Shakespeare that may have

16

come rather new to you." He had himself just underscored in the *Tempest* what struck him forcibly:

> *Urchins*
> *Shall, for the vast of Night that they may work,*
> *All exercise on thee.*

He could not exist without poetry, eternal poetry, and dropped all else to pick up his Spenser, which opened at the lines:

> *The noble heart that harbors virtuous thought,*
> *And is with child of glorious great intent,*
> *Can never rest until it forth have brought*
> *Th' eternal brood of glory excellent—*

An omen! Forthwith he set out his inkwell and took up his crowquill to rebegin "Endymion." He was urged on by the pleasant prospect of exchanging verses with Reynolds in a delightful place marked near the old castle. This "Endymion," long planned, must be as rich as Spenser, as light as Ariel, as bewitching as *A Midsummer Night's Dream.* He looked at the beginning:

> *A thing of beauty is a joy forever.*

In his heart he thanked Henry Stephens, a hospital class-mate, who had heard him read first, "A thing of beauty is a constant joy." Stephens had said, "It's good, John; but—well—it wants something." He had rewritten and asked, "How now, Henry?" Stephens smiled, "It will live for-ever."

Now, sitting there in Canterbury House, he read on:

> *yes, in spite of all*
> *Some shape of beauty moves away the pall*
> *From our dark spirits.*

But his spirits remained unfree; he was too indisposed, or

disinclined, to resume the poem. He walked out to the ivied
ruins, climbed the steps, bared his head to the breeze and sun,
forgot he was a poet, and returned to the house, sparkling,
hair curling about his face. "Such eyes the young man has!"
Mrs. Cook met him on the way in and reported to her parlor
maid.

> *Therefore, 'tis with full happiness that I*
> *Will trace the story of Endymion—*

he went on, hoping to write many verses before the daisies
were hidden in deep herbage; and, before the bees hummed
about the clover, he must be near the middle of his story.
And, then:

> *let autumn bold,*
> *With universal tinge of sober gold,*
> *Be all about me when I make an end.*

Imagined scenes transferred through his flying pen spread
themselves over his paper. Might the Muse let a portion of
ethereal dew fall on his head and unmew his soul:

> *that I may dare, in wayfaring,*
> *To stammer where old Chaucer used to sing.*

Chaucer. Tom loved the first English poet even as he himself
loved. He wished Tom were here. He laid aside the sheets,
but returned after a walk up and down the room and wrote
rapidly on. He grinned when he saw he had put down a
reminiscence of Wordsworth:

> *By the dim echoes of old Triton's horn.*

Never mind. Let be. And he entered into the creation of a
"Hymn to Pan." "It's good, very good," He chanted aloud
the Hymn and approved his work.

Before the week ended he was exhausted. The food was
not wholesome. He thought so much about his poem and

about poetry he could not sleep. He was, for John Keats, too much alone and "obliged to be in continual burning of thought as an only resource." Wordsworth had written about the

> *inward eye*
> *Which is the bliss of solitude*

Doubtless the great man must by nature be a solitary; John Keats was not. He was finding in solitude no inward eye at all blissful but a hot intensity that charred his mind and soul.

After a week or ten days, he wrote, "I fear I am becoming not over capable in my 'upper stories.'" He thought he would like his old lodgings at Margate, "where despite the barrenness I might contrive to do without trees." Down in the mouth from loneliness, he confessed himself, and asked, "Why should I be a poet? So great a thing, so great to be famed as one." Surely, to be a poet, a poet of the first order, was beyond his power of attainment. He would give up. Give up? Ambition and pride struck back, "It is disgraceful to fail, even in a huge attempt." Banishing the very thought of failure, packing his boxes—with the addition of the Shakespeare portrait, which kindly Mrs. Cook gave him— he left for Margate, a hundred and fifty miles away.

He was not happy until Tom arrived.

II. *Junketing to Canterbury, Hastings, Oxford.*
Endymion

"ALREADY I have caught a more healthy countenance from your coming!" The stage had set Tom down at the inn only this morning, and now they faced each other across the table in Keats's room.

"Why back to Margate?" Tom's question ended in a laugh at John's posture of a dandy taking snuff, flicking back an imaginary ruffle, and replacing the lid of his box with hauteur.

"Because," he replied *in propria persona,* "I like old things best. Things I know. New scenes are well enough but not if one is alone. I believed I should feel more at home here than at Carisbrooke—desolate spot—" Keats's eyes warmed. Thrusting long fingers through his gold-brown mop of hair, he went on with a delightful grin, "What I really needed, Tom, was you."

"Yet in your sonnet on 'Solitude' you preferred 'Nature's observatory'—"

"And also a kindred spirit. Nobody has yet pointed out that my little address to solitude converts itself into an Irish Bull."

"Not quite," protested Tom. He caught the humor in his brother's eye, and walked to the window. "It's as treeless as ever." The bare headland stretched out to the sea.

"We'll make excursions to Canterbury, Ramsgate. We might go back to London along the Canterbury Pilgrims' Road."

20

"Have we money for larks?" Anxiety wrote itself over a face John saw too worn, too haggard. Tom was not well, and he loved Tom better than anybody else.

"I can get money," he spoke confidently. "My publishers are good fellows." He invested his tones with fictitious cheer. Damn Abbey! Letting him have ample funds at Guy's, and now withholding—

"That's well," and Tom held out his hands for the neatly ordered sheets of "Endymion" John was fishing from the table drawer, and settled himself among pillows.

Keats at the table watched his face; it would betray pleasure or disappointment more than his words—that gentle, melancholy face, yet mobile and lighted by eyes of peculiarly mild lambency. "It's only a beginning, so far—" He broke off when he saw Tom already turning a page. He carried on his idea silently: only a pin's point of a beginning. So many pin points to a bodkin point; so many bodkins to make a spear bright enough to throw any light on posterity. Hunt might like that figure!

Tom exclaimed, questioned, approved, and flew on. After he laid down the pages he gazed at his brother half-worshipfully, wholly with pride: "It's a beautiful and, I believe, a great work."

"Much uphill journeying ahead—and, even so, a possible missing of the goal," but he bloomed with renewed confidence as he laid the sheets on the baize cover. Tom got up, put them in the drawer, and sat down at one side to write a letter. Ah, this was like old times! Keats happily finished his letter to Leigh Hunt, signing himself in a rare burst of gayety and fellow-feeling, "John Keats alias Junkets." His friends had played upon his name, alluding to fairy-lore associations—"How faery Mab the junkets eat"—and his love for jaunts, "junketing about." One had added, "And it shows your vein better than 'John Keats.'"

21

"Here's a letter from Haydon"; the May 11 post arrived while they were sealing their letters, Keats with the big red carnelian "J.K." at the end of his fob. A moment or so later he was reading aloud, "Don't despair, collect incident, study character, read Shakespeare, and trust in Providence—and you will do—you must—you shall—"

"Odd fellow," Tom ventured. "Wasn't his being a vegetarian all a pretense—though he is so great a Christian?"

"Can you blame him greatly?" Keats laughed at the memory. "Here were Shelley and Hunt chasing around a few nondescript vegetables on their plates, while Haydon, bless us, felt impelled to follow their noble examples. So well he succeeded in shifting over from a strong meat diet, he grew suspect and somebody set a trap to catch him, followed him out of the house plump into a coffee shop. He was digging into a rare juicy steak."

The brothers smiled appreciatively. "He has a few words to say of Hunt—" Keats had taken up Haydon's letter again: "He advises me to beware of the delusions and sophistications ripping up the talent and respectability of our friend Leigh Hunt. 'He will go out of the world the victim of his own weakness and the dupe of his own self-delusions—'

"I wonder," said Keats as if he had got the tail of an idea; he was thinking of Haydon.

Hunt doubtless deceives himself, thought Tom.

"There is no greater sin," his brother declared, "than to flatter oneself into an idea of being a great poet."

"You could not be guilty of such self-flattery," Tom smiled, and conveyed a double meaning in his words.

"I could never be deceived about myself in that way," Keats was sure.

Tom picked up a volume of Shakespeare from the heap in the corner. "Open it, John." The pages fell apart at *Love's Labour's Lost*. " 'Let fame, that all hunt after in their lives,' " Keats read so far and stopped. "I might make a pun on 'hunt,' but I'll read on." He finished the speech of Ferdinand, wondering whether he might buy with his breath the honor that would make him heir of all eternity. He had begun a letter, "My dear Haydon," for whom he quoted the passage. He felt himself far below Haydon, but to think he had not the right to couple himself with the artist in the wish that "Fame live register'd upon our brazen tombs" would be death; he hoped their tombs might be near neighbors. Aware "the endeavour of this present breath will soon be over," though feeling himself like "one that gathers samphire, dreadful trade," from the high cliffs of poesy, yet when he heard Tom read *Plutarch's Lives,* he felt that some of those lives were mice compared to his own.

He had been reading *King Lear,* here hard by the cliffs of Dover, and the play had taken his soul with grappling hooks. Tragic to an almost unbearable degree, it left the reader in a serene mood. He made out the reason to his own satisfaction: "The excellence of every art is its intensity, capable of making all disagreeables evaporate, from their being in close relationship with Beauty and Truth."

Again, he was reading and writing eight hours a day, always arduously reattacking "Endymion" where he had left off. Centered in Shakespeare and in his own poem, he quoted Shakespeare, absorbing lines, whole passages, and through the alchemy he did not understand but accepted as a sign of his poetic endowment he was enriching "Endymion" from the magnificent vitality of a man alive these two hundred years.

"You're speaking in Shakespeare's rhythm, John," Tom remarked, in their talk and walk along the shore.

"If a good genius over me preside," Keats answered in offhand iambics, "I trust it may be he."

23

"You see—" Tom began, but John was twinkling. "Oh, you fraud," he wound up.

"Seriously," said Keats. "I was just writing Haydon that I shall never read any other book much except Shakespeare. The Stratford man throws all small deer into their humbler places."

His spirit wholly elate, since Tom kept him rooted in reality, fell at a disquieting letter from George. "Money troubles will follow us for some time to come." Tom was silent; John had but taken up his pen.

Unable to swing into the strain of his numbers, Keats nervously got up, thrust on his old cap and handed over Tom's. "Let's walk." They made for a chophouse. "I can understand," said he ruefully, "why Coleridge never completed 'Kubla Khan.' Nearly twenty years ago, and he will never finish it."

"Some tailor chap—with a bill—wasn't it?"

"From Porlock," Keats agreed absently. "He never did return, he never could return," his tones were of despair for Coleridge, "to the magic of that interrupted melody and vision. But I must," he was again centered in his own worries, "I will finish 'Endymion.' "

"You will," Tom spoke firmly.

But his spirit was too fevered for writing and he revoked his plan of finishing by autumn. In his new depression he was glad a time must come when the fading of this insubstantial pageant would "leave not a rack behind." The baneful morbidity had some share of good: "It would enable me at any time to look with an obstinate eye on the devil himself— ay, to be as proud of being the lowest of the human race as Alfred could be in being of the highest. I feel confident I should have been a Rebel Angel had the opportunity been mine."

"Rhodomontade," some of his friends would have said. Not Tom.

Perhaps he swaggered a trifle, he chuckled to himself. He had but written an intimation of being ready to die in six hours if plans could be brought to conclusions; yet in the *Tempest* he had underscored:

> *As I hope*
> *For quiet days, fair issue, and long life.*

Tom knew he was at odds with himself and urged him into gossip. They spoke of the stir being made by the Manuscript from St. Helena (*Manuscrit venu de St. Hélène*) and of Haydon's remarks upon it in a recent issue of the *Examiner*. "I was reading *Antony and Cleopatra* when the *Examiner* arrived," Keats had written in effect, and had spoken of several speeches being applicable to passages chosen for comment by Haydon. "But how differently does Buonaparte bear his fate from Antony!" Keats had exclaimed.

2

"Good fellows, Tom!" he waved a note extracted from a London letter, this middle of May. "I assured you Taylor and Hessey would advance something on royalty."

"You were lucky in getting away from Olliers'," congratulated Tom.

"They wouldn't have had me," Keats confessed. "And Dick Woodhouse is the reason for John Taylor's generosity. Both Mistessey and Taylor swear by Dick's judgment. He's a good literary adviser," he ended in a fine humor.

Covering gratitude under lightness of manner, more real he acknowledged to himself than he had experienced since the arrival of George's letter, he wrote: "I am extremely indebted to you for your liberality in the shape of manufactured rag value £20 and shall immediately proceed to destroy some of the minor heads of that spring-headed Hydra the Dun—To conquer which the Knight need have no sword, shield, cuirass, cuisses, herbadgeon, spear, casque, greves, pauldron, spurs, chevron, or any other scaly commodity, but he need only take the Bank Note of Faith and Cash of Salvation, and set out against the monster invoking the aid of no Archimago or Uganda—and finger me the paper light as the Sibyl's leaves in Virgil, whereat the fiend skulks off with his tail between his legs." With these cullings from Shakespeare, Ephesians, "The Faerie Queene," and the Amadis of Gaul, he knew Woodhouse would be pleased, "and maybe Taylor, a well-read man."

After more of this sprightliness, he dropped to the matter-of-fact. He had gone at his poem day by day for a month when, finding his brain so overwrought he had in it neither rhyme nor reason, he had given up work for a few days. He had a swimming in his head and a feeling of mental debauch. Tomorrow, however, May 17, he would begin the work of his second month on "Endymion." This very evening he was setting out for Canterbury where, he hoped, the remembrance of Chaucer would set him forward "like a billiard ball." Even as he acknowledged the loan, Tom was packing up their bags and boxes. They could pay their debts here and go where there were trees.

Before night they were on top of the departing coach. Two hours or so afterward, Keats broke off a discussion with, "See the spires ahead!" A trifle later they were climbing down near the cathedral, at an inn not too far from oak and thorn.

"Here I stick until Book One is off hand," and for the third time since leaving London Keats began to unpack.

"I'll see that you take your walk and study the inside of the fane . . .

26

Junketing to Canterbury, Hastings, Oxford

And specially from every shires ende
Of Engelond to Caunterbury they wende."

"Did Shakespeare ever come here?" asked Keats. . . .
Toward the end of the month he wrote line 992:

They stept into the boat and launch'd from land,

and gave the final passages to Tom, who pronounced all of
the first Book successful.

"You are more weary, John, than you know," said he. "I
propose to return to the city while you go to the shore—
somewhere near St. Leonards."

Keats thought he would like to see the battlefield of Hastings. Maybe the village of Bo-Peep, in the outskirts of St.
Leonards, would be refreshing and inexpensive. "But I'll
be along home soon," he promised.

This time he stood below while the stage moved off with
Tom. Tom had been coughing and was thinner.

3

With George Felton Mathew's review of his *Poems,* in
the *European Magazine* for May, he was not wholly pleased.
The poetical beauties of the volume reminded the reviewer
much of the elegant and romantic Spenser and, knowing
G.F.M. was his friend, Keats read with gusto these words
and those declaring, "The author has a fine ear for grand,
elaborate, and abstracted music of nature." But he frowned
at the pronouncement, "Till I heard Chapman speak out
loud and bold" a bad line. "Not only as it breaks the meta-
phor, but as it blows out the whole sonnet into an unseemly
hyperbole." That clause and the conclusion drew astonishment ending in a wide grin. The author could ultimately
hope, the reviewer asserted in a highly *ex cathedra* man-

27

ner, "to bind his brows with the glorious sunbeams of immortality."

"How do I go about binding my brows with sunbeams?" Keats laid down the review.

At Hastings he met a lady who made him forget everything else but themselves, while he "warmed with her and kissed her." The harbor was pleasant, and so he wrote Tom, "but my money is low. I shall be with you and George by the end of the first week in June."

By the tenth he was at Number One, Well Walk. "Mrs. Bentley is a kind, motherly soul," Tom assured him.

"What of the noisy children?" asked Keats.

"Out much of the time," said George, "though in rainy weather their stockings do, of a truth, smell rather strong."

"George," Keats asked bluntly. "How much money should we have—all or singly?"

"From the estate?"

"Yes. After all was settled." His tone was urgent.

"It isn't settled; that's the difficulty," George told them. "Our fortune is in chancery. We should have had something like fifteen hundred pounds, every one of us, including Fanny. But you, John, used a good part of your share in medical training"—John raised his eyes to heaven—"and you, dear Tom, have been ill and so used some of yours. Still, if we could get what is ours, we should do, we could manage."

"Abbey will never let me have anything," said Keats, "so long as he can avoid paying it. You remember what happened when I told him I was determined to be a poet."

"We know," George returned warmly, "and his prophecy that you would speedily terminate your 'inconsiderate enterprise' is so far, Tom and I are glad to say, unfulfilled."

Keats had told his brothers, at the time, of the scene, still vivid to him. He had gone, with his book, *Poems,* to his ex-guardian and offered it as proof of ability. Abbey, knee-breeched and white-stockinged, leaning stiffly from his chair, awkwardly received the volume. He was not, he would have said, a book fancier. "I will look at it, John," he promised, "because it is your writing. Otherwise, I would never trouble my head with any such thing."

With equal vividness the sequel flashed before Keats. "What did you think of my poems, sir?" Not doubting his critical acumen, the stout gentleman had replied, "It reminds me of the Quaker's horse, which was hard to catch and good for nothing when he was caught—so your book is hard to understand and good for nothing when it is understood." By delivering himself of that comparison, he put himself forever out of sympathy with John Keats.

"What will he make of 'Endymion'!" Keats envisioned profound puzzlement.

"And yet, John, he manages our finances. We must see what we can do."

They must have money. That was a fact not to be dismissed.

"I shall not put up much longer," George surprised them by saying, "with the overbearing of Abbey's Mr. Hodgkinson."

"But he is only the junior member of Abbey and Cock!" Tom exclaimed.

"So much the worse. He is in Abbey's confidence, under his control. I am not inclined, moreover, to the life of a tea-dealer in Pancras Lane." To his still wide-eyed brothers he added, "No more inclined than you, John, to the profession of medicine."

Tom said nothing. "What will you do?" asked John.

"If Georgiana will marry me and go with me to America —and I think she will—I shall try my fortune there. Maybe in Birkbeck's Colony. I like the earth—"

29

"But it's London you know." John emphasized "know."
"I like the idea of becoming a planter or of something to
do with forestry—I'm ready for the new continent." He was
becoming, in his enthusiasm, almost oratorical.

"We shall miss you," Tom was more gently melancholy
than ever.

"Why not come along?" George invited briskly.

Unable to say another word, Tom shook his head miserably.

"I don't believe I should like America," said Keats
thoughtfully. "But I'll tell you what. I'll come for a visit
after you and Georgiana are well settled." He had not
grasped that George was serious.

At this moment money was the pressing need. Abashed,
chagrined, at calling upon new friends again so shortly, John
sat down and began a sheet, "My dear Sirs: I must endeavor
to lose my maidenhead with respect to money matters as soon
as possible—" He paused and leaning on his hand considered.
The reply of Taylor and Hessey, spoken or unspoken, must
be that he had already lost it. But he went on—he could not
waste that sheet of paper—informing them of a couple of
duns that had opened upon him "with a cry most untunable."
He was keeping 25 good notes in his fob, but they were to
write with. Again, he felt his virginity come strong upon him,
while he requested a 20 pounds and 10 pounds. Somehow, it
seemed less, dividing it so.

When £30 fell out of the sealed letter a day or so later,
he told himself, "Now I can go on," and once more days and
nights aided him, "like legion'd soldiers." In that month or
so, urging his hero towards the depths of the ocean, often he
recalled the line in Spenser which, when he first heard
Charles Clarke read it, had given him the sense of power and
vastness: "sea-shouldering whales." He had cried out then,

30

"What an image!" and Charles said later, "You looked big and burly, yourself, when you spoke."

He read aloud his couplet closing Book Two:

"The visions of the earth were gone and fled—
He saw the giant sea above his head.

I rather think that last line can keep Spenser's company," he said to Tom.

"It can," Tom beamed from his pillows. He was too much in bed these days. "But I enjoy reading more when lying back comfortably," he apologized. "Now you're half through?" He still thought "Endymion" a masterpiece.

"Not what I yearn to do; but, by heaven, it's my best now." Eager for a change of scene, he spoke of an invitation he had received from Benjamin Bailey, undergraduate theologian at Oxford. "I met him when he stopped with Caius— Jack Reynolds, you know—at the beginning of the Long Vacation."

"Also a Miltonian and Wordsworthian?" Tom remembered.

"The same. He is in London again, on the way back from Cambridgeshire, where he's been visiting his family. He says there will be few students at Oxford now—and in short I should find it well enough at Magdalen Hall."

"Sort of chap you can work with—live with?" Tom had drawn aside the curtain and was looking out upon Well Walk.

"Quite. He's reading divinity, a man who will study as hard as I shall write."

"Run along. You need a change for the third Book. When George is ready for Paris I'll go with him."

On the third of September, Keats with Bailey "disembarked from his Whipship's coach, the 'Defiance,'" near Magdalen tower.

Soon he was feeling at home, comfortable enough, among

31

colleges, halls, stalls, with plenty of trees, thank God, plenty of books, and plenty of snuff and segars. And clear streams! He had never seen so many together—"more in number than your eyelashes," he told Reynolds—as at Oxford.

Every morning he thought how fortunate he was to be here when, after breakfast, Bailey sported his oak and they sat down opposite each other at the same table or, occasionally, at separate desks. They worked until two or three o'clock—only pausing for a stretch and chat now and then—before going out for exercise. He was writing fifty lines a day, as easily as if this new friend were Tom, as regularly as he wrote to his family, the Reynolds girls, Reynolds, and Haydon. Bailey liked his poetry and daily heard him read what he had brought forth as naturally as a tree bears leaves. On the fourth or fifth day when he came to these lines in the story of Glaucus:

> *Suddenly*
> *He woke as from a trance; his snow-white brows*
> *Went arching up, and like two magic ploughs*
> *Furrow'd deep wrinkles in his forehead large—*

he looked upward, furrowing his own brow. Bailey intent upon the "magic ploughs," silently commented, "In your hands they have turned up so much of the rich soil of fairyland."

Every day beside the Isis, Keats remarked, "Thank God, no rain yet." Always he felt better in bright weather. As they walked, he learned that Bailey was in love with Mariane Reynolds, now on vacation at Littlehampton with her sister Jane. Out of rollicking spirits, he wrote them playfully, reporting in his airiest mood a brief conversation between himself and Bailey. In the study was a picture of Jeremy Taylor, befitting the abode of a divinity student. "Bailey," Keats had declared, "your author of *Holy Living and Holy Dying* always threatens to rap me with that book."

"It is," Bailey had stared at the engraving as if for the first time, "held rather menacingly." "So my head is in imminent danger," Keats concluded his account to Jane. In reply to his question whether she preferred Juliet or Imogen, she had said Imogen. Well, she was right, he would have been disappointed at hearing her say Juliet. Yet, for himself, he felt so great a yearning for Juliet, he would rather follow her into Pandemonium than Imogen into Paradise. . . . "In what mood and accompaniment do you like the sea best? It is very fine in the morning when the sun,

> *Opening on Neptune with fair blessed beams,*
> *Turns into yellow gold his salt sea streams.*"

But Jane might think him attitudinizing. He paused to construct a jingle: "And superb when

> *The sun from Meridian height*
> *Illumines the depth of the sea,*
> *And the fishes beginning to sweat,*
> *Cry, 'Damn it! How hot we shall be!'* "

Too patently funny. Reverting to his first mood, "Don't you think there's something extremely fine after sunset . . . when the waters are ebbing and the horizon a mystery?"

Nowadays he rarely thought of anything connected with apothecary-doctor years; but he had promised Mrs. Dilke a little box of medicine. He wished Jane to say he had not forgiven himself for not having sent it. "Junkets" reappeared and sat a moment concocting a nonsensical array of fun and pun. Had he remained at Hampstead, he "would have made precious havoc with Mrs. Dilke's house and furniture: would have eaten her clothes pegs, fried her cabbages, fricasseed her radishes, ragouted her onions—"

"You are displaying no mean knowledge of cookery, Keats," Bailey smiled when hearing this paragraph read aloud. "Negatively, that is."

33

Keats wrote on—"belaboured her beat root, outstripped her scarlet runners, parlezvou'd with her french beans . . . dis*organ*ized her piano, dislocated her candle-sticks, turned out her maid to grass and astonished Brown." Even if Brown lived in his part of the house all to himself, there was little that escaped his shrewd eyes. But this reflection he kept to himself.

He would always be grateful that her brother Jack— whom he considered his brother also—had made known to him so real a fellow as Bailey. "He delights me in the selfish and (please God) the disinterested part of my disposition."

Breaking off, he looked out upon the waning summer and thought of Bailey, reminding himself that he sat as at a feast when Bailey read the works of the old poets. A necessary attribute for a parson's calling was a good voice, and Bailey had it. He, Keats, interrupted only now and then to say, "That was nice," in an undertone, not to break the flow. Bailey's enthusiasm for his calling and for all things good was exalted, though his frame was not robust nor his spirit untorn.

One day Bailey broke off, when something read recalled one of their acquaintances. They spoke awhile of the man and Bailey said, "Keats, you allow for people's faults more than any man I ever knew." When he raised a just-what-do-you-mean face, Bailey added, "Though not where an act of wrong or oppression is at stake."

He finished his letter to Jane. In the diction of Wordsworth's "Ode" he had intimated he was far inland; but in reality he was at the bottom of the sea with Endymion, whom he had hauled there with "unrelenting perseverance."

Another day Bailey spoke of religion. "You are no scoffer; you are no infidel." Keats remained silent. "You are a liberal," Bailey went on. "Your flowing tie and the low-turned collar—"

"I was trying to say, Bailey, I know and respect your feelings and principles. Surely, I could not offend you, and"—he lightly touched the black ribbon tie under his neat collar— "even sartorially, I am now less radical."

Bailey approved the change. "Promise me one thing, then, Keats—" his religion urged him to rescue a possibly errant sheep—"promise me you will never scoff at religion. I've heard some of those. . . ."

All this conversation, part of Bailey's lifework, touched too near the quick for himself, thought Keats. Quickly he replied, "I promise," and then reminding himself that he never broke a promise: How cheap are those who do scoff and sneer. But this he did not speak aloud.

Bailey said no more then but later remarked, "I think you do not like Wordsworth in the full-length portrait, as it were, as I do—a Christian poet, one of great imagination, of great philosophy—"

"But, my friend," Keats interrupted, "is there anything finer than the noble passage in the 'Lines on Tintern Abbey'?" He quoted softly:

"that blessed mood,
In which the burthen of the mystery,
In which the heavy and the weary weight
Of all this unintelligible world
Is lightened."

Bailey had no reply for that, and presently asked, "Which of his passages strikes you most deeply?"

Again, he quoted:

"Not for these I raise
The song of thanks and praise;
But for those obstinate questionings
Of sense and outward things,
Fallings from us, vanishings;

35

Forever Young

Blank misgivings of a creature
Moving about in worlds not realized,
High instincts before which our mortal nature
Did tremble like a guilty thing surprised."

"And why this passage, Keats?"

"I feel it to be so true of myself in the first part. And the last lines I see as quite awful in their application to a guilty, finite creature like man, in the appalling nature of the feeling they suggest to a thoughtful person."

"What of the *Lyrical Ballads*, as a whole? Their place in literature?"

"They represent the dawn of a new era—if we can drag ourselves away from eighteenth-century formalism. They have led the way for us who are younger. Take the poem, 'She dwelt among the untrodden ways,' which I believe came a year or two after the *Lyrical Ballads*, however:

She lived unknown, and few yet know
When Lucy ceased to be;
But she is in her grave, and Oh,
The difference to me.

The simplicity of that last line is the most perfect pathos."

From "The Excursion" Keats pointed out instances where better taste might have prevailed:

"Fancy fetched
Even from the blazing chariot of the sun
A beardless youth, who touched a golden lute
And filled the illumined groves with ravishment.

The description of Apollo should have ended at the 'golden lute,' " he averred, "and Wordsworth should have left it to the imagination to complete the picture—how he filled the 'illumined groves.' "

36

He spoke then of Chatterton, chanting the "Roundelay Song" by the Minstrels of Aella:
" 'Come with acorn cuppe and thorne,' " he chanted in his best voice for the lines.

> *"Drain my hertys blood away;*
> *Life and all its goods I scorne;*
> *Dance by night and feast by day.*

Isn't the first line charming?"

"No more," said Bailey, "than are many of your 'Endymion' passages."

Keats got up, bowed awkwardly, and entered into a favorite "abstraction." "The principle of melody, I dare think," he began, walking back and forth in the study, "is not thoroughly understood. Nowhere less than in the management of open and closed vowels."

Bailey was not sure he got the meaning but certainly understood that vowels should be so managed as not to clash with one another, marring the melody, and should be interchanged like differing notes of music to prevent monotony. "Unless, of course," Keats added, "monotony of effect is for some reason desirable." He illustrated with one of his preferred quotations—"Singing masons building roofs of gold" —wherein the humming of the bees seemed to him enhanced by the "short *i*" sounds. "If I had studied music," he wound up, "I have some notions of the combinations of sounds by which I think I might have done something as original as in my poetry."

A trifle later they were rowing on the Isis, soon drifting into a secluded backwater where they talked and read. "Let's call this sheltered nook for Reynolds," suggested Keats. "Agreed," said Bailey. "It shall henceforth be 'Reynolds's Cove.' "

Here at Oxford, Keats began to feel a definite responsibility toward his sister Fanny. Not permitted often to see her, he felt the more her lack of brotherly attention, her confinement to so restricted a way of living. Who were her acquaintances? Why, chiefly, birds, books, and flowers! That is, when not in Miss Kaley's school—for she never got away from the Abbeys. He was not sure of her needs or wishes or pleasures; but he might help her toward some enjoyment at which not even her guardians could cavil. Was she still at the Cinderella-and-glass-slipper stage, or had she arrived at interest in Moore's *Almanack?* Would she prefer the *History of King Pepin* to *Pilgrim's Progress?* He did not know. They had hardly been together since she had arrived—if she had arrived—at the age of reflection.

His duty presented itself to him more and more forcibly. After a few letters, he might learn to adapt his enjoyment to hers. They must, he felt and told her so, become intimately acquainted that, as she grew up—she was now, "umm, yes, fourteen"—he might love her as his only sister and confide in her as his dearest friend. Already he was thinking in language he conceived perhaps fitted to her liking. He drew toward him a sheet of paper on which he set down as much of his poem as he knew her capable of understanding.

"Many years ago"—this would do if she was still in the fairy-story age—"there was a young handsome shepherd who fed his flocks on a mountain's side called Latmos—he was a very contemplative sort of person and lived solitary among the trees and plains little thinking that such a beautiful creature as the moon was growing mad in love with him. However, so it was; and when he was asleep on the grass, she used to come down from heaven and admire him excessively for a long time; and at last could not refrain from carrying him away in her arms to the top of that high Latmos while he was a-dreaming. But I daresay you have read this and all the other beautiful tales which have come down from the ancient

38

times of that beautiful Greece. If you have not, let me know, and I will tell you more at large of others quite as delightful."

He thought this paragraph would be a test. If hers was yet only the mind of a little girl, she would tell him, unaware, through or between her answering lines. If the paragraph were for a young woman, not for the little outgrown girl, next time he might convey to her something of what Endymion said to Peona in answering the question, "Wherein lies happiness?" He would have her believe happiness is

> *in that which becks*
> *Our ready minds to fellowship divine,*
> *A fellowship with essence; till we shine,*
> *Full alchemized and free of space.*

Turning from Fanny, his thoughts concentrated on his attempt to show how the spirit of man rises to happiness, passing through the "more ponderous and bulky worth" of friendship and its steady splendor to the very top, where hangs the orbed drop of light that is love. Could Fanny, his Peona sister, understand what he had said? Melting into the radiance of love, and so becoming a part of love?

> *who, of men, can tell*
> *That flowers would bloom, or that green fruit would swell*
> *To melting pulp, that fish would have bright mail,*
> *The earth its dower of river, wood, and vale,*
> *The meadows runnels, runnels pebble-stones,*
> *The seed its harvest, or the lute its tones,*
> *Tones ravishment, or ravishment its sweet,*
> *If human souls did never kiss and greet?*

He would be at Oxford, he roused himself to tell her, until he had finished the third Book of his story, not more than three weeks longer he hoped, and then she would see

him. "How do you like Miss Taylors' *Essays in Rhyme?*"
He had sent her a copy inscribed, "John Keats to His Dear
Sister," thinking it suitable to her age and remembering her
liking "those pleasant little things the original poems," by
the same authors.

On his desk in Magdalen Hall, he told her, lay a letter
from George and Tom, in Paris. "They both send their loves
to you." And he had written George requesting him, "as you
wish I should, to write to you." After commenting on French
as inferior to our native speech, he ended: "Now Fanny you
must write soon—and write all you think about, never mind
what—only let me have a good deal of your writing— You
need not do it all at once—be two or three or four days about
it, and let it be a diary of your little life. You will preserve
all my letters and I will secure yours—and thus in the course
of time we shall each of us have a good bundle—which, hereafter, when things may have strangely altered and God knows
what happened, we may read over together and look with
pleasure on times past—that now are to come." He liked
that idea of looking forward and from the vantage of the
future looking backward.

He told Bailey about his sister, of her being for some
reason "withholden" from him, of her schooling, her
guardian.

"Will she have literary aspirations?" Bailey wondered.

"I hope not such as Elizabeth Montagu has," snorted
Keats. "I look on *her* as pre-eminent among those lacking in
feminine modesty."

"Elizabeth is probably not related to Mary Awbrey, Mrs.
Montagu—" Keats pricked up his ears. "I have Katherine
Philips' verses here"; Bailey searched out the volume by the
Matchless Orinda and placed it in his friend's hands. Keats
flashed through the volume, coming back to the lines to
Mary Awbrey. "How charming!" he exclaimed.

Bailey swelled and rose—in his own eyes. To have set Keats on to something new!

Toward the end of September, Keats wrote Reynolds of the discovery, copying the ten stanzas, which he hoped Jack had not read. On the blue-stocking tribe he delivered himself with gusto: he had a little itch toward personal talk and "a few neighborly remarks to make."

"The world, and especially our England, has, within the last thirty years been vexed and teased by a set of devils, whom I detest so much that I almost hunger after an acherontic promotion to a torturer, purposely for their accommodation. These devils are a set of women who"—he aptly recalled a snatch from *Love's Labour's Lost*—"having taken a snack or luncheon of literary scraps, set themselves up for towers of Babel in languages, Sapphos in poetry, Euclids in geometry—and everything in nothing." No, he did not admire Elizabeth Montagu.

He had now finished eight hundred lines of the third Book of "Endymion." Only Bailey had seen the part composed since he came to Oxford; he anticipated reading it to Reynolds. He handed his letter to Bailey, who "crossed" it, "There is one passage of Keats's 3rd Book which beats all he has written. It is on death (11.258-280). He wrote it last night." He had returned to that part of the poem after nearing line 800. "Is it," Keats wondered, "because Bailey is a theologue or because he has a feeling for poetry that he likes these lines?" He was rather sure Reynolds would care less for them, and—not to put his friend still in Christ's Hospital into a sad frame of mind—he amused him with nonsense rhymes in the manner of Wordsworth's "style of school exercises."

> *The Gothic looks solemn*
> *The plain Doric column*
> *Supports an old Bishop and Crosier;*

41

Forever Young

The mouldering arch,
Shaded o'er by a larch—

Now what the devil rhymed appropriately with "Crosier"?
"Lives next door to Wilson the hosier," he finished Stanza I
more or less triumphantly if untruly.

"Then there are the black trenchers or common hats,"
which might well go in as local color, also the singing of the
chantry boy and the rule of the Chancellor. In Stanza III
he must mention the trees. He wrote and lay back and
chortled:

And plenty of fat deer for parsons;
And when it is venison,
Short is the benison,—
Then each on a leg or thigh fastens.

"Parsons and fastens!" Jack would mouth at him the
abominable distortions.

Seriously, whether among the books in Bailey's neat study,
strolling under umbrageous trees, or idling on the Isis, he
felt himself a part of this seat of learning; but he was, he
hoped, too philosophic to regret he could not have spent five
years here—not with Hammond, not at Guy's and St.
Thomas's.

Around the middle of September he had been requested by
Haydon to look up a young man at Magdalen College who,
when Haydon had seen him there, was copying the altarpiece
by Ribalta. If he had ambition and the promise of power, and
if a friend or friends could assist him up to London and support him for a year, Haydon would train him without remuneration. Through the Magdalen porter Keats got his
address and asked him to call.

Charles Cripps came in, bearing a copy of "Mary Queen
of Scots," which Keats took up eagerly—one of his best-loved

42

paintings. It seemed to him that Cripps was guilty of certain faults but might become a "neat brush."

"Should you care to study with Benjamin Haydon—that is, if there were some means of support for you in London?"

"Certainly, I should like to study with Haydon, but I know of nobody to help."

"A man of great executing powers at twenty," reflected Keats, "with a look and a speech almost stupid is sure to do something." And, surely, he would take fire at Haydon's gigantic picture.

After some talk, Keats and Bailey "stummed up a sort of contrivance," whereby he might study, and Keats wrote at once to Haydon. He was done with the third Book of his "Endymion" when he wrote Haydon, September 28, and felt that his ideas were running low. He would like to write the subject thoroughly again. But he was weary of it and believed he would do better to begin a new romance, which he had in his eye for next summer. All the good from this summer's employment was the fruit of experience, which he hoped to gather in his next undertaking.

When he could no longer delay returning to London, not even the thought of a reunion with Tom and George could reconcile him wholly to leaving this reposeful scene of study and simple exercise. One thing only could have been better, and Bailey was proposing it now. "What do you say, Keats, to an excursion of a day or two at Stratford?"

"There is nothing I should like so well," and they booked top seats.

"You will enjoy Anne Hathaway's cottage, the old church, and the River Avon, also." Bailey spoke after they had marked the first autumn tints in oak and beech.

Keats was in a sort of contented, happy reverie, when they visited the house and stood in the small "low attic apartment," the walls of which were literally blackened by inscriptions of names of "numbers numberless." They scrawled theirs and went along to the church. There they were pestered by a commonplace showman of the neighborhood who refused to let them study the interior in their own fashion.

Looking at the simple statue in Shakespeare's corner, Keats felt that despite its rude execution it could not be neglected. "Do you know what, Bailey? I shouldn't wonder if it's the best likeness of the many extant—but none are very authentic —of the myriad-minded Shakespeare."

Bailey's pleasure was chiefly in his friend's enjoyment. "It is of that quiet kind," he said to himself, "which is so much a part of his gentle nature."

Immediately after returning to Oxford, Keats continued alone to London.

III. With Brothers, at Well Walk. With Shakespeare and Endymion at Burford Bridge. "The Immortal Dinner"

AT Well Walk in October, the three were again together. "For the first time in six months," remarked Tom.

"You felt a mighty preference, you temporary Parisians, for things English." John put an arm around each as they stood there in one of the little rooms at the Bentleys'. "Or so I gather from your letters."

"Meadows, people, towns, churches, books—everything, as I wrote you," admitted George. And Tom added, "We saw plays—and understood the language—"

"Why not?" challenged John. "It's not equal to the Italian."

"Cathedrals, art galleries, to say naught of lamplighters and dancing masters," Tom went on, "and the oddest washerwomen—*blanchisseuses.*"

"But your boxing? You took over a set of gloves."

They confessed there'd been too much else to do, but George declared he had kept in condition. "A man must be very fit to bear life in America," he suspected, and thought he would go soon for a bout in Chancery Lane.

"How much," challenged John quickly, cannily, "did you lose at *rouge et noir?*"

George laughed. Tom said, seriously, "Not much, but too much for people of our condition." And George apologized,

45

"We were always going to win, you know." And the questions speedily turned toward the oldest brother.

"You've finished your third Book?" George wanted to know. "May I read it now?" begged Tom.

"I'm off to see Abbey, in Pancras Lane," George set his hat at the proper tilt and dashed out for the stagecoach.

Keats picked up a parcel. "From Bailey to Mariane Reynolds. I must deliver it today and see sundry of our friends. But not before you say somewhat of my 'Endymion.' " He drew out his portfolio.

Tom glanced at the bundle. "Sits the wind in that quarter?" and his brother thought so.

He watched Tom's interest over the beginning—

> *There are who lord it o'er their fellow-men*
> *With most prevailing tinsel—*

deepen to absorption while Tom sank into the story of Glaucus, here and there reading aloud a line or passage for joy of hearing the melody and showing he got on. Keats was writing letters—too much suspense he could not bear—but often he cut an eye at the shifting pages, which at last Tom squared neatly. "Scholarship and depth, and not only sea depth," he punned mildly. "It's true poetry. An advance in many senses, John. Oxford was good for you." He disturbed the sheets for the lines beginning:

> *Old rusted anchors, helmets, breast-plates large*
> *Of gone sea-warriors; brazen beaks and targe;*

and read aloud a dozen verses following. "It brings back Virgil."

Glowing, Keats took up the portfolio, thinking to get Reynolds' opinion. At the door on his way out, he heard Tom repeating, "Death fell a weeping in his charnel-house."

At Lamb's Conduit Street, Jack was not at home; but Jane

46

and Mariane were there, much improved after the outing at Littlehampton. Mariane especially had no undue plumpness in her face but, as he would write Bailey, "comes me healthy and angular to the chin." Jemmie Rice, who had been well throughout a tour, was ill.

Keats got on top of the stage to Hampstead Heath and particularly to the Vale of Health and Hunt's cottage. Hunt was at home and Shelley was with him. The meeting was a trifle awkward for Keats. Sensitive to Shelley's kindness, "Somehow, I cannot meet him halfway." Because he knew Shelley born to the estate of gentleman? "No, O, no! I refused to visit him that I might have my own unfettered scope." So he assured himself then and Bailey afterward. "But he has charm"; he was listening, for the most part, to the others. "Though his voice is high, almost to effeminacy, and he eats almost nothing."

Shelley inquired politely about "Endymion," hoping to see it soon.

"It will not be ready, I fear, before winter." Keats thanked him and left for Haydon's house, near at hand in Lisson Grove.

Haydon greeted him effusively, as one returned from a long odyssey.

"Why is your Jerusalem not advancing?" The big canvas was not a line or color forward.

"How can it?" the artist shouted. "Hunt walks up and down the room, criticizing the heads unmercifully." Keats stared. Was Hunt annoyed that he had not been included among the figures? Here, Haydon had moved to Paddington that he might be near Hunt—*et cui fine?* A paltry state of affairs!

My world seems at outs, even in so brief a time, thought Keats. What had happened?

"Better not show your poem to Hunt," urged Haydon.

47

Keats raised eloquent brows.

"He will soon make it appear," the artist spoke feelingly, "that he has done half of it for you!"

"Ah!" but he still questioned with his eyes.

"I saw Reynolds who told me this for a fact. Hunt met him in the theater the other day. 'Hunt,' said Jack, 'Junkets is getting on to the completion of four thousand lines.' 'Ah,' replied Hunt, 'but for me they would have been seven thousand.' Now, Keats, if he said this to Reynolds what will he be saying to others?" And he added, "A lady has written me, asking me to caution you."

Disgusted with all this pettiness, Keats vowed never to know another writer except Wordsworth. For a fact, Hunt had once asked, "Why endeavor after a long poem?" Keats would answer that lovers of poetry liked a little region where they might pick and choose, a region in which images are so numerous that many are forgotten and found new in a second reading, food for a week's stroll in the summer. Also, "A long poem is the test of invention, the polar star of poetry, as fancy is the sails and imagination the rudder." Gathering strength in arguing, "Who of our great poets ever wrote short pieces? That is, in the shape of tales."

Yet, after all, who was he to argue! He had best wind up "Endymion." He hoped Apollo was not angry with him for a certain mockery at Hunt's this spring past. While drinking claret they had been inspired to the bacchanal notion of crowning themselves. He himself chose leaves from vines climbing about the cottage and Hunt searched the yard for laurel. While they wrote sonnets, Jane and Mariane Reynolds came in with their sister Charlotte. Hunt removed his homemade wreath, but Keats declared, "I will take mine off for no human being!" and, seeing the girls were mirthful over their aspects, addressed his second sonnet "To the Ladies Who Saw Me Crowned." In a "Hymn to Apollo,"

48

he had confessed himself "a blank idiot" for mocking the
god of the golden fire, the god who had perhaps not scorched
him only because he was a worm "too low crawling, for
death."

Whatever a man might do, his world would talk. He had
not listened to Hunt's attempted dissuasion; but knowing
ones might trace in his poem emendations and amputations by
the man who wrote the "Story of Rimini." Yet this was but
a day's annoyance, he reflected, finally getting off the coach
with the third Book, and he would not honor it with so many
words except to those who had at heart his welfare and good
repute. He spoke to Tom and wrote to Bailey, as one of such
friends.

Of these, Bailey appeared to him the best. "When you are
settled," he wrote, "I will come and take a peep at your
church—your house—try whether I shall have grown too
lusty for my chair—by the fireside—" He had already told
Bailey he would like to see him comfortable with a little
Peona wife, for it appeared that his friend had got a curacy.
But now the Bishop of Lincoln had somehow interfered.
That a miter, Keats exclaimed in a letter of early November,
should cover a man guilty of the most coxcombical, tyrannical, and indolent impertinence! Yet there sat the Bishop in
his palace, self-willed yawning impudence in the shape of
conscience sinking him into a smashed frog putrefying, while
Bailey lived in a continual struggle against the suffocation of
accidents. "O, for a remedy against such wrongs!" he lamented, "recourse somewhat human, independent of the
great consolations of religion!" But come . . . come. "You
have, I know, a sort of pride which would kick the devil on
the jawbone and make him drunk with the kick." He, Keats,
would take Bailey's hand that they might walk up the
mountain of common sense and look down on that parcel of
knaves and fools. "Many a mitre is moving among them."

At home with George and Tom he was happy enough or would be if Tom were looking well. The two of them might go to Lisbon. Lack of health, lack of harmony—how could he write many lines? "In this world there is no quiet—nothing but teasing and snubbing and vexation." He had been junketing around too much, found out too many things to disturb his peace.

When he read *Blackwood's Edinburgh Magazine* for October, 1817, he saw that Hunt was in for it. "The Cockney School of Poetry," in this first philippic, blazed away against him, depreciating his wife, his poetry, his habits, his company, his conversation. "I don't mind the thing so much," he wrote Bailey, "but if he—this writer who takes refuge under the snake-like sibilance of Z—should go to such lengths with me as he has done with Hunt, I must infallibly call him to account." He felt his fists clenching as they had clenched against Hammond four or five years ago. "I don't relish his abuse."

Sitting there, pen poised to go on with his letter, he reconsidered the review of his first book by Hunt in the *Examiner* for the sixth and thirteenth of July. Some of the phrases came back to him: he had "reveled in poetry for its own sake." Hunt had smoked his imitations. Why not? Had they not talked more than once of Spenser, Shakespeare, Wordsworth? But Hunt had declared him of sensitive temperament, fine ear, fancy, and imagination at will, with "an intense feeling of eternal Beauty in its most natural and least expressible simplicity." Yet he remembered just as well faults pointed out by Hunt: "the tendency to notice everything too indiscriminately, without an eye to proportion and effect"; the lack of a sense of "proper variety of versification, without a due consideration of its principles."

He had not been troubled by these adverse comments, with which he was not in agreement. Just as well if Hunt did not praise too greatly his own discovery! And the notice, he knew, had been kindly enough by comparison with that in the *Eclectic Review* for September of this 1817, which regretted that a young man of "vivid imagination and fine talents should have fallen into so bad hands and to have been flattered into the resolution to publish verses he would gladly forget." And when this October, *Constable's Scots and Edinburgh Magazine* saw in Keats what he himself liked to believe he was—a disciple of Spenser—but warned him against Hazlitt and Hunt and their ideas—when he read this review he objected less than ever that Hunt had not warmly championed his first volume. This critic said if he took his way alone, he might succeed.

"He's right," said Keats. "And I will take my way alone."

"Endymion" was still an incubus on his shoulders. In late November he was still writing on the fourth Book, still teased by the affairs of young Cripps—for whom no plans had yet been perfected for study with Haydon—and more than anything else he was worried over Tom. Sawrey, the specialist, declared the boy must go to Devonshire, and speedily. George would go with him; John would take George's place with the invalid later on. They journeyed to Teignmouth; Keats to Burford Bridge Inn, at Dorking.

He walked up Box Hill, saw the moon, came back to his room and wrote "some lines," before taking up Shakespeare's *Sonnets*. They would cheer him in a measure for the loss of George and Tom, for the unease over dissensions among friends. Never before had he found in the *Sonnets* such beauties—"fine things said unintentionally."

"Is this to be borne?" he challenged Reynolds. "Hark ye!

When lofty trees I see barren of leaves
Which erst from heat did canopy the herd,
And summer's green all girded up in sheaves,
Borne on the bier with white and bristly beard—"

51

Shakespeare had left nothing to say about nothing or anything: "For look at snails, you know what he says about
snails, you know where he talks about 'cockled snails'—well,
in one of these sonnets he says—the chap slips into—no! I
lie! this is in the 'Venus and Adonis'; the simile brought it
to my mind. Audi—

> *As the snail, whose tender horns being hit,*
> *Shrinks back into his shelly cave with pain,*
> *And there all smothered up in shade doth sit,*
> *Long after fearing to put forth again:*
> *So at his bloody view her eyes are fled,*
> *Into the deep dark caverns of her head."*

And as he read Shakespeare, he found the motto for "Endymion": "The stretched metre of an antique song." Other
fine phrases he quoted for Reynolds: "Time's antique pen,"
"April's first born flowers," and "death's eternal cold."

Jack should learn to look unconcerned at his heart's vex-
ations. "They never surprise me—Lord! a man should have
the fine point of his soul taken off to become fit for this
world." He, himself, he was amused to think, had never been
hard hit.

Impishly, he rounded out his letter with a series of phrases
he'd wager would put the fellow's mouth agape: " 'I suppose
you do not lack—send me a few—lend me thy hand to laugh
a little.' " Would Caius spot that from *Henry IV?* " 'Send
me a little pullet sperm' "; *that* he might remember from
the *Merry Wives of Windsor,* but never " 'a few finch
eggs' " from *Troilus and Cressida.*

After more nonsense he sent remembrances to each of the
card-playing club. "I'd like," he told himself, "nothing
better right now than a good game of loo."

More hard feelings among friends! Haydon, it appeared
from Bailey, had hurt the young theologian by a communica-

52

tion over the Cripps business. Bailey was much cut up. "What occasions the greater part of the world's quarrels?" Keats now addressed himself to Bailey. "Simply this, two minds meet and do not understand each other time enough to prevent any shock or surprise at the conduct of either party—as soon as I had known Haydon three days I had got enough of his character not to have been surprised at such a letter as he has hurt you with." What would Bailey think of Keats in connection with Haydon, this statement accepted? Again, he explained: he himself did not feel it a principle to drop acquaintance with Haydon—though with Bailey it would have been an imperious feeling. He hoped Bailey would not think of it. Meantime, Keats would write to Cripps and request that young man to tell of his goings on from time to time.

For full justice to a subject touching this particular, he needed five years and three volumes octavo, but he could say one thing that had pressed upon him lately and increased his own humility. "Men of genius are great as certain ethereal chemicals operating on the mass of neutral intellect —but they have not any individuality, and determined character." He was excusing neither himself nor Haydon. He had said something like this before and would say so hereafter. "I am certain of nothing but the holiness of the heart's affections and the truth of the imagination. What the imagination seizes as beauty must be truth—whether it existed before or not—for I have the same idea of all our passions as of love; they are all in their sublime, creative of essential beauty. . . . The imagination may be compared to Adam's dream—he woke and found it truth."

He sat back, lifting the wings of his own imagination. What may one not make of that idea? "He awoke and found it truth." Let be, let be. He must copy "Endymion," "and write five hundred more lines."

Returning to Bailey, he spoke of another favorite speculation: "We shall enjoy ourselves hereafter by having what we called happiness on earth repeated in a finer tone and so repeated." But he reflected lightly, "La, la! Bailey will like this—coming from me!"

So Jane and Mariane had told Bailey that John Keats had sacrificed his health for the sake of Tom's? "I do not think my brother's illness connected with mine," he replied to that. Anyway, he and Bailey had discussed their ailments at Oxford. "You know more of the real cause than they do nor have I any chance of being rack'd as you have been." Bailey knew Keats had needed mercury and he had taken it and reported sometime back that it had improved his health.

He reverted to happiness, upon which he had never counted. "I look not for it if it be not in the present hour—nothing startles me beyond the moment. The setting sun will always set me to rights—or if a sparrow come before my window, I take part in its existence and pick about the gravel."

Would this existence be repeated in a finer tone, and so happiness? "No traveller returns," he quoted softly. At Reynolds' the other evening they had talked about ghosts. He had listened, alert for their opinions and stories, but lacking the sort of belief that would enable him to contribute so much as one episode of a revenant's behavior.

2

Alone here at Burford Bridge, for all the moonlight on Box Hill, he grew distrait. Not sorry when Reynolds, who had been reviewing for the *Champion* asked him to come to town for the reappearance of Edmund Kean, he shot back. To comment upon his most admired Thespian, that was something worth doing. And *Richard the Third!*

On the fifteenth of December he sat in his stall at Drury Lane, waiting for the return of the tragedian. "In *Richard* he is his sword's dear cousin," he measured and compared, "in *Hamlet* his footing is germane to the platform. In *Macbeth* his eye laughs siege to scorn; in *Othello* he is welcome to Cyprus. In *Timon* he is of the palace—of Athens—of the woods. . . ." He left the theater in a dream, a particular dream gradually emerging from the general spell—a dream of seeing the actor in a drama of heroic cast by John Keats.

Thursday the eighteenth he went again, when Kean acted Luke, in *Riches*, a poor version of Massinger's *City Madam*. John watched trait succeeding trait: hypocritical self-possession, caution, pride, cruelty, avarice—but the excellence "which at this moment weighs upon us is the elegance, gracefulness, and music of elocution. . . . There is an indescribable *gusto* in his voice, by which we feel that the utterer is thinking of the past and future while speaking of the instant. When he says, in *Othello*, 'Put up your bright swords, for the dew will rust them,' we feel that his throat had commanded where swords were thick as reeds. . . ."

He left the playhouse to walk and talk with Charles Wells, later to write for Sunday's *Champion*. The two plays were so vastly different, he saw no way of unifying them in one brief comment. He must keep to space limitation but must say a word in general of Kean's acting. "His two characters of the week comprising the utmost of quiet and turbulence, I will use as an invitation to do so."

No sooner had he read, Monday, his comment in the *Champion* for the twenty-first than he was setting out again for the theater. He was on tiptoe, ready to see the first performance of *Richard Duke of York*. Just what would this drama be? Soon after he and his friend were seated he saw, looking over the program, that *King Henry VI*, Parts I, II, and III, had been butchered to make an English holiday and a character for Kean's interpretation.

Opening with the Temple Garden scene, the play progressed through lines recognizably not Shakespeare's, other lines badly altered, and speeches transferred from one character to another. Keats found himself curious. Who had done this snipping up and changing? Accepting it, however, as a compilation, he remarked in the intermission, "The men are too hastily introduced and despatched, and their language clipped too closely."

"Make that point," suggested Wells; "it's a fact."

"And where is Talbot?" Seeing nothing of that man, he remarked, was like "walking among the Elgin marbles and seeing an empty place where the Theseus had reclined." Yes, he would use that comparison.

The curtain rose and the drama went on. Now he felt the too-great modernizing of the poetry, the progressing by fits and starts and the inlay of facts—facts, not facets—of different color: "We can see the cracks which the joiner's hand could not help leaving." Still, he discovered ingenuity in the chopping-up, eking-out and cementing-together. And while Kean with naturalness held the focus from the string of gas lamps along the apron front, Keats saw "The workings of Richard's mind are brought out, as it were, by the hand of the anatomist, and all the useless parts are cut away and laid aside." Undoubtedly, Kean had had a hand in the compiling of *Richard Duke of York*, if indeed he had not done all the work. What a part he had constructed for his limelight supremacy!

He and Wells walked out through the surging throng, that was vocal with praise of Kean, on past the line of carriages. The coachmen cleverly restrained the horses as group after group ascended and the footmen slammed doors, driving off while the next liveried turnout moved forward. "A great night!" they heard somebody say.

Before setting down his review on paper, his literary conscience directed him to read all of *Henry VI*. What more logical than after reading he thought of Shakespeare rather than of Kean? He believed the man of Avon intended to write a complete dramatic chronicle history of England, the three parts of *Henry VI* falling between the two *Richards*. All three parts were vigorous but Shakespeare's hand was tied by necessary adherence to facts. This restriction to the high road did not permit Shakespeare to turn down leafy and winding lanes, or to break wildly and at once into the breathing fields. So he must say in his review. He said also, "The poetry is for the most part ironed and manacled with a chain of facts, and cannot get free; it cannot escape from the prison house of history, nor often moved without our being disturbed with the clanking of its fetters. Poetry must be free! It is of the air, not of the earth; and the higher it soars, the nearer it gets to its home."

Only then he reverted to the acting. "Kean stands like a tower." He smiled at remembering the concentration of lamp-beams on that tower. "He is 'all power, passion, self-will.'" If he were to single out a favorite part, he would choose that in which Richard parts with his son, young Rutland, just before the battle. "It was pathetic to oppression," he wrote. "Our hearts swelled with the feeling of tears, which is a deeper feeling than the starting of them in the eye." And "his death was very great." But, he added, Kean always "dies as erring men do die. . . . It is an extinguishment, not a decay. . . . The very eyelid dies. The acting of Kean is Shakespearian—he will understand full what we mean." He ended on Shakespeare, "the only lonely and perfectly happy creature God ever formed. He could never have a mate—being most unmatchable."

To George and Tom, meanwhile, he had sent a copy of the *Champion* for the twenty-first, and a recent *Examiner*. Two or three weeks they had been down there in Teignmouth, with perhaps little news from London. They would be amused by the trial of William Hone, publisher, on the eighteenth, nineteenth, and twentieth of December, for having published "impious, profane, and scandalous libels." Hone's "Not Guilty," he wrote them, "is a thing which not to have been would have dulled still more Liberty's emblazoning."

Besides theater-going, he had also been, with Charles Wells, to see Benjamin West's "Death on the Pale Horse." Wonderful, he thought, considering the artist's age, "but there is nothing to be intense upon; no women one feels mad to kiss, no face swelling into reality."

"I've been going out too much," he told himself before telling his brothers. He had dined pleasantly with Haydon, on another day with Horace Smith and Horace's brothers, also the book collector Thomas Hill; Edward DuBois, editor and man of letters. And a stamp commissioner, one John Kingston.

He had taken no very active part in the conversation. Recalling that evening, he saw these men in their true light as wits—not Kingston, to be sure—and was convinced of the great superiority of humor over wit. They were all alike, their manners alike; they all knew the fashionable world; they were mannered in eating and drinking, "in their mere handling a decanter." They had talked of Kean and his low company. " 'Would I were with that company instead of yours.' said I to myself." Such acquaintance would never do for him, yet he had promised to go to Reynolds' on Wednesday, Christmas Eve.

On Boxing Night, December 26, he walked with Brown and Dilke, his Wentworth Place friends, to the Christmas pantomime, *Don Giovanni*, and wrote a sort of criticism of it for the *Champion* of January 4. Talking with Dilke on qualities that form a man of achievement, he had thought of one that Shakespeare "possessed so enormously," Negative Capability—"that is, the capability of being in uncertainties, mysteries, doubts, without any irritable reaching after fact and reason."

He was disturbed that Shelley's *Laon and Cythna*, just out, was being objected to. Now it was being converted into the *Revolt of Islam* and would be published around the middle of January.

On the last day of 1817, Keats met Wordsworth walking on Hampstead Heath.

3

Three days before, on the twenty-eighth, he walked into Haydon's painting room where a number of men had already gathered. "Christ's Entry into Jerusalem" towered as background for Lamb, Wordsworth, Landseer, Thomas Monkhouse and, notably, the stamp commissioner, Kingston.

The Lake Poet was amiable, Keats saw; and Lamb, full of spirits of another kind even before the advance of dinner, sparkled half-clownishly, half-maliciously. They talked, gloriously talked, on Homer, Shakespeare, Milton, and Virgil, and turning to Keats somebody politely mentioned his article of that day on Kean as Richard Duke of York.

While Keats replied, Haydon turned to another of the company, "See that eager, inspired look, his light-brown hair flowing over his ears, his fine hands clasping that volume—"

Lamb got merrier and wittier, "and his fun in the midst of Wordsworth's solemn intonations of oratory was like the sarcasm and wit of the fool in the intervals of Lear's passion." Lamb's merriment approached a climax: he made a

speech in which he suddenly said, "I vote Haydon absent!
Let's drink his health!" He attacked Wordsworth, rascally
old Lake Poet, for calling Voltaire dull. They had been
appraising the heads on the giant canvas, and Wordsworth
was much pleased with his. "There is a state of mind when
the French writer is dull," someone countered. But Lamb
held to his admiration and said nothing about the likeness of
the man from Rydal Mount. "Here's Voltaire—the Messiah
of the French nation and a very proper one, too."

Keats, near the bookshelves which he was exploring, heard
Lamb bawl out, "Why did you include the head of Sir Isaac
Newton?" And without waiting for explanation, continued,
"He was a fellow who believed nothing unless it was as clear
as the three sides of a triangle." Then turning around and
discovering Keats among the books, he seized upon the review of the twenty-first. "You said, yes, you said, 'The goblin
is driven from the hearth, and the rainbow is robbed of its
mystery.' Who robbed us of that mystery? Old Newton, by
reducing the arch to nothing more than an array of prismatic
colors." This or something like it, he said, and Keats thought
it wise to agree. For he was thinking, "Lamb is on the down-
hill side of tipsydom." In the end they all drank Newton's
health and confusion to mathematics. Even Wordsworth,
who could not but see he was foremost of the contemporary
and other comparatively late figures in the painting, good-
humoredly and laughingly gave himself up to the evening.

When other friends came in with young Ritchie, Haydon
introduced him as a "gentleman going to Africa." Keats
looked up with interest: George and Tom had met him in
Paris. Lamb, who had seemed sunk in his cups, suddenly
roared out, "Who is the gentleman we are going to lose?"
Everybody drank the victim's health, in which the 'victim'
himself joined. Keats was grateful when Ritchie turned to
him and inquired, "How and where is your brother Tom?"

60

Keats explained, adding, "I hope soon to see him." One would remember Tom, he felt proudly.

Though a stranger to Haydon, Kingston had appeared earlier in the day and begged the privilege of an introduction to Wordsworth. "Seeing him a gentleman, I instantly asked him to come to our party," he was accounting for the entrance to those not so near the group including the commissioner. Unfortunately, he neglected to mention either name or occupation of Commissioner Kingston.

After a few moments while the younger men were momentarily quieted by this alien presence, Keats—who had met Kingston and was not wholly unobservant of proceedings —saw the commissioner look up, look down, and heard him ask Wordsworth, "Don't you think, sir, Milton was a great genius?" Keats looked at Haydon; Wordsworth looked at the commissioner. Lamb, presumably asleep by the fire, woke up. "Pray, sir, did you say Milton was a great genius?"

"No, sir," Keats heard Kingston reply. "I asked Mr. Wordsworth if he were not."

And to Keats's incredulous ears, Lamb commented, "Oh, then you are a silly fellow."

"Charles, my dear Charles," Wordsworth reproved. . . . But Lamb had returned to his dozing, seemingly unaware of any confusion he had created.

The commissioner broke the awful pause. "Don't you think Newton a great genius?"

Haydon could stand it no longer. Keats, still by the bookcase, put his head into the volumes. Ritchie chortled. Wordsworth, dumfounded, appeared to be asking himself, "Who is this man?"

At this moment, Lamb got up and, taking down a candle, approached Kingston. "Sir, will you allow me to look at your phrenological development?" He then turned his back on

Kingston and at every question the poor fellow ventured, he chanted:

> *"Diddle, diddle, dumpling, my son John*
> *Went to bed with his breeches on."*

By this time the commissioner had deduced that Wordsworth did not know who he was, and remarked, "I have had the honor of some correspondence with you, Mr. Wordsworth."

"With me, sir?" exclaimed the great man. "Not that I remember."

"Don't you, sir? I am a Comptroller of Stamps."

In the dead silence that ensued, the commissioner evidently saw he had said enough. He had, quite enough for a poet who was seeking a local comptrollership.

Before Wordsworth could reply, Lamb sang out:

> *"Hey diddle diddle*
> *The cat and the fiddle."*

And again Wordsworth rebuked softly, "My dear Charles."

Once more Lamb chanted: " 'Diddle diddle dumpling, my son John,' " and, rising, begged, "Do let me have another look at that gentleman's organs."

Keats and Haydon managed to coax him into another room and to shut the door, behind which they gave way to inextinguishable laughter.

Lamb eyed them fatuously, "I wanted to show you wh-a-at-sort-fellow he waas," Keats heard him saying, "with my candle."

Monkhouse came in and tried to persuade Lamb to go home. Haydon and Keats rejoined the larger party but the commissioner or comptroller was hornet-mad. They soothed and smiled and apologized and asked him to stay for supper.

He remained, in somewhat ruffled dignity, but held no animosity and the company parted in good humor. At supper Keats thought, I am astonishing him with a pertinacity in favor of drinking, and kept his glasses knowingly at work.

Throughout the meal, Lamb continued to struggle and to call out now and then, "Who is that fellow? Allow me to see his organs once more."

"It was a night worthy of the Elizabethan Age," declared Haydon afterward, "and yet not a word passed that an apostle might not have listened to."

Before they separated, Keats asked Ritchie, "Will you carry a copy of my *Endymion* to the desert of Sahara and fling it in the midst?"

"Most certainly," smiled Ritchie, and Keats sent him one of the first copies.

Wordsworth had not hurt himself with the commissioner. He had constantly chided Lamb, and of that fact Kingston was as mindful as Keats.

"Will you not dine with me, sir?" he asked Wordsworth, and included the man who had seemed somewhat less boisterous than most of the party.

Before the day arrived, Keats said to himself, "I don't like that place," and sent his excuse.

Instead, he would call on the Lake Poet in Mortimer Street, Saturday, January third.

IV. Well Walk; Endymion

BEFORE that day, however, he went with grudging permission from Richard Abbey to call on Fanny at Walthamstow. There they sat, a girl of fourteen, whose character was yet unformed, a pretty child in her simple dress ending in a ruffle; Abbey, stuffy in white cotton stockings and knee breeches; Mrs. Abbey, matronly, entirely under her husband's thumb. Or so Keats thought, Keats—his linen stock fresh, sleeves white under half-closed brown coat cuffs.

From some bright remark of Fanny's he had just said to himself, "She will be quick!" when he heard Mrs. Abbey attacking his family. "The Keatses are indolent—they were born so, and it will ever be in them."

She turned to her husband and Fanny whispered, "If it is born with us, how can we help it?" Keats raised his brows. With a glance at her guardians, she pleaded, "I so much want a medal of the Princess Charlotte."

"Loyal Fanny," smiled her brother. "Are you," he asked in a lowered tone, "keeping your diary?" But he saw the Abbeys exchange glances, and talked of something else.

Abbey sat on, glum, rarely speaking but at length awkwardly contriving to let John know he had no business there. Keats went away but managed to see Fanny twice in the holidays.

On Saturday, the third of January, he called on Wordsworth, and waited some time before a door opened to admit the Lake Poet, in full dress, from stiff high collar to knee breeches and silk stockings.

64

"I am in a Great Hurry, Mr. Keats," the man from Cumberland received the younger man's bow. "I am About to Dine," and Keats disliked his self-importance—"with a Commissioner of Stamps."

Against rising anger, Keats remarked, "I would not delay you one instant, sir," and was leaving when Mrs. Wordsworth and Dorothy entered. They sat down and Wordsworth, excusing himself, asked somewhat more cordially, "Will you be so good as to dine with us the day after tomorrow?" Keats murmured that he would be happy. . . .

On that evening he found the poet warmly human. "We shall have your poems bound," he said. Mrs. Wordsworth added that cloth from one of her gowns—probably a blue-gray silk—would provide the binding. When Keats looked his astonishment, she smilingly assured him it was the custom in their household so to use her discarded dresses. After dinner, Keats rushed to Severn's home where, elatedly, he described the party.

Sunday, the fourth, meantime, appeared the *Champion* that contained his final reviews: the first on *Retribution, or the Chieftain's Daughter;* the other on the pantomime, *Don Giovanni.* Reading his comment on the drama, he confessed he had been able to rouse in himself none of the enthusiasm he had felt for Kean in *Richard.* Convinced of his dislike for this sort of hack-work, aware that as theatrical critic he could be at his best only when the best—Shakespeare—was interpreted by best actors, he determined to do no more such criticism.

As he sat there at his desk, he heard Charles Wells and Joseph Severn below, merrily gusting in for dinner.

He brought out a bottle of claret and one of port, sufficient to set them off boisterously on a "concert," himself imitating the bassoon. From four o'clock to ten they kept steadily at this fun-making, in which they pretended to be the several musical instruments chosen.

In a lull of the "music," Wells poured out claret and offered "To your brothers!" Bottoms gleamed in the candle-light.

"To Peter Pindar!" proposed Severn.

"What—why—old Wolcot? Never mind—to Peter Pindar!" and so on to draining the last glasses and voices hoarse from "performing." Severn was in fine feather, over an order from the Emperor of Russia for some drawings.

While they were talking about Henry Stephens and the odoriferous first gallery at the playhouse, Keats remarked with a twinkle in his voice, which his guests saw in his eyes, "I wonder careful folks would go there."

"Why?" demanded Wells, foreseeing something good. Severn looked interrogation.

"Although it's but a shilling, still you have to pay through the nose!"

"Bravo, Junkets! Best thing you were ever guilty of," and they regretted the last of the wine.

Next morning he wrote to his brothers about this party, also of his "initiation," through Jemmie Rice, into a "set" or little band of young men. "They call drinking deep 'dying scarlet,' and when you breathe in your watering, they bid you cry hem and play it off—they call good wine 'a pretty tipple,' and call getting a child knocking out an apple; stopping at a tavern they call 'hanging out.' " "Where do you sup?" he illustrated, is "Where do you hang out?"

That very morning, Monday, he had called at Sawrey's place in Bedford Row, High Holborn. "I have come to consult you about Tom," he had said, and when Sawrey asked for latest symptoms, "He spits blood; he has palpitations." He thought the doctor not at all "put out," and he himself was relieved, believing Tom in a favorable place there on "the Edge" in Teignmouth, enjoying fine effects of salt air.

The boys would be interested to know he would dine with Wordsworth that evening, had dined with Haslam, was getting to be good friends with Charles Dilke, and that Charles Brown was still absent. He himself had been to a dance at Redhall's, where he drank deep and won 10.6 at cutting for half-guineas. Recalling that evening, he saw and heard again what he summarized to his brothers.

The ladies had retired from the supper table. Young Squibs offered a toast to "Mater Omnium."

"I understand nothing but plain English," lisped Redhall, little innocent man, with a powdered, upright head. And Keats, recollecting also the eight dozens ranged on the kitchen stairs, thought he understood too little about the quantity of wine a few men could consume.

"Say the word out plain, then," urged Rice.

Squibs said it, whereupon an inquiry followed about its derivation. Two parsons and grammarians were settling the question in true parson-scholarly style when Squibs, interrupting, remarked: "I always understood it to be a root and not a derivative!" More jests had followed on other elemental and bawdy subjects. Oddly enough, Bailey enjoyed the evening.

Ever since he had left his brothers Keats had been finishing and copying "Endymion." When Wells told him Tom was licking his chops in expectation of reading a first copy, he felt a qualm at so much racketing and junketing about. He had not kept his good resolutions and, for a fact, gallivanting and carousing had done nothing to make him feel over-well. Conscience-smitten, he wrote Taylor he would be at 91 New Bond Street in four days, with the first Book, written out fair and revised for the press, but he did not finish for ten days and got so much of his copy in only around January 20.

Young Cripps was yet on his mind. Haydon thought the artist's work improving and Cripps himself wished to be bound to Haydon. But a hundred and fifty to two hundred pounds would be needed in subscriptions. Keats prepared a copy of subscribers' names including everybody he thought might get him five pounds. He ended his letter to Haydon: "There are three things to rejoice at in this age—The Excursion, your pictures, and Hazlitt's depth of taste."

Unable to break off his gadding, he went Monday, January 12, with Wells to see *John Bull* but, escaping from "the dirty hole" of the theater, borrowed Brown's life-ticket to Drury Lane, for another performance of *Richard III*. Later, they returned to the first playhouse. *John Bull* was over, and *Bombastes Furioso* and a Review were scheduled. "Like to go behind the scenes?" asked Wells.

"Can you manage it?" Keats had not been hitherto in this Green Room. It was under the stage and there they were threatened over and over to be turned out by the oily scene-shifters. Gallant bucks, pressed against the wall, were rapping their boots with thorn sticks.

Wells engaged in conversation "a little painted trollop" who had played Mary. "I failed in that part," said she, and illogically—she was dressed as a Quaker for the Review— "I'm damned if I play a serious part again as long as I live."

Keats and Wells returned to their seats for the Review and heard one fellow begin a song. "But an unlucky finger point from the gallery sent him off like a shot." Another was dressed to kill, for the king in *Bombastes,* but the thing was not played. There was nothing left but to observe the antics of the orchestra who, after playing the overture three times, went into a country dance and then into "boonsome pot-house."

2

"That sort of probity which such men as Bailey possess does hold and grasp the tip-top of any spiritual honors that can be paid to anything in this world." So Keats wrote his brothers, January 13, adding that he wrote with a grateful heart, "in that I had not a brother who did not feel and credit me for a deeper feeling and devotion for his uprightness than for any marks of genius however splendid."

Friendships around him were strained to breaking. Reynolds, who had been invited to Haydon's dinner on December 28, had not gone, nor had he sent explanation of his absence. Haydon, always supersensitive, wrote a sharp letter, followed by one in "palliation." Reynolds felt the second aggravated the first, and answered Haydon cuttingly, "exposing to himself all his own weaknesses," said Keats, "and going on to an excess which, whether it is just or no, is what I would fain have unsaid; the fact is they are both in the right and both in the wrong."

"Why are the Hunts 'at outs' with Haydon?" George and Tom wanted to know.

Mrs. Hunt, John wrote them, had the habit of borrowing from her near neighbors, the Haydons. The last time she had asked the loan of silver, Haydon requested, "Please let us have it back by—" naming a day, "if possible." She had promised. When she failed to return it, Haydon sent for and got it. But Hunt then marched over to Haydon's home and remarked, "I am sorry you have treated my wife so indelicately about the silver." One word led to another and shortly they had parted forever!

"All I hope," Keats concluded his version of the serio-comic affair, "is at some time to bring them all together again."

Perplexed by continued animosity between the men, he was moved to write Bailey: "Men should bear with each other. There lives not the man who may not be cut up, aye, hashed to pieces on his weakest side. The best of men have but a portion of good in them—a kind of spiritual yeast in their frames which creates the ferment of existence—by which a man is propelled to act and strive and buffet with circumstance. The sure way, Bailey, is first to know a man's faults, and then be passive—if after that he insensibly draws you towards him then you have no power to break the link." He did not forget to tell his Magdalen friend that Cripps was improving "very fast."

He had been, he said, in a state of chaos, and reported his involvement in the many events about him; but, belatedly, he had been "squat at Hampstead," copying "Endymion."

And now that the make-up of the book was being considered, Taylor asked, "What about a drawing for the frontispiece? We might publish in quarto if Haydon would make one from some event in your poem."

Pleased with the idea, Keats left his copy and hurried on to Haydon, whom he found at work.

Haydon was flattered, though, his heart only in the heroic, Keats knew he would not have considered such work except for a friend.

"What would you like yourself, dear chap?"

"My next poem in all likelihood will be 'Hyperion' "; he was struck by the notion that Haydon would like that epic flight better. "There the artist will have a greater choice."

"You mean—" Haydon caught the idea.

"The nature of 'Hyperion' will enable me to treat it in a more naked and Grecian manner. The hero of 'Endymion,' being mortal, is led on—like Buonaparte—by circumstance. Apollo, in 'Hyperion,' being a foreseeing god, will shape his actions like one."

70

Haydon, mixing colors thoughtfully on his palette, then asked, "How about an engraving of your head, which I would do with all my might. Would that answer Taylor's idea? It would be, I think, effectual; and I have not done it for any other human being."

Keats would think about it. Haydon had already made a life mask. Perhaps that might serve now or later.

On the twenty-third, he wrote, "Your proposal pleases me, and, believe me, I would not have my head in the shop-windows from any hand but yours—no, by Apelles!" He wasn't punning.

While they exchanged letters on the frontispiece Keats, though still revising and copying, was hearing Hazlitt at the Surrey Institute. The first day was that on which he delivered the first Book to Taylor and Hessey; he arrived at the hall too late for the lecture but not too late to be pounced upon joyfully by certain of his "set": Charles Wells, John Hunt and son, Bewick, John Landseer with his sons Thomas, Charles, and Edwin, and Hazlitt himself. Overjoyed at his reception, he forgot to be cautious and walked over one evening, with Book I, to visit Leigh Hunt; after all, Hunt was the best critic he knew. On leaving he drew the sheets from his pocket and, somewhat diffidently, offered them. "Will you tell me if it has any merit?"

Hunt accepted the script and, laying it aside, picked up a small packet. "Should you like to see a well-authenticated lock of Milton's hair?"

Keats glowed, as he fingered gently the reddish curl, and when he heard Hunt suggesting, "Why not some verses on the subject?" he sat down and began at once:

Chief of organic numbers!

But the ode did not go so well. "I will do better," he said—

71

Forever Young

*"When every childish fashion
Has vanished from my rhyme."*

He left Hunt deep in "Endymion" and walked home, aware a little change was taking place in his intellect. Once he had been addicted to passiveness; now he could not bear to be uninterested or unemployed. His only worry was Tom, still spitting blood.

At his table, sitting down to read *King Lear* once again, he felt the need for the prologue of a sonnet. Into the final four lines he poured the essence of this intellectual change:

> *When I am through the old oak-forest gone,*
> *Let me not wander in a barren dream,*
> *But when I am consumed with the fire,*
> *Give me new phoenix-wings to fly at my desire.*

Perhaps the fact that he was dropping one book from his brain but freed him for another burden. So be it.

On calling again to see Hunt, he was somewhat dashed. "He's in a hypercritical mood," he told himself, when Hunt declared Endymion unnatural "and the conversation much too high-flown for brother and sister."

"But," protested Keats, "they are overshadowed by a supernatural power. They could not possibly speak like your Francesca in your 'Rimini.' And what about Caliban's poetry?"

"Why, Junkets," Hunt countered by veering, "did you not show me your poetry sooner?"

Keats said nothing, but smiled and took back his first Book. "You are already disposed to dissect and anatomize any trip or slip I may have made," he thought, after he closed Hunt's door behind him. "I could have written nothing with your special brand of criticism curbing whatever genius I may pos-

72

sess." Having the critic read after the event was another matter.

"The fact is he and Shelley are hurt," he wrote George and Tom, "at my not showing them the affair officiously. . . . But who's afraid? Ay, Tom! Demme if I am."

Yet he missed dropping in at Hunt's, as in other days. He liked not loneliness! He would never be a poet if he must be alone. He was probably different, he suspected, from all other poets in that he preferred writing with a friend, or even friends, about him. He acquired the habit of taking his paper to Dilke's and copying there.

When proofs began to come in and he saw in cold, impersonal print some of his lines, a strong critical sense asserted itself. "These lines, as they now stand, about Happiness," he wrote Taylor, "have rung in my ears like a 'chime a mending.'" Certain verses appeared to him "the very contrary of blessed," and he offered as substitute a certain passage beginning with line 777, hoping it would be "more eligible." He wondered how he could have seemed to rely on what Taylor must have thought mere words, "but I assure you that when I wrote it, it was a regular stepping of the imagination towards a truth." The new lines were necessary; they were his first step toward the chief attempt in the drama—"the playing of different natures with joy and sorrow."

This critical spirit he indulged even more strongly when Reynolds sent him two sonnets on Robin Hood. "His first sonnet is the better on account of the first line," and he read aloud:

"The trees in Sherwood Forest are old and good";

also for the fifth line:

"No arrow found—foil'd of its antler'd food."

73

Oh, but the second sonnet! The eighth line ran:

His greenwood beauty sits, tender and true.

"Tender and true!" What a quicksand. . . . He wrote firmly, "We must cut this and not be rattlesnaked into any more of the like."

He was, further, penetrating Wordsworth's weakness. "For the sake of a few fine imaginative or domestic passages, are we to be bullied into a certain philosophy engendered in the whims of an egotist?" Poetry should be great and unobtrusive. . . . He would have no more of Wordsworth or Hunt in particular. Why should we be teased "with Wordsworth's 'Matthew with a bough of wilding in his hand,' when we can have Jaques 'under an oak'?" Though not denying Wordsworth's grandeur and Hunt's merit, he would have grandeur uncontaminated and unobtrusive. "Let us have the old poets and Robin Hood." In return for "the dish of filberts," he enclosed a "few catkins," to J.H.R. "In answer to his Robin Hood Sonnets." The merry lines on Robin Hood, Maid Marian, and the Mermaid Tavern fell lightly from his quill. He had dropped the weight of revising Book II, which he hoped to bring tomorrow, Wednesday, the fourth of February, for Jack to read. Meantime, he was copying, on the hill.

Three days earlier he had written Reynolds, enclosing:

O blush not so, O blush not so—

intending to follow it with prose. But the sun was shining, and he was incited by Milton's "Hence, vain deluding joys," to begin:

Hence, burgundy, claret and port—

and to beg Caius's forgiveness for ranting. In that letter he enclosed as well "a serious sonnet":

74

Well Walk; Endymion

When I have fears that I may cease to be—

wondering whether it was worthy to rank with Shakespeare's or whether too obvious an imitation.

When he called at the Reynolds home, according to his hope, he saw Reynolds receive a letter from the artist. It would be, he thought, but decent to say a word for Reynolds to Haydon. He wrote, after going back to Well Walk, "Reynolds is very unwell—he has all kinds of very distressing symptoms, and I am on this account rather glad that he has not spare time for one of our right sort meetings—he would go too far for his health." After this good deed—what he hoped was a good deed—he must write Taylor he could not get around today with his second Book. He needed a day to look it over. He had been diligent in the Cripps affair and, though he did not so inform his publisher, he was going to Covent Garden that night, February 5, for the opening of Milman's *Fazio*.

But before he returned to Well Walk, that Wednesday, the fourth, he had gone with Reynolds to the Novellos, "the land of Harpsicols." There, he and Shelley and Hunt had written sonnets on the Nile. His own, revised and dated the sixth, he began:

> *Son of the old moon-mountains African!*
> *Stream of the Pyramid and Crocodile!*

Shelley's, he was well aware, was superior. The poet called it "Ozymandias," and it set out with promise of a story—clever that!

> *"I met a traveller from an antique land,"*

he quoted. . . . Why, even Hunt's sonnet was better than his own! Did Shelley somehow cramp his fingers? His mind still lingering on the Nile neighborhood, he signed the letter to Haydon, "Yours like a Pyramid."

75

Ahead of his printer, he played around again. Thomas Richards told him, "Your poems are known in the West Country and are being imitated. I saw a clever copy of verses with a motto from your Sonnet to George."

"La! La! I am imitated?" He spoke mockingly but oh, he was pleased!

Richards told others, or else the imminent appearance of *Endymion* was reason for invitations. "I am in the highway of being introduced to a squad of people," he wrote to Teignmouth, "Peter Pindar, Mrs. Opie, Mrs. Scott. Mr. Robinson, a great friend of Coleridge's called on me." Honors were rushing thickly upon him. "What think you? Am I to be crowned in the Capitol, am I to be made a Mandarin?" Oh, no! He was to be invited to a party at Ollier's to keep Shakespeare's birthday. "Shakespeare would stare to see me there."

February 11, he heard Hazlitt on Thomson, Cowper, and Crabbe, praising the first two, but giving Crabbe "an unmerciful licking." Along with these details, he copied some lines from Horace Smith's manuscript exposing the Methodists. He would refuse, however, to dine with Smith, on the plea of going to Devon, and having much work to do before setting out.

Yet he delayed leaving town. He went to the British Gallery, where Wilkie's "Bathsheba" had been condemned, where he thought Stark's "Penning the Flock" and "Lambeth, Looking toward Westminster Bridge" were "nice"; but he could not bear the American Washington Allston's "Uriel." He visited Reynolds, in a hot and parched room, among the tongues of women, from which the sick man needed to get away. I wish he would move to my friend Butler's for at least a short time, Keats thought, recalling the boy who had entered as surgeon's pupil at Guy's one day before himself. Also, he saw much of Dilke and Brown, so

76

near his rooms in Hampstead; both had been "kind" to him.

"We are very thick," he reported, and but for them could not have remained alone where he was.

Hazlitt's latest had been on Gray, Collins, and Young; he had also given, in Keats's opinion, a fine piece of criticism on Swift, Voltaire, and Rabelais. His treatment of Chatterton had been disappointing. . . . Wordsworth, whom he had frequently seen, had left town. He had made a bad impression wherever he went by his egotism, vanity, and bigotry. But his wife was beautiful and his sister was enchanting. "Oh, that he had not fit with a Warrener!" Keats exclaimed to Haydon. In short, it was a pity Wordsworth had dined at Kingston's.

"Endymion" was running its slow way through the hands of the printers, this February. He had got the third Book copied and had begun the last. In telling some of these details to Tom and George, he said, "I do not like to write a short letter to you, or you would have had one *long* before." But he did not underscore. They would be on the alert for his outrageous puns.

3

In these days he was thinking much on the subject and nature of poetry. "I think poetry should surprise by a fine excess," he wrote, "and not by singularity. It should strike the reader as a wording of his own highest thoughts, and appear almost a remembrance."

In the second place, "Its touches of beauty should never be halfway thereby making the reader breathless instead of content: the rise, the progress, the setting of imagery should like the sun come natural to him—shine over him and set soberly although in magnificence leaving him in the luxury of twilight.—But it is easier to think what poetry should be than to write it—and this leads me to another axiom. . . . If poetry comes not as naturally as the leaves to a tree it had better not come at all. However it may be with me, I cannot help looking into new countries with 'O, for a muse of fire to ascend!' If Endymion serves me as a pioneer, perhaps I ought to be content." He wondered whether his friends noticed any change in his life; if so, they would attribute it to humbleness, rather than pride, a cowering under the wings of great poets, rather than to bitterness that he was not appreciated.

A week back reflecting on the powers of poesy, he wrote: "I had an idea that a man might pass a very pleasant life in this manner—Let him on a certain day read a certain passage of full poesy or distilled prose, and let him wander with it, and reflect upon it, and bring home to it, and prophesy upon it, and dream upon it until it becomes stale—But when will it do so? Never." Any one grand and spiritual passage might serve as a starting post towards all the "two-and-thirty palaces of delight."

V. Teignmouth: Nursing Tom. Endymion Published. Well Walk

HAIR blown about his face, coat globuled with icy drops, Keats stepped in at Taylor's home, 91 New Bond Street, Sunday, the first of March. From a bulging pocket he drew corrected proofs. "George will be in soon with the third Book."

"You are leaving town?" Taylor had been making disturbed sounds over his wetness.

"At once. George has returned to London and Tom needs me at Teignmouth."

"But, Keats, man, you will take an inside seat? This blustery lion-entrance of the month—"

"I ride on top," Keats spoke untroubled, "and shall be quite comfortable with a plaid." After a few more words about "Endymion" he went away.

Taylor, distressed, shook his head and muttered, "Too bad. He shouldn't go in such weather, but if go he must he should ride within." So long a journey would be, of course, far less expensive on the outside. The House had advanced, moreover, much to so young a poet; he himself could not offer further royalty. Now if this had been the Fleet Street office and Hessey had been in—

" 'Blow, blow, thou winter wind!' " Keats repeated more than once, March second, drawing toward Devonshire. In the strongest gusts he wondered whether the coach would be blown over, whether he would be blown off and under,

79

whether the trees swaying beside the road would crash down upon horses, vehicle, and passengers.

He escaped and got off at Teignmouth splashed yet not so uncomfortable as he might have been. "What a county!" he looked about the dreary coaching stop. "Rainy, misty, snowy, foggy, haily, floody, muddy, slipshod," and did not remind himself that London must be quite as bad, but concentrated on getting to Number 20, the Strand.

"If Tom seems to you much worse," George had cautioned, "you will not of course show him you think so." To Keats's question, he had replied, "Sometimes bad, occasionally better."

The maid showed him into the tiny sitting room, where Tom was pathetically happy over his arrival. He had expected nothing, nobody, in the objurgated weather, five more days of which kept them fast indoors. "I am of a mind to see downs and dales, and to take you out for short rambles," Keats looked at the continued downpour. "But it's all propitious for writing."

By Saturday, the fourteenth, he had copied in a fair hand his fourth Book. "I wish it was all done," he wrote Reynolds, "for I want to forget it and make my mind free for something else."

Such of the inhabitants as he saw in the first week evoked his strong dislike: "Degenerated race, pulvis ipecac. Simplex —a strong dose." "Dwindled Englishmen are not fine." "A Devonshirer standing on his native hills is not a distinct object—he does not show against the light." Touched off by Shakespeare's Seven Ages of Man, he composed a sonnet, "Four seasons fill the measure of the year." It was, he knew, monotonous and slate-colored as the weather, with only the word "coves" to hint at the locality in which he had written.

Yet something of fine spirits and playfulness struggled through his anxiety over Tom in the mildewing, mushroomy

80

days. Before he left London he visited Reynolds, suffering from an injury to his right foot. Brown was there and told of an old accident to himself. A stone from the wall of a roof had fallen on his leg—which he feared he would lose. "I would sooner have a harmless piece of herculaneum sent me quietly as a present than ever so modern a chimney pot tumbled onto my head," he now assured Reynolds. Since hearing of Brown's accident he had had an "aversion to a dose of parapet."

News from home was at least not depressing. George had left the third Book at Taylor and Hessey's, with directions that proofs be sent to Charles Cowden Clarke, at Clerkenwell, where he was staying with his sister, Mrs. Towers. Meantime, here he himself sat at his desk by the window overlooking "a pretty valley—pretty cliffs, pretty brooks, pretty meadows, pretty trees, both standing as they were created and blown down as they are uncreated."

While he revised and copied the last of "Endymion," Tom read from a black letter Chaucer of 1596, which they had found in a bookshop in a sally between showers. "We'll have it 'bounden gothique,'" said John. "It will go a little way to unmodernize."

Tom read aloud:

"*Somwhat he lipsed, for his wantownesse,*
To make his Englissh sweete upon his tonge."

"If lisping was objectionable in an old monk, how much more so in a young lady. Yes, she lisps."

"The Jeffrey girls have been most kind to us all," Keats remarked.

"O, yes. Very kind. Their mother, too." A moment later he added, to bring Keats's face about from the window, "I daresay they thought George eligible, John."

John looked inquiry.

81

"It's nothing. They were very good friends but he has most tactfully written decisive, if regretful, farewells."

John was about to turn again to the window, when Tom remarked, as if irrelevantly, "He told them how handsome you are."

Keats laughed, thoroughly appreciating George's predicament. "A pity all this green is amphibious," again he spoke from the casement. "The flowers wait for the rain twice a day as the mussels do for the tide."

Remembering a book he had read to his mother, in her long illness, he wrote Reynolds, "I am getting among scenery whence I intend to tip you the Damosel Radcliffe," and as the *Mysteries of Udolpho* returned more vividly, "I'll cavern you, and grotto you, and waterfall you, and wood you, and water, you, and tremendous-sound you, and solitude you." He was not so spirited as he might seem, despite his promise to be witty on salt-fish—a specialty of the town—for Reynolds was still in the hospital and Tom, for all his red cheeks, was not improving.

Before the eighteenth of March he could not deny that his brother was worse and so wrote to George, in Pancras Lane. By return post, George hoped and trusted "your kind supervision will prevent any violent bleeding in future."

The truth is, John thought ruefully at this sign of dependence George reposed in him, we don't understand the treatment of this disease.

Propped up among his pillows, Tom called out, "What does George say?"

"He encloses twenty pounds"—Keats held up the note for Tom to see—"and remarks that he will keep regular accounts." He did not add, " 'for the sake of justice and a future proper understanding I intend calculating the probable amount Tom and I are indebted to you.' " Tom knew and George knew that anything of his was also theirs.

"George is better able to manage old Abbey than I am— or was," he went on. "Our guardian always esteemed George's business nature."

Turning back to the letter, he added, "Georgiana sends her *respects* to me, as usual, and her *best wishes* to you." He approved entirely of Georgiana. "I hope they can be married soon."

"But you and I shall still be together?" Tom spoke wistfully.

"Always!" John came over to draw the cover about a body ever frailer, thinner, increasingly racked by coughing. It was hard to keep the bedclothes in order.

The publishers were in immediate want of the last bit of "Endymion"—including the Preface. All, including the dedication and the title page, he sent March 21, and at once lifted his shoulders, flung up his head and went to a fair:

> *Over the hill and over the dale,*
> *And over the bourn to Dawlish.*

This poem of twenty lines he enclosed to Jemmie Rice in a longish letter of the twenty-fourth, containing at least one pun—which Rice would know how to value: "I have seen everything but the wind—and that, they say, becomes visible by taking a dose of acorns or sleeping one night in a hog trough with your tail to the Sow Sow West." La, this was as bad as the "bit o' brothrell" he had sent Haydon!

Next day he wrote Reynolds, mostly in verse. His regained freedom had gone to his head, literally, provoking humorous thoughts and pictures to offset those more serious. Junkets had had a vision—half-asleep or half-dreaming—of Voltaire in casque and shield, Alexander wearing a nightcap, old Socrates tying his cravat, Hazlitt playing with Miss Edgeworth's cat, and "Junius Brutus pretty well so-so." John Keats had had another sort of vision:

The sacrifice goes on; the pontiff knife
Gleams in the sun; the milk-white heifer lows,
The pipes go shrilly, the libation flows:
A white sail shows above the green-head cliff,
Moves round the point and throws her anchor stiff.
The mariners join hymn with those on land.—

He hoped Reynolds would be pleased with the "Enchanted Castle." His subject beguiling him subconsciously into recalling "Kubla Khan," he wrote for the close of his own "pleasure dome," that was half Merlin's hall, half dream:

—like a beauteous woman's large blue eyes
Gone mad through olden songs and poesies.

He became philosophical:

It is a flaw
In happiness to see beyond our bourn—
It forces us in summer skies to mourn:
It spoils the singing of the nightingale.

The mood deepened. He saw:

Too far into the sea, where every maw
The greater on the less feeds evermore:—
But I saw too distinct into the core
Of an eternal fierce destruction,
And so from happiness I far was gone.
Still am I sick of it: and though today
I've gathered young spring leaves, and flowers gay
Of periwinkle and wild strawberry,
Still do I that most fierce destruction see,
The shark at savage prey—the hawk at pounce,
The gentle robin, like a pard or ounce,
Ravening a worm.

And yet, as Reynolds knew, he'd rather be a clapping bell to a Kamchatkan missionary church than to be left with these horrid moods.

"Tom is getting greatly better," he reported yet felt his own mood balance day after day between the gay and the grave.

Playfully, he wrote to Haydon: "The hedges by this time," it was the eighth of April, "are beginning to leaf. Cats are becoming vociferous. Young ladies that wear watches are always looking at them.—Women about forty-five think the season very backward.—Ladies' mares have but half an allowance of food." Playfully, he visited the girls at the bonnet shop across the way, jested with Atkins the coachman, Simmons the barber.

Seriously, he talked to Bartlett the surgeon, wrote Haydon, "Your picture is a part of myself," but confessed to knowing so little the emphasis of painting: "The innumerable compositions and decompositions which take place between the intellect and its thousand materials before it arrives at that trembling, delicate and snail-horn perception of beauty."

Of everyday life and plans he wrote Haydon he hoped to set off shortly, knapsack at back, to tour North England and part of Scotland. Though he did not say so, he had been invited to come along with Charles Brown. They had hoped Severn and Haslam would be with them, but neither of these could manage. Severn said he hadn't enough money for even so modest a trip and, besides, he was loath to cut himself adrift from what seemed the only safe course to progress in art. But he, Keats, would clamber through clouds and somehow exist—would see all Europe at lowest expense.

Discouraging, annoying opinions from London. His Preface to *Endymion* was unworthy the volume, they intimated, a bad business. He referred to his first book of poems in that Preface; he apologized for fighting under disadvantages; his steps had been uncertain; the poem must be considered an endeavor rather than an accomplished thing; he should have kept it back a year or two—and so on. To be sure, he had not considered sufficiently his publishers; but, well, what of it? Was it not his book?

On reading a letter from Reynolds, however, he gave in. "Since you all agree that the thing is bad, it must be so." Yet he must say something for himself: "Look it over again and examine into the motives, the seeds from which any one sentence sprung.—I have not the slightest feel of humility towards the public—or to anything in existence—but the Eternal Being, the principle of beauty, and the memory of great men."

He looked upon the public as an enemy, and a preface was written to that enemy, whom he could not address without feelings of hostility. It would not be in character, he sat there inspecting his mind and heart, if he addressed an enemy in subdued style; to multitudes he hated the idea of being humble. "I never wrote one single line of poetry," he told Reynolds, "with the least shadow of public thought." Well, he would think about changing the Preface, but if the idea continued repugnant to him, he would not write another.

And they did not approve his dedication! He read it again: "Inscribed,/with every feeling of pride and regret/and with 'a bowed mind'/to the memory of/the most English of Poets except Shakespeare/Thomas Chatterton."

Very well, then: If the new Preface desired did not reach London in four or five days, "tell Taylor to publish it without a Preface, and let the dedication simply stand, 'Inscribed to the memory of Thomas Chatterton.' "

He wrote the new Preface. Next day. "Do let the Printer's Devil cook it, and let me be as the 'casing air,' " he wrote Reynolds, while rain fell and kept on falling. Drops beating on the windowpane gave him the same sensation as a quart of cold water offered to revive a half-drowned devil; even

86

the roots of the earth seemed rotten, cold, drenched. How different from last April, when on his way to the Isle of Wight he saw the first gleam of yellow furze! As late as the twenty-seventh of March he felt drowned and rotted like a grain of wheat. He could not get to Kent's Cave at Babbicombe though, earlier in the month one rarely beautiful day, he had clambered over the rocks as far as the village. And on a short walk, a day or so after that tramp, he had found a lane banked on each side with primroses.

On the twenty-fourth, he opened a small flat parcel. *Endymion!* "I am more happy in Tom's pleasure in seeing it," he felt in his weary soul, "than I am for myself." But he read through the volume carefully, praising the publishers' and printers' work. "It is," he said to Tom, "very free from faults." Racing through with some sense of elation, despite himself, he corrected one blunder—a stupid confusion of pronouns for Tellus and Ocean—that demanded a single line erratum leaf, which would appear in first copies henceforth. Another thing amused him. He had written "tiptop quietude," and Taylor had deleted the word, substituting "utmost." Keats reached out for his quill, restored "tiptop," read the line aloud, and laughed. Why, he had all unwittingly used slang! He corrected his own correction by deleting the line in which he asked for restoration of "tiptop." Altogether, he was concerned over some twenty errors, which he set forth in his letter to Taylor.

2

While his physical self was caring for Tom, walking, observing, talking to the neighbors and particularly to Sarah, Fanny, and Mary Ann Jeffrey, his mentality was undergoing further change. He could have no enjoyment in this world but continual drinking of knowledge: he had left behind all cavalierdom; and if he must be immortal, he hoped it would be after he had taken a little water of Lethe to forget some of his schoolboy days and others since then. Any worthy pursuit must do some good for the world. To this end he had arrived. Some did good through their society, or wit, or benevolence; some with power of conferring pleasure and good humor on all they met. . . . "There is but one way for me: the road lies through application, study, and thought." So he opened his mind to Taylor.

And to Reynolds, he wrote: "I compare human life to a large mansion of many apartments, two of which only I can describe, the doors of the rest being as yet shut upon me. The first we step into we call the infant or thoughtless chamber, in which we remain as long as we do not think. We remain there a long while." . . . At length, impelled by the awakening of the thinking principle, "we no sooner get into the second chamber, which I shall call the chamber of maiden thought, than we become intoxicated with the light and the atmosphere; we see nothing but pleasant wonders, and think of delaying there forever in delight." But one's nerves become convinced that this "world is full of misery and heartbreak, pain, sickness, and oppression." And so it is that the chamber of maiden thought becomes darkened "and at the same time on all sides of it many doors are set open—but all dark—all leading to dark passages."

He thought himself and Reynolds now in this state. "We feel the 'burden of the mystery.' To this point was Wordsworth come, as far as I can conceive, when he wrote 'Tintern Abbey,' and it seems to me that his genius is explorative of those dark passages." Again, he was convicted of Wordsworth's genius and superiority in depth to Milton, though conceding that this greater depth depended more upon the general and gregarious advances of intellect, than individual greatness of mind. . . . "He did not think into the human heart as Wordsworth has done."

But there is a third chamber of life: a lucky and gentle one —"stored with the wine of love and the bread of friendship."

He planned for some months of work and study here in Teignmouth. Tom had been helped by the lung specialist, Dr. Turton, and believed in a period of sunny days he was getting well. Keats thereupon wrote George for certain books, declaring he would learn Greek and Italian and in other ways prepare himself in a year for taking the metaphysical road best in the opinion of Hazlitt. Also he ordered down his folio Shakespeare—which contained sheets of paper with stanzas of "Isabella," or the "Pot of Basil." He had finished the poem here by the sea and sent it all to George, from whom it would go on to Reynolds.

Within a week, he was surrendering the idea of staying longer at Teignmouth, more than ever disturbed, in too uneasy a state for writing. Tom had been a whole night without a wink of sleep and was overburdened with fever. Again, he appeared better, and only then Keats unbosomed himself to the invalid friend in Christ's Hospital, hoping Reynolds, too, had been "again around the Common without any effect but refreshment." Here was an apt occasion for remarking he was glad he had not given away his medical books: "An extensive knowledge is needful to thinking people—it takes away the heat and fever; and helps, by widening speculation, to ease the burden of the mystery: a thing I begin to understand a little."

Wordsworth, to be sure, had hurt him by remarking, "A pretty piece of paganism!" He remembered the hurt—after he had walked up and down the room chanting his "Hymn to Pan" for the poet from the Cumberlands. Yet he could not, would not, obliterate the influence of the man who wrote of the "Burden of the Mystery." It had cut too deeply into

89

his mind. On the third of May, he copied for Reynolds some lines he had written on May Day to "Mother of Hermes! and still youthful Maia."

The leaves were out now, but Tom was spitting blood and wanted to go home. Before they left Number 20, and "the Edge," Keats had from Haydon a note praising *Endymion*— "the most delightful thing of the time."

3

"Lord, what a journey I had and what a relief to be at the end of it!" John was sitting with George on his favorite bench in Well Walk, while Tom slept in his old room. "I could not have stood it much longer."

"Tell me how," George spoke sympathetically, "it was so bad."

"I had all I could manage in keeping Tom protected and as free from suffering as possible. It's a long way, you well know, and the many changes were hard on the poor boy."

"You could not, of course, stop to see Bailey," George stated rather than asked.

"No, oh, no. We came by chaise to Honiton—and so far Tom held up remarkably. But the stops and changes after setting out by coach at that town were agony to his frame. Leaving him a moment to dash in to some inn for a cup of hot tea or glass of milk, trusting our parcels were in the right place, managing not to get left behind while Tom went on— oh, you fancy!"

"I fear he is worse," said George sadly.

"But he is happy to be with the Bentleys, even to see the children—and Mrs. Bentley is kindness itself." John ended hopefully, "And we are together again."

George hesitated. "Not for long. Georgiana and I shall soon be setting out for the banks of the Mississippi," and added they hoped to be married around the end of the month.

Keats felt a sudden dismay merging into dumb passivity. They talked a trifle longer before he excused himself to write the Jeffrey girls. He wished they might come for a little while. "But lauk," he told them in early June, "we haven't got any female friend in the house. Tom is taken for a madman and I, being somewhat stunted, am taken for nothing." By that day George and Georgiana were living in their own place.

"I am in that temper that if I were under water," he wrote Bailey in late May, "I would scarcely kick to come to the top." He felt no spur at George's going to America, "and am almost stony-hearted about his wedding." He continued his rounds, nonetheless, dining at Haydon's on the twenty-fourth, meeting there Barnes, Hazlitt, and Wilkie. Across the fields from smoky London, Severn strolled for talk on the bench or farther walking beyond Highgate Woods and Hampstead Weald.

On the tenth of June, he wrote: "Now I am never alone without rejoicing that there is such a thing as death—without placing my ultimate in the glory of dying for a great human purpose. Perhaps if my affairs were in a different state, I should not have written the above—you shall judge—I have two brothers: one is driven by the 'burden of society' to America; the other, with an exquisite love of life, is in a lingering state." Love for his brothers, he said, because he had suffered early misfortunes and then loss of parents, had grown into an affection 'passing the love of women.' Thought of his brothers always had stifled the impression any woman might otherwise have made upon him. He had, however, a sister and must not follow George to America or Tom to the grave. Life must be undergone. In lighter mood, he wrote, "I certainly derive a consolation from the thought of writing one or two more poems before it ceases."

He still meant to tramp with Brown, but he was leaving it all to that friend—itinerary, things to be packed, everything—and he would accept Brown's decisions.

Endymion, entered at Stationers' Hall, May nineteenth, had as yet no reviews. The *Edinburgh* had blown up Leigh Hunt again and had spoken of "Mister John Keats" as "the amiable but infatuated bardling." He was not so much interested in presenting copies of his new book as he had been in giving out *Poems* a year ago. But he asked his publishers to send Tom a bound copy and Mrs. Reynolds one carrying the line he wrote to be pasted in, "With J.K.'s best respects."

"Remember me to Hessey," he was finishing a note to Taylor, "saying I hope he'll *cary* his point." The pun arose from some discussion over their publication of Cary's *Dante.* He was going to take the three small volumes in his knapsack, for they would go "into the aptest corner."

He was about to be off with Brown for four months in the North. He believed Tom was slightly better. In any event, for both their sakes, he must escape.

VI. Pointing His Nose to the North and West

BETWEEN Finsbury and Moorgate on the east and Aldersgate on the west, Lad's Lane was near the Poultry where the brothers once lived; and the Poultry was near Finsbury Pavement, where all were born. Here, in Lad's Lane, before half past eleven on Monday, June 22, 1818, at the Inn of the Swan and Two Necks, stood John, George, and Georgiana; and Charles Brown. They were incommoded by no great amount of luggage: George had shipped boxes, barrels, and crates by goods-coaches; John and his friend had only their knapsacks, plaids, and the suits they wore.

All got on top, for Liverpool. There they would separate, the married pair soon to sail for Philadelphia, thence overland to Cincinnati, and to Birkbeck's Colony. The tramping tourists would make for the north of England and Scotland, "to gorge wonders." Tom, at home, was under the care of Mrs. Bentley and Dr. Sawrey.

The coach stopped at St. Albans for dinner. Keats proposed calling upon Henry Stephens, fellow-student of Guy's Hospital days, now a practicing physician in the Redbourne neighborhood. He received his friend warmly and greeted cordially the couple Keats introduced with brotherly pride. "You've no attendant, no surgeon's case," he observed, "but that kit is larger, and you have a friend." He would have gone along with them but patients held him back.

"What have you got there?" he asked, on hearing they were to walk four months.

"Three small volumes, a shirt and nightcap," Keats

grinned. "New stockings, underwear, hairbrush, toothbrush, comb and towels—anything else, Brown?"

"I have a guidebook," Brown indicated his somewhat bulkier sack.

"They are small enough," smiled Stephens, "but they'll seem more, I warrant you, many a day."

"I forgot to mention inkstand, paper, and pens," Keats added.

Interested in the American venture, Stephens chatted to George about the Colony, and all sat down to dinner in festive mood. They were soon off again, uneventfully arriving at the Crown Inn, Liverpool, for the night of the twenty-third. On the twenty-fourth, leaving before the others were up, John and Charles—pointing their noses to the north—continued by stage forty or fifty miles to Lancaster.

"I forgot to inquire what vessel will be next to sail, in all probability," remarked Keats.

Brown, seeing his thoughts would lie backward for some distance, diverted them to the practical. "Has George ample funds for a long venture in America?" he asked, casually enough.

"Something like 1100 pounds," Keats thought. "To get that he waited for his twenty-first birthday, the last day of this February."

"But he has been in business," returned the economically minded Brown. "Has he saved nothing?" he was still casual, as if talking to pass the time.

"Not of late. He resigned from Abbey, Cock and Company and has been studying this American project. And," he added boyishly, "courting Georgiana."

Brown was silent.

Presently Keats went on. "He has repaid me for money I furnished him when he was under age—seventy pounds or so. He spoke of keeping regular accounts, but we all shared what we could get from our guardian."

Brown nodded, and waved toward a lark. They watched its flight vanish in the blue, and Keats resumed where he had left off. "It's unlucky to be the eldest of brothers who cannot live on small incomes." He mentioned certain expenses, emphasizing rather his elder brothership than the boys' spending. "All this is in confidence, Brown," suddenly he bent his falcon gaze on his companion, waking up to the thinking aloud he had indulged.

Again Brown nodded assent, as if the matter were at once confidential and yet of momentary importance to himself.

"Abbey's House acknowledged this June 4 they owed me £500. I owe them a little something for tea, chocolate, and cocoa for the three of us in three years—some thirty pounds, perhaps."

At Lancaster a contested election denied the rural peace they had hoped to encounter throughout the tour. They put up at a private house for the night.

Looking out through the early dawn, which seemed no dawn, at four o'clock, Keats remarked, "It's raining." "It would be"; Brown turned over. At seven Keats declared it was only misting and urged Brown to get up. "Let's move on." The mist became a downpour and Brown, consulting patience from Samson Agonistes, thought they'd better put up under a spreading tree.

When a trifle later walking through Lancashire, they saw, past the River Dee and Point of Air, the mountains of Wales, Keats's spirits rose. At Lancaster Castle he was full of comparisons. "No splendid long flight of stairs," he declared, "like that at Carisbrooke ascending to the old stone keep." He ran long fingers through hair curling from moisture and took up his knapsack.

"We'll try to reach Morecambe Bay," said Brown shutting the guidebook, "for breakfast."

"Anywhere, anywhere, good Charles, so it be soon." Rain fell again but they walked on, under their plaids. Morecambe Bay, shut from view by the mist, was gloomy enough. After eating they trudged on, bearing inland, to Burton-in-Kendal, where this second night they also ran into crowded inns. Partisans of Lowther, contesting with Brougham, were protected by militia. Keats's feet were smarting, his sack weighed a ton, but they continued to End Moor. "Seventeen miles for the day!" Keats drew out paper, ink, and quills to write Tom. "Here beginneth my journal," his plan being to combine daybook entries with thoughts for and to his brother. Fagged, he managed now only seventy words or so, and put it away to send after he had rolled up a goodly length. He would write to others when he could but Tom—Tom was following this tour in imagination and Tom came first.

Resting in the common room of the inn, they were fascinated by a sodden old toper. "Staggers like a bear on its hind feet," remarked Brown. "He stands in the shape of a drachm," Keats made in the air the apothecary's sign, ℨ, wondering whether Brown would catch the pun.

Just here the old man, Richard Bradshaw, or Radshaw, introduced himself and asked, his nose in Brown's face, "Do —you sell spect-ta-cles?"

"No; we're on a walking tour"; whereat Mr. Bradshaw stared unbelievingly.

They walked on to Kendal where, at table, they were seated with a soldier who had been in all the wars, he said, for seventeen years.

"All this century, then," observed Keats.

"That is true, my boy," and the veteran spoke of his Napoleonic campaigns.

Hooking over shoulder the straps of their impedimenta,

they now turned northwest to Bowness-on-Windermere. In this walk of nine miles through scenery ever more beautiful and rugged, they paused often to look at the lake which, at every turn, presented new and charming aspects.

Keats, who to this point had compared every view unfavorably with Devonshire—forgetting certain strictures formerly made against that country of dales and downs and tors—now saw a picture that evoked, "How can I believe in that? Surely, it cannot be!" A mountain peak, beneath which floated a silver cloud, a small island green with foliage and surrounded by water of a most entrancing hue.

Brown smiled. He believed this Lake country had more of the sort of thing Keats could scarcely credit.

So it was. "No view in the world can equal it! It must surpass all Italy." But a hundred yards farther on, catching the distant extremity of the lake, "No; it is more and more wonderfully beautiful!"

Brown was receiving impressions of his own: the trees far and near, the grass immediately around them, fern and furze in luxuriant growth. Not a mist but an imperceptible vapor bestowed a mellow, soft tint over mountains on the opposite side and at the remote end of the water.

Keats sank into a taciturn mood, one of contemplation: "These views of most noble tenderness can never fade away; they make one forget the divisions of life: age, youth, poverty, riches. They refine one's sensual vision into a sort of North Star which can never cease to be open-lidded and stedfast over the wonders of the Great Power." Something of this feeling he would write to Tom.

For dinner they stopped at the White Lion, at Bowness-on-the-Lake. Keats rowed out to one of the islands for trout, kept in porous boxes, which were broiled and soon agreeably provoking their nostrils. Travel-stained, in collars without stiffening or ties, boots scuffed and dusty, both felt a "down-the-nose" look of certain guests.

Keats turned the full power of his eyes upon more than one of these gentry and had the satisfaction of seeing the look glide off. "The miasma of London," said he. "That this place, Brown, should be contaminated with bucks and soldiers and women of fashion. And hatband ignorance."

Brown saw the signal in the hazel, falcon eyes. "Do you enjoy your whisky?" he asked.

"Prime enough," and they finished their meal.

"Do you know Wordsworth?" Keats asked of the waiter.

"Yes, sir. He was here only a few days back, canvassing for the Lowthers."

"How far to his place—to Rydal?"

"Six or seven miles, sir," and the waiter staggered out with very empty dishes. Many dishes.

"Wordsworth against Brougham," Keats spoke in disappointment and anger. "Yet that family has always been his friend." His feeling was still regnant when, before leaving the hotel, he wrote Tom: "Lord Wordsworth instead of being in retirement has himself and his house full in the thick of fashionable visitors quite convenient to be pointed at all summer long."

Continuing that afternoon along the east shore of Windermere, up the valley of the Rothay, they were so drunk on scenery before coming to Rydal Water as to require a little pause. Throwing aside burdens, they rested and lost themselves in wonder. "I think," said Keats after some minutes, "I should like to read you my 'Isabella' just here," and fished about for his script. Soon he began:

"Fair Isabel, poor simple Isabel—"

while Brown listened, wishing to goodness he could read his verses better. But the story and the craftsmanship swept him along, and what elocution lacked eyes supplied. They are wine-dark, thought Brown, while the poem rose to a climax and when Keats ended:

"O cruelty,
To steal my basil-pot away from me!"

he was ready with warm praise, and asked to see parts for a second reading.

"You would have been a rebel against those existing affairs, Keats," and he read aloud the stanzas beginning:

"With her two brothers the fair lady dwelt,"

and ending:

"Why in the name of glory were they proud?"

"I am," replied Keats, "a rebel against such things as weary hands sweltering, loins melting into blood from the whip-lash—against all gainful cowardice."

They resumed tramping and soon covered the fourteen miles to "Wynandermere," seeing the mountains grow and heighten before them. After twenty-three miles that single day they felt no ill effects from the climb. "Why, so many miles here," remarked Keats, "are not so much as the four from Hampstead to London!"

"Mountain air," pronounced Brown. "You'll feel results when we drop to the valley."

"Still rather misty," said Keats, "but I have an amazing partiality for mountains in the clouds."

Loughrigg swelling up before them all the way, they continued to Ambleside. "Almost thirty miles in one day! I never walked so far, never."

"Anything like this in Devon?" challenged Brown, while they paused for a new rise.

"Never! Anything in Wales?"

99

Brown probably forgot the magnificence of Snowdon and the wild road leading to it from the east, for he replied, "Nothing comparable."

"How beautiful the lake, its wooded shores, and islands!" Keats continued to marvel. "The green arches over our heads, these long slender spikes of foxglove. And all the while Kirkstone and other large hills nestled together in a sort of gray black mist."

In Ambleside they stopped at Salutation Inn and were almost immediately asleep.

Next day, the twenty-seventh, they felt like sleeping as late as six o'clock.

"It would not be seemly, I daresay," Keats spoke cynically, "to call on Lord Wordsworth too early. We can call this a day of rest."

"There's a waterfall about here," Brown consulted the guide. "Stock Ghyll Force, it's called. Shall we walk out to get a view?"

They missed the direct path, fortunately, and found the fall by its noise, "buried in trees in the bottom of the valley —the stream itself interesting throughout with 'mazy error over pendant shades.' But Milton meant a smooth river," said Keats, "this is buffeting all the way on a rocky bed, ever various."

To Brown he remarked, "This is the first waterfall I ever saw."

"A small fellow," Brown smiled.

"Beyond my expectations, even so." Standing a little below the head, about halfway down the first fall, he watched it "streaming down two more descents to the depth of nearly fifty feet."

"George will see finer ones. I'll not describe to him a teapot spout—" but Keats continued his observation of the different falls: "the first darting down the slate-rock like an

100

arrow; the second spreading out like a fan; the third dashed into a mist—and the one on the other side of the rock a sort of mixture of all these."

Moving away a space, they saw the whole cataract, "more mild, streaming silverly between the trees." They passed beyond the roar while Keats meditated on what most astonished him: "the tone, the coloring, the slate, the moss, the rockweed; . . . the intellect, the countenance. This countenance or intellectual tone must surpass every imagination and defy any remembrance."

Back at Ambleside, he completed his first installment to Tom. "I shall learn poetry here," he wrote, "and shall henceforth write more than ever, for the abstract endeavor of being able to add a mite to that mass of beauty which is harvested from these grand materials, by the finest spirits, and put into ethereal existence for the relish of one's fellows." Living through his eyes, he felt that his imagination, surpassed, was at rest. Because he believed descriptions bad at all times, he apologized for the word-picture of the fall: "I did not intend to give you any, but how can I help it?" After all, Tom might taste some of the pleasures he was having and could taste without the fatigue Brown and he endured.

"After eating a monstrous breakfast," he posted his letter, and they were off for Rydal.

Wordsworth was not at home. None of his family was at home. Keats wrote a note and stuck it over Dorothy's portrait. Drawn to the parlor window, he gazed at the scene down Windermere. "Lord! What a view for a poet."

"A glorious situation," Brown agreed.

Visiting two more waterfalls, they went along by Rydal Water and Grasmere through the Vale of Grasmere, through a defile of the mountains into Cumberland, and so to the foot of Helvellyn. The summit lay four miles off, rise above rise. Here at the foot, Keats would write George that he had

101

seen Kirkstone, Loughrigg, and Silver Howe, and had recognized from afar Wordsworth's "ancient woman seated on Helm-crag." Putting himself in George's place, he thought of the ennui and fatigue the couple would undergo; "but you will have an inexhaustible astonishment . . . you will be cheered on from day to day."

"I wonder if they've sailed," remarked Brown.

"Who can say? They have if a ship has raised anchor." And thinking of their possible homesickness, he would have his series to Tom copied and sent by the first packet George would have from England.

He would be glad, there at the foot of Helvellyn, to know what humor sister George was in, that he might please her with a sonnet or pun or riddle or ballad. Perhaps she might wish an acrostic, and he began:

> *Give me your patience, sister, while I frame*
> *Enitials verse-wise of your golden name.*

Finishing the twenty-one lines for Georgiana Augusta Keats, he fell into bed.

Next morning, Sunday, they trudged eight miles to Keswick, on Derwent Water, before breakfast. Mist forbade a climb up Helvellyn but that day they made the ten-mile circuit around the lake, pausing at the Falls of Lodore. Keats made his way easily among the streams and about the fragments of rock and would have got to the top of the Falls but slipped one leg "into a squashy hole." Again the "intellect" of the place charmed him: for delightful accompaniment to the water the perpendicular rocky walls were "all fledged with ash and other beautiful trees." On they walked to the south end of the lake, where the mountains of Borrowdale were as fine as anything they had seen, and so arrived back at the caravansary. There Keats wrote George he had been a week without news of his family and was ready to "drop like a hawk on the post-office at Carlisle."

"Have you written to Stephens?" Brown wanted to know. "We owe him a few thanks—"

"When could I write? I'm a day behind with Tom. Then how am I to manage Fanny and two or three others I've promised?"

Brown set out his own paper, pens, and ink. In this order. Then he bethought himself to look at the guide. "There's a fine Druid temple near here," he discovered. "Are you stout enough for it?"

"Any time for such a wur-r-r-k," but he thought after dinner would be the best. "How far?"

"Matter of a mile and a half."

Soon they were speculating on the aged stones in the midst of clustering mountains. "Vale of St. John," Brown indicated the opening.

"Beautiful name. Beauty everywhere," breathed Keats. "Even the fag up hill too near dinner is rendered void at this sight."

"Perfect of its kind," thought Brown.

"There can be only one of this kind," said Keats.

Early next morning, the twenty-ninth, they got off before breakfast to climb Skiddaw with two "very good sort of fellows."

"A glorious day!" Keats was all unacquainted with the vagaries and sudden shifts of weather in the Lake region.

"Mist may come down any moment," said one of the men. "Best climb while we can." They "fagged and tugged," pausing here and there to rest and observe the far landscape. "Over there's the Scotch coast," the same man waved toward the northwest.

"But the water? Is that the Irish Sea?" Keats stood rapt.

"The Irish Sea," and while the other pointed out surrounding mountains, "Helvellyn, Saddleback, Scawfell," Keats was thinking of young Edward King and Lycidas. He came back to the present when the other, waving toward the south, told him, "Hills beyond Lancaster."

Keats had never been so high. They were almost upon the summit when mist descended and the air bit cold. They drew out brandy flasks. "Mind ye," Keats reported to Tom, "mixed with mountain water." All four responded to the elevation as to a cold bath. "I felt," wrote Keats, "as if I was going to a tournament."

Disappointed at not getting to the top, Brown remarked of the descent, "It's a sad jolt trotting down a mountain. A man's inside seems mixing together."

At the Keswick hostelry they had breakfast, rested, and wrote—Keats telling Tom of the climb. On this last day of June, then, they were headed for Ireby, oldest town in Cumberland. "They're having a country dancing school at the Inn," he heard as they entered, and delightedly paused to watch the gyrations and leapings. Burns in mind, he saw it was "no new cotillion fresh from France. No; they kickit and jumpit with mettle extraordinary, and whiskit and friskit, and toed it and go'd it, and twirl'd it and wheel'd it, and stamped it, and sweated it, tattooing the floor like mad."

"Not much like our London efforts," commented Brown.

"About the same as leisurely stirring a cup of tea and beating up a batter pudding." His eyes on the rows of boys and girls, Keats wished he could attain the Highland Fling. "See the exquisite mouth of that lassie!" he exclaimed. "This is what I like better than scenery." And when his more settled companion lifted an inquiring eyebrow, he explained. "I never felt so near the glory of patriotism, the glory of making by any means a country happier." Like the Greek religion, this was a thing of joy and he loved it.

For all the remark at Ireby, nonetheless he wrote Tom he

was a creature of rivers, lakes, and mountains. They moved too quickly from place to place to become learned in village affairs. From the inn called The Sun, they walked to Wigton and from Wigton to Carlisle, up to which they had covered one hundred fourteen miles, merely tired in the thighs and a little blistered. "We shall ride 38 miles to Dumfries, where we shall linger awhile about Nithsdale and Galloway." At Carlisle, he found a letter from "Sister George," which he stowed away for Tom.

2

From the old, whitewashed streets of Carlisle, the ancient castle and cathedral—which, Keats observed, did not appear very fine—they rode the first day of July past Solway Firth and the Cheviot Hills to Dumfries.

On top of the coach, they had for companion a Scot who pointed out Burns's tomb. "There! De ye see it, amang the trees—white, wi' a roond tap."

"Where does Mrs. Burns live?" asked Brown.

"In Dumfries—whaur but?" he retorted.

All along for miles they had passed numbers of men and women going to the horse fair at Dumfries: "the women nearly all barefoot, with their shoes and clean stockings in hand."

"How beautiful the girls' uncramped feet against the grass!" exclaimed Keats. "But why the footwear? A symbol?"

"Ready to put on and look smart in the towns," Brown told him.

They got down at the inn, where they had "whuskey." "Wull ye hae a toddy?" asked the innkeeper. "What's that?" asked Keats. "Whuskey mixed wi' sugar and water," he was told. A very pretty drink and, he recalled, much praised by Burns. They had the toddy.

While the sun set among clouds hovering over rounded hills, they made for the churchyard corner. Keats sat down on a flat stone and wrote a sonnet, "On Visiting the Tomb of Burns," while everything seemed "beautiful, cold-strange— as in a dream."

Early next morning they left their trappings at the inn while out to find the red sandstone ruins of Lincluden. "Wings put crosswise on their breasts," Keats spoke softly in the chapel, gazing intently at a frieze of angels, while Brown read from the guide.

On the way back he remarked, "I say, old chap, your knapsack has worn through the seams of your coat."

"Then at last it must to the tailor's," and Brown went out with the garment while Keats sat down to write to Fanny. His sister, he thought, would be interested in the barefoot girls, and the cottages that had no exit for smoke but the door. She would be wide-eyed at hearing they had been taken for spectacle sellers, razor sellers, and traveling jewelers. He implied their lives would be worth little in so notable a whisky country should they be challenged as excisemen.

"Here's your jacket," and Brown was back before he had time to say more about the ruins of Lincluden than that they were "fine."

"Fortified at all points!" and he got into his coat. Putting up Fanny's letter, he was ready for Galloway.

After Dalbeattie and Auchencairn, the scenery of Kirk-cudbrightshire, "very wild with craggy hills," high moors, and blue inlets burst upon them. They crossed so many sparkling streams, Brown fell into reminiscences of boyhood.

"I myself fished in a fashion"; Keats grinned at the memory. "Often I would wake early in the morning and slip off

106

to the brook. Mostly small minnows, but sometimes miller's thumb or tickleback."

"This angling, I judge, was not far from Hampstead Heath," ventured Brown.

" 'And I seyde his opinioun was goode.' But dinna lauch at our Hampstead streams, mon." He was getting the hang of the dialect. "Dinna forgit the Fleet rises there; remind yersel' that Holborn means Hole-born—"

"What did you do with your small fry?" laughed Brown.

"Kept them in three washing-tubs," and he fell silent, constructing a jingle of childhood and of this journey to send Fanny.

Brown was impelled to remark, "You are aware this is the country of Guy Mannering—"

"Ah, I haven't the honor of knowing book or hero." How different, he thought, his "set" and the world of Scott.

"Here's the story," which so impressed Keats he dashed off a ballad, "Old Meg she was a gipsey," that he would enclose to his sister. With fine insouciance he added, "If you like these sort of ballads, I will now and then scribble one for you." At Kirkcudbright it was that he wrote out the four stanzas, "There was a naughty boy." Oh, they would make her smile.

Still the cottages poured forth smoke, and Keats continued with Brown the tirade begun on discovering so poor a country. "I thank Providence I am not a Scot, nor related to a Scot"—he cut his eye sidelong at Brown, who declared himself so related—"nor in any way connected with them."

Brown laughed. "See what Ireland has in store. Everything hereabouts is clean and neat."

"Now the cottages in the vales of Devonshire—"

"Keats, Keats! What of the rain you encountered in Devon?" Brown referred to descriptions he had read from Teignmouth.

His companion's face was humorously abashed but uncompromising. "You well know 'tis distance lends enchantment."

"I'll be harking to what you say of Scotland after seeing the Paddies," promised Brown.

"We dined yesterday," Keats recalled, "on dirty bacon, dirtier eggs and dirtiest potatoes." He concluded, then, his merry epistle to Fanny, though so fatigued, "When I am asleep you might sew my nose to my great toe and trundle me round the town like a hoop without waking me." With his Gargantuan appetite, "A ham goes but a very little way and fowls are like larks to me . . . I can eat a bull's head as easily as I used to do bulls' eyes. I take a whole string of pork sausages down as easily as a pen'orth of lady's fingers. Oh, dear, I must soon be contented with an acre or two of oaten cake, a hogshead of milk and a clothes' basket of eggs, morning, noon, and night when I get among the Highlanders." They had walked sixty miles since he began this letter at Dumfries, and he was closing at Newton Stewart six miles from Wigtown, where he would drop it into the post office.

Always he remembered Tom. While Brown copied the "Meg Merrilies" ballad, Keats began, at Auchencairn, July 3, to tell his brother of Kirkcudbrightshire, before going on with the letter to his sister. On the fifth, he got back to Tom, "Our lady of yesterday said very few southrens passed these ways. The children jabber away as in a foreign language." What varieties of entertainment they met he indicated by saying that after dirty food a day or so back, "we breakfast this morning in a nice carpeted room with sofa, hair-bottomed chairs and green baized mahogany."

From Wigtown, they moved on to Glen Luce, for the most part over flat, bleak heath, interrupted now and then by a morass out of which peats had been cut, and which perhaps exhibited the verdure of a few water plants. But there

108

were birds: gulls, larks, robins, and God knew what others for Keats to follow in their direct or swooping flights—

> *showing their black and golden wings,*
> *Pausing upon ther yellow flutterings—*

or high in air sleeping on level wings outspread.

They slept the night at Glen Luce, continuing on the morning of the sixth to Port Patrick though making a detour to see ruins "scarcely worth the while," and in a burning sun were sweltering toward Stranraer when overtaken by the mail coach. They hailed it, got on for the two miles to the Port and took the first packet for Donaghadee, some twenty miles across the Channel.

At ease in the little boat, their heavy weights thrown aside, they rested among changing views, and upon hearing voices in song strolled to the source.

"Beguilement for the passengers," and Keats searched for coins. "Seem to be poor old fellows."

Brown looking at the two added, "And poor stuff."

"Hark ye," said Keats. " 'Tother one's striking up the 'Battle of the Boyne,' " and they heard him through. Both sang of Robin Huid, chanting a refrain which stuck in Keats's memory:

> *"Before the king you shall go, go, go,*
> *Before the king you shall go."*

"There are your Irish," They were at the rail, watching the shore approach, when Brown introduced the population in view.

"Poor, destitute, not interested in work"—and Keats, eying the mob, believed him right.

But their landlord's chambermaid was "fair, kind, and ready to laugh, because she is out of the horrible dominion of the Scotch kirk." For a fact, the Scotch were formed into "regular phalanges of savers and gainers," and hence their country presented a greater appearance of comfort than that of their Irish neighbors. "But," Keats said in his letter to Tom, "I would sooner be a wild deer than a Scotch girl under the dominion of the kirk, and I would sooner be a wild hog than be the occasion of a poor creature's penance before these execrable elders." The kirkmen had banished puns and laughing and kissing. "I should make a full stop at kissing for after that there should be a paren*t*-thesis: and go on to remind you of the fate of Burns." Tom would like the jest.

"What of the Giants Causeway?" he inquired. Brown was taking out paper, pens, and ink.

"Only forty-eight miles," heading his sheet. "Shall we walk it?"

"I have heard," cautioned Keats, "that Irish miles are of great length."

The distance was seventy English miles. They gave up the trip. "Anyway, it's expensive, this life in Ireland. Dear as the hotel in the Piazza of Covent Garden." This from Keats, who went on, "How about a night at Belfast? Not far, and we could get back next day in time for the packet."

That walk gave them all they wished to see, and Keats admitted handsomely that even though a Scotch cottage might have no proper chimney flue, it was a palace to an Irish hut. "Here's a bog!" And a little later, "What could be drearier, blacker, danker, flatter, and spongier?"

"And here are men," Brown told him, "making their living on it." A number of poor, dirty creatures were cutting and carting peat. After three miles of struggling through the morass, the two breathed more freely until nearing Belfast they heard the play of a shuttle. "Most disgusting of all noises," Keats was thinking of the wretched weavers.

"Laugh of a monkey is not pretty," challenged Brown.

"Also the chatter of women alone and the scream of a macaw. No, the shuttle is worst."

At a "miserable house of entertainment" between Donaghadee and Belfast, they found two men over whisky glasses —a laborer and a drunken weaver. They were complaining of treatment received in England.

"Art a Frenchman?" The laborer was staring at Keats's handsome face and gold-touched hair.

The other hinted at bounty money and was ready to take it.

"What a tremendous difficulty," Keats's political interest prompted, "is the improvement of the condition of such people."

On the return from Belfast: "What in the name of humanity is that?" He stared at a procession headed toward them.

"A kind of sedan chair," offered Brown.

"A dog kennel, rather, placed upon poles from moldy fencing."

Nearing the party, they saw two ragged girls carrying along the chair-kennel in which sat an old, old hag. Squat and squalid like a half-starved ape, a pipe in her mouth and looking out with a round-eyed, skinny-lidded inanity. Slowly her head wobbled from side to side. Squab and lean and puffing out smoke.

"Duchess of Dunghill!" Keats labeled, while the trio passed on toward Belfast. "What a thing would be a history of her life and sensations." He would write Tom about the Duchess.

111

VII. Scotland. Too Exhausted to Finish the Tour

BACK at Port Patrick, July 9, after studying the map and calculating distances, they headed for Ayr and Glasgow by Cairn Ryan, Stranraer, Ballantrae, Girvan, Kirkoswald, and Maybole. From Cairn Ryan their road lay "half-way up the sides of a green mountainous shore, full of clefts of verdure, and eternally varying," to a large and beautiful glen seven miles long, finely wooded in parts, a mountain stream winding down it, full of happily situated cottages and musical with lowing cattle. Ploddingly they ascended, to see Ailsa Rock towering before them. "It strikes me overwhelmingly"; Keats threw back his head, bare to the ocean winds, holding fast to his fur cap. "Really, I am a little alarmed."

Brown re-covered his own half-bald head and remarked, "Yet it's fifteen miles off." Softly the mist dropped down.

Keats fell silent, inspired to the sonnet, "Hearken thou craggy ocean pyramid." Now and again looking toward the mighty sea-column, he ended the poem, later declaring that in the soft rain Ailsa had given him the complete idea of a deluge.

At Ballantrae, July 10, they paused by a bridge to watch a procession that proved to be a Scotch wedding. Still in the mood for ballads, Keats began, "Ah, ken ye what I met the day," and wrote forty-odd lines.

"Capital dialect!" praised Brown.

"Hoot, mon! I've not read my Bobbie Burns in vain or

112

heard Hazlitt lecture on his vairse, or" his fellow-tramp made a sweeping gesture, "hearkened to these inhabitants so many days for naught."

All along to Girvan, thirteen miles farther on, Ailsa was still beside the two, "like the sun or moon. But there are other mountains over there—" they had paused at a rise and he waved westward—"black and huge over the sea."

"They are of Arran," explained Brown, who had consulted the guide, "and here, nearer home, is Kintyre."

"How was it," Keats wondered, "those mountains did not beckon Burns to some grand attempt at epic?" The peaks stood out clear on this rare day, "notched against the sky."

"An everyday commonplace to him," said Brown.

"Beauty never grows commonplace!"

After a restful night at Girvan, they asked how far to Kirkoswald.

"Eight miles, sir. Thank you, sir." The maid curtsied and scurried back to mop and brush.

"Come along, Keats. Here's your stick. I have the guide," and again they set out before breakfast. At Kirkoswald in his journal-letter Keats wrote his ideas on the difference between Scotch and Irish. "English point of view?" queried Brown.

"We're getting on for Ayr." Keats studied the map.

"But the text indicates ruins we must see." They walked four miles—stopping at Crossraguel Abbey where winding stairway and watchtower drew further comparison with Carisbrooke—before dinner at Maybole.

The country had entranced them with increasing beauty and grandeur. "I'd no idea," panted Keats on a climb; "it's as rich as Devon."

"Yes. Burns did not see what he had. He was a plough-man, accustomed to hills as so much inconvenience in getting about—" Brown heaved sympathetically. "At this moment I quite appreciate his preference for mice and field daisies."

113

Quite suddenly, they bore down upon Ayr and the steep-arched Brig o' Doon. " 'Tis the sweetest river I ever saw." Keats drew out his snuffbox, while they paused on the keystone of the Brig to look up and down the stream as far as they could see. Luxuriantly fine trees overhung the banks, behind which they saw a pleasant heath.

Eying his knapsack, dropped at his feet, Brown groaned, "Another hole in it!"

A few minutes afterward they looked through the windows of Kirk Alloway, scene of the witches' and warlocks' dance, and shortly ran into Burns's birthplace. "Thatched with straw and with rooms for the beasties," Brown observed.

"What do we here?" Keats thought the low-sitting house very humble for such a poet.

"You know how Bobbie would best be celebrated," Brown reminded. So they drank stiff toddies held aloft to the former owner of the cottage. A sonnet, composed while he was tired and "warm with old barleybree," his pulse "light with pledging a great soul," was—Keats felt—valueless. That liquor had misted his brain.

The guardian was a nuisance of an old chap. When he was called to the door, Keats remarked, "D'ye ken what? That fellow is a great bore—fuz, fuzzy, fuzziest."

Brown raised his eyebrows—and his toddy.

"He drinks five glasses for the quarter and twelve for the hour," Keats slightly misquoted "Christabel." "A mahogany-faced old jackass, who knew Burns. He ought to have been kicked for having spoken to him." He had a grievance of his own. "I can understand only five words in a hundred of what he says."

"Cant, Cant, Cant!" he wrote Reynolds. "It is enough to give a spirit the guts-ache. That flat dog made me write a flat sonnet. So I destroyed it." But Brown had copied it.

Reynolds knew Burns was one of his admirations. "One

song of his is of more worth to you than all I could think for a year in his native country. His misery is a dead weight upon the nimbleness of one's quill. I tried to forget it, to drink toddy without any care, to write a merry sonnet. It won't do: he talked with bitches, he drank with blackguards, he was miserable." As if we were God's spies, he thought, we can see horribly clear in the works of such a man his whole life.

On matrimony and death he wrote: "I have spoken to you against marriage, but it was general; the prospect in those matters has been to me so blank that I have not been unwilling to die. I would not now, for I have inducements to life: I must see my little nephews in America and I must see you marry your lovely wife. My sensations are sometimes deadened for weeks together—but, believe me, I have more than once yearned for the time of your happiness to come, as much as I could myself after the lips of Juliet." And he remarked to Reynolds on how attached he had become to Georgiana.

"Tell my friends I do all I can for them, that is, drink their healths in toddy."

At Kingswells July 12, they dined with a traveler with whom they fell to talking about Kean. "I have seen him," said the traveler, "in *Othello the Jew*—I mean, er, er, er, the *Jew in Shylock*."

Seeing he was lost in vague ideas about the *Jew in Othello, Shylock in the Jew, Shylock in Othello,* &c, &c, yet still satisfied with himself, he strolled to the window and whistled abortively.

"Now," chuckled Keats, "he'll go and tell people he's seen Malvolio in the *Countess,* Twelfth Night in *Midsummer Night's Dream,*" and spun out a list of absurdities.

2

Rain held them up on the thirteenth after a dozen miles on the road, but let them into Glasgow at the end of the day. They had crossed the bridge when Brown, looking back, ejaculated, "The whole population is turning to wonder at us!" They walked on, meeting a drunk, who faced Keats. He was thrust off. "I ha'e seen all foreigners bu-u-t I never saw the like o' ye!" He fell into step beside the two until Keats said gently, "I shall call an officer and turn you over to the police if you do not leave us."

Before breakfast on the fourteenth he finished his long letter to Tom: "Take care of yourself. I mean in not being vexed or bothered at anything. God bless you!"

He was weary. The banks of the Clyde were "extremely beautiful," the north end of Loch Lomond "grand in excess," but no felicities of phrase fell from his lips. He began to understand that one may be among mountains too long to exclaim upon their grandeur. They were still being stared at, he and Brown, while boats on the Loch and barouches along the shore roads marred the romance. He could wish for a fleet of chivalry barges, with trumpets and banners to die away into the blue place among the mountains, and he sketched the scene for Tom. "The water was a fine blue, silver'd, and the mountains a dark purple, the sun setting aslant behind them. Meantime, the head of Ben Lomond was covered with a rich pink cloud." On the boat they rested. "This pause restores the scenery"—Brown waved an encompassing arm. "Good as a house-maid's cloth for the windowpanes," Keats thought. They did not climb Ben Lomond; the price was too high and another day of rest more to their liking.

On the seventeenth they were up at four and walked fifteen miles, "through two tremendous glens," before eating. In the early morning they walked through Glencroe, mellow

116

sounds of sheep, bells, and dogs descending from misty heights close above. For some time, they saw nothing. Two objects then came in sight, creeping like emmets among the crags. They saw from the guide that "Rest and Be Thankful" stood near the end of the first glen. It sounded so sweet an inn they walked on. "Only a stone seat, Brown," Keats called back to his friend still plodding upward.

Towards nightfall they approached Loch Awe in solemn majestic scenery, every step creating a new picture. "See those islands on the lake!" Brown waved his stick. "And each with a beautiful ruin," Keats had already discovered. Just off the salt water of Loch Fine, they stopped for food, the inn window opposite the lake. Keats had a bath, fiendishly pursued by gadflies, as both had been much of the time since leaving Lad's Lane.

Around the Loch they came upon Inverary and the castle of the Duke of Argyll. "Band playing over there." They heard two or three tunes, but said Keats, "Nothing can stifle the horrors of a solo on the bagpipe. Will the beast never have done?"

In the town they saw a playbill on the hoardings. "Kotzebue's *Stranger*," read Keats. "Shall we see it?"

"My feet must be favored. Knocked up completely by these infernal new shoes."

"I told you—" but at Brown's humorous regard of his outrageous footwear, Keats chuckled. "Very well. You stay at the inn and I'll to the Barn."

There he damned the wretched play. Even the bagpipe accompaniment and the players were not worse. In ironical mood, he wrote:

Of late two dainties were before me plac'd.

Brown wrote, resting his abused feet on a chair. Keats wrote. To Bailey he spoke of women. He was certain he had

117

not the right feeling for them; he could not be just. "Is it because they fall so far beneath my boyish imagination?" When a schoolboy he thought a fair woman a pure goddess. "My mind was a soft nest in which some one of them slept, though she knew it not—I have no right to expect more than this reality. I thought them ethereal above men—I find them perhaps equal—great by comparison is very small." Among women he had evil thoughts, malice, spleen, could neither speak nor be silent. "I am in a hurry to be gone." How was he to get over this trouble? "The only way is to find out the root of the evil and so cure it. . . . After all, I do think better of womankind than to suppose they care whether Mister John Keats five feet high likes them or not."

On the eighteenth and nineteenth they found accommodations so bad they were in no mood for anything. On the second day the one still scarcely able to walk and the other feeling the effects of too much coarse food, they trudged twenty miles down the side of Loch Awe, catching a glimpse now and then of an indolently moving eagle. For supper they were served eggs and oatcake. "I can scarcely bear the taste of it, Brown. We've eaten about ten eggs, each, this day." For next day's dinner they had a small chicken and a good bottle of port. "But more oatcake!" It stuck in Keats's throat.

"Why should so beautiful a country be so poor?" asked Brown. "Why can't craggy mountains and granite rocks bear corn, wine, oil?" A hardy fellow, he had overcome to a degree his distaste for oats but saw his younger, more delicate companion—not well enough for fatigue and privation— "gagging" at the sight.

Now at Ford, detained by rain, they stopped before going on to Kilmelfort, between Loch Craignish and the sea just opposite Long Island (Luing). The few people they saw "gabbled away Gaelic at a vast rate."

118

"Not many kilts in Argyllshire."

"At Fort William a man is not admitted into society without one." Brown raised question marks in his friend's eyes.

"The ladies have a horror at the indecency of breeches." He did not smile, but his eyes twinkled. As for Keats he thought he might do a little observing when he arrived at Fort William.

"You know what, Brown?" he was gazing floorward in their room at Kilmelfort. "You can see right through the chinks into the ground rooms." They were comfortable here and waited for snuff the old grandmother was making for them. They were "out" and none was to be had except this homemade brand. The guid wife of the inn, stockingless, wore a pair of old shoes. A number of young girls were barefoot. There, a little thing driving cows down a slope; another, at the cowhouse door, was rather pretty, but "fac'd all up to the ankles in dirt." The language here was largely Gaelic; the Testament on a chest of drawers in a room adjoining theirs was in Gaelic; whisky men chattered Gaelic till one o'clock.

On the twenty-first they walked fifteen miles in a soaking rain to Oban. There Keats fell upon white bread, "like a sparrow." Opposite to the Isle of Mull, they were now so near Staffa and Iona they asked how much to cross over. One of the boatmen uppishly replied, "Seven guineas."

"Like paying sixpence for an apple at the playhouse," compared Keats. "Let's get on to Fort William tomorrow morning." But one of the men followed, "A great pity ye won't see the curiosities."

After bargaining, he agreed to guide them across the Isle of Mull. They crossed a ferry to the Isle of Kerrera, a short distance away, and after nine miles on a second boat stepped out on Mull. They made for the middle of the Isle, en route to Staffa and Iona, walked with tucked-up breeches and held

119

their stockings high in hand. "Over heath and rock and river and bog," they came that July 22 to the home of a family speaking no word but Gaelic. The smoke in the cottage was so dense—the door was lower than Keats's shoulders—rafters and turf-thatch were black. Faces were all but invisible, and the guests' eyes were much incommoded for traveling. Everybody was kind, making them more comfortable than they could have fancied. They slept in their clothes, with some blankets, while the guide snored away at arm's length on another bed.

"Can it be rougher in America?" Keats lifted his head from a letter to Bailey, whom he was telling of the young woman met yesterday when the guide lost his bearings. Without a word, she had thrown on her cloak "and walked a mile in a missling rain and splashy way to put us right."

"Much worse," Brown thought. "That's a pioneer land, fresh from the savages."

"Nonetheless, if I live three more years I expect to pass a whole year with George," and Keats returned to his letter. "I shall be prudent and more careful of my health than I have been," he wrote in hope of such a visit.

All this time, Brown was writing "volumes of adventures" to Dilke. Every evening after settling down for the night's lodging, he affronted the "indolence and luxury" of Keats— stretched out on a couple of chairs, taking snuff or reading Cary's *Dante*—by pulling out of his knapsack in unvarying order: paper, pens, ink. "If he would only change about a little," wrote his young friend amusedly. "Why not sometimes take out his pens first?" But, he closed his letter, "I might as well tell a hen to hold up her head before she drinks instead of afterwards." While Brown wrote, he copied out forty-eight lines he had written:

"There is a joy in footing slow across a silent plain," glancing at recent scenes and ending with a prayer.

Next day they struck a better path and the guide proclaimed himself a good fellow by two songs in Gaelic. One was about Mr. Brown who had been drowned, an elegy by his widow; the other, a Jacobin lay on Charles Stuart. Brown's professed interest in genealogy—he believed his grandmother came from Luing—kept about him a fascinated crowd. "I think you are a relation," he remarked to a lady who had been a Miss Brown. ("Indeed," said Keats wickedly, "I think so from the likeness.") Brown "jawed with the old woman, flattered a young one, kissed a child who was afraid of his spectacles, and finally drank a pint of milk." Keats watched them handling the eyeglasses, "as we do a sensitive leaf."

At the end of thirty-seven miles across the Isle of Mull, they sailed to Iona or Icolmkill.

No sooner had they stepped ashore, near the old nunnery, than Allan Maclean introduced himself as schoolmaster of the island, and offered his services as guide. They walked part way uphill from the landing, Maclean talking of St. Columba and his work in the place, so many centuries ago. Keats was enthralled. "And what does 'Icolmkill' signify?"

" 'Columba,' signifying 'dove,' is 'colm' in Gaelic," Maclean told him. " 'Kill' means 'church,' and 'I' is as good as 'island,' so 'Icolmkill' means the 'island of St. Columba's church.' "

They turned to the right, where ruins of the cathedral to the dovelike saint reared their broken arches above "compact rows" of graves and one stone cross as old as St. Columba himself.

"Who are in these graves?" Keats was studying the plot.

"You must know that in the course of years this island came to be considered the most holy ground of the north," Maclean watched the rapt eyes of his interrogator and shining spectacles of the older visitor. "They say sixty-one kings

121

are buried here: forty-eight Scotch from Fergus to Macbeth, eight Irish, four Norwegian, and one French." There was no external evidence that so many who lived in a long ago past lay there. But tombs of more recent Highland chieftains bore effigies, face upwards, in complete armor, black and moss-covered from age.

"How rich in antiquities!" Keats's words drew a wrinkle of appreciation from the master.

Afterward, when walking back toward the shore, Keats picked up some Scotch pebbles and dropped them in his pocket. "Rather shabby, I fear," he explained to Brown, "but I think my sister may like them."

It occurred to him that he was of a thirst, and he asked whether Maclean would join them at a little public. Allan Maclean would and did. He liked his whisky. Politely setting down his glass, he was pressed to take another—and a third.

"You can hire a boat from here to Staffa," he told them, "and have the men land you at Loch Nakgal (Loch na Keal) afterward. You would walk but half the distance to Oban, and the ganging would be better."

An intermission in bad weather let them land at Fingal's Cave. Keats looked about. "I am puzzled," he confessed, "how to give Tom an idea of this structure." He worked out a figure. "Suppose the giants who rebelled against Jove," he wrote, "had taken a whole mass of black columns and bound them together like a bundle of matches, and then with immense axes had made a cavern in the body of these columns —such is Fingal's Cave except that the sea has done the work of excavations and is continually dashing there—so that we walk along the sides of the cave on the pillars which are left as if for convenient stairs. The roof is arched somewhat Gothic wise, and the length of some of the side pillars is fifty feet. About the island you might set an army of men each on a pillar." As he studied the formation of the basaltic isle, he felt its solemnity and grandeur. "It far surpasses the finest cathedral in these respects," he said to Brown, who replied he had just been jotting down that no one could have an evil thought in such a place.

3

On the return to Oban they saw a swarm of sea gulls attacking a shoal of herring, now and then a porpoise heaving about among them for his supper.

"Brown, look! The water is spangled with scales."

"So great," said Brown, "has been the destruction by the gulls."

From wading ankle deep in bogs, acrid smoke in poor cottages, and exposure in open boats, Keats was suffering from a sore throat when they returned to Oban. "We'd best stay here a day or two," suggested Brown, who did not like the look his friend was wearing. In the pause, they took walks only along the shore, exclaiming when the mist rose, over the Paps of Jura to the south and all the enchanting coastline toward the west. But at Fort William there would be, probably, a letter from Tom; Keats was first to urge moving on. His throat was more comfortable but while so wretched he was longing for a cup of tea in Well Walk. Yet, he resolved, he would weather out this summer: he was happier than if he had time to be glum. "Still there will be theatres at home," he remembered, "and I expect to study hard." He began to realize George would be with him no more, but refused to face Tom's leaving. . . .

He enclosed his poem on Staffa, "Not Aladdin magian," when he wrote Tom on the twenty-sixth. He had attempted to expand his impressions:

123

Forever Young

This was architected thus
By the great Oceanus,
Here his mighty waters play
Hollow organs all the day—

this cathedral of the sea, which only the sea would "war down."

"Thirty-eight miles to Fort William, at the foot of Ben Nevis," Brown spoke from the depths of the guide. "We skirt Loch Linnhe all along. Can we make it easily in three days?"

"We must be fit for Ben Nevis."

"Let's set out on the thirtieth, then. We should do the twenty-six miles to Ballachulish in one day. If not, no matter."

On the first day of August, they tramped into Fort William after continued bad weather. To get warm and sleep a long night through was Keats's chief desire—and need. But next morning he was up betimes.

"It will be fair the day," the innkeeper told them. "Ye'll see Auld Ben. But ye maun tak a man an' a dog along wi' ye." Both were near at hand, the guide in tartan and cap, "Ma tam," he called it.

Again with fag and tug and a glass of whisky each, they gained the first rise. Keats's knowledge that 4,300 feet lay between the Fort at sea level and the top of the mountain spurred him to the unusual task of climbing this, the highest peak in Great Britain. "On that account," he promised himself, "I'll never ascend another in this empire."

"Save your breath," counseled Brown.

"It is almost—it is—like a fly crawling up a wall," he looked up. "Why, there's a tremendous chap still high above us." He gasped.

"Ach, mon, thot's a lang wa' fram the tap"; the guide

124

walked effortlessly. Now they were in a valley of heath enclosing a loch, but presently climbed again, gaining the line above all vegetation, Keats panting, feeling the pain in his throat. "Twa, three miles o' this," the guide casually dismayed the outlanders. Struggling, they gained the vantage they had foolishly thought the summit. "That crag above is the end?"

"Na, na!" The guide strode on, followed by the dog.

From the crag they walked in a mist, on large loose stones, "thousands of acres," past patches of snow and a chasm "completely glutted with it." Keats looked down, felt dizzy, and used ears instead of eyes, while they threw stones and waited for the resounding echoes that responded "in fine style."

"The mist has lifted but the clouds—" Keats watched them opening and shutting at intervals, "like large dome curtains."

Through loophole views they saw the region below, east, west, north, south. "The most new thing of all is the sudden leap of the eye from the extremity of what appears a plain into so vast a distance," wrote Keats. At the moment he asked the guide, "How did this large heap of stones come to be here?"

"Soldiers of artillery piled 'em," he was informed, and climbed on top for the pleasure of feeling himself higher than Ben Nevis himself. There he composed a sonnet.

All had expected the glimpse of a red deer but saw not one, and the dog languished for something to do. "I think of the loose stones going down," Keats spoke as they took another whisky and turned backs on the summit. Coming up they had crawled sometimes on all fours, again used sticks and legs, jumped here and boggled there. "A weel," the guide had encouraged, "dinna forgit that Mrs. Cameron, the fattest woman in all Invernesshire made the ascent." They had felt humbled but just at this moment had no inclination to take headers down the steep slopes.

125

"The woman had her sarvants," the guide smiled as at a memory.

Keats concocted a dialogue between Mrs. Cameron and Ben Nevis, the stout lady beginning to speak after taking a glass "as she was tolerably seated at ease."

"How old was she?" he asked of the tartan and tam.

"Feefty yair, if a day. She aye had her sarvants," he repeated, "but she aye had hersel'."

"Should have hired Sisyphus—"

"Wha, sir?"

" 'Up the high hill he heaves a huge, round'—Mrs. Cameron." He went on with his nonsensical dialogue.

His throat ached horribly. "What surprises me," he said, "is how the lady got down again." He did not speak aloud but thinking how vile the descent, how it shook him all to pieces, how tired he was, he managed with the others to reach the inn. Immediately, he went to sleep, drifting off to a dimly challenging voice telling him how to improve that sonnet conceived on the mountain:

Read me a lesson, Muse, and speak it loud.

His throat still hurt at Inverness, to which they hurried, walking over sixty miles in three days. There he was cheered by letters from Tom, Fanny, and Dilke. Resting, August 6, he wrote to Mrs. Wylie, who had made so great a sacrifice for George's happiness. He was, besides, grateful on his own account. She had expressed solicitude in fearing that a traveler, whose fate she had read, crushed by a precipice fall in Kirkcudbrightshire, might have been himself. He touched the catastrophe as brightly as possible for one who needed to be reassured and diverted from the tragic.

He put his hand to his throat. Brown was eying him: "Fevered, he has lost weight—too much—in this venture.

126

Worse than he'll admit. I must do something." Excusing himself, he left his friend at the table bent over letters.

"I must leave joking," Keats finished the imaginary Jonas of the fall. "I have been werry romantic, indeed, among the mountains and lakes. I have got wet through, day after day; eaten oat-cake and drunk whiskey; walked up to my knees in bog; got a sore throat; gone to Icolmkill and Staffa . . . went up Ben Nevis and—N.B. came down again. Sometimes when I am rather tired I lean rather languishingly on a rock, and long for some famous beauty to get down from her palfrey in passing, approach me with—her saddle-bags and give me—a dozen or two capital roast-beef sandwiches."

He paused to calculate the distance they had traveled, and wound up by informing her that besides riding about four hundred miles they had walked above six hundred.

Brown came back. "Your cold is so much worse, Keats. I've called a doctor."

He was not sorry at Brown's taking matters in hand. Nothing they had experienced since the wretched Isle of Mull episode had helped him to shake off the cold, hoarseness, or pain. He folded and sealed his letter, lay down, and drew up the blanket, glad of rest. Soon he heard Brown saying, "Here's the physician," and held out his wrist to the man with the watch.

The verdict was instant and short. "You're much too fevered to continue walking."

He woke feeling better but without desire to go on. "Will you promise to continue your tramp, Brown?" He could not bear that the seasoned walker might discontinue the tour.

"Shall I walk in Perthshire and counties back to Carlisle— where I should see Bailey, even without you—in solitude? And think, Keats, of the disappointment you'll suffer in losing my company."

"A great loss, and, to make it worse, I'll lose the country.

127

You must promise to see it for us both." He well knew Brown's house was let for almost two months longer. He got the promise.

"I'll arrange that you travel to London on a ship of some kind. After mountains, the sea air will be a welcome change." He went out and discovering the smack *George*, Walter Strachan, Master, would sail August 10, engaged Keats's passage.

VIII. *Home, a Charmian and the Reviews.*
A Dying Brother

ADVISED by the captain to be alert for change of sailing, Brown said they'd best get along to Cromarty. By coach they went to Beauley Abbey, where Keats wrote "Stanzas on Some Skulls," and on to the *George,* which sailed August 8. Brown did what he could for his fellow-tramp, shouldered pack and resumed schedule.

A qualm now and then when the smack was well out at sea reminded the unexpectedly homing seafarer of what Georgiana had but recently undergone. "There's a seasick lady," he smiled despite sympathy for one who rushed from the crowded cabin. She could not hold up her head before the *George* swung into the Thames, while he soon acquired sea legs. He was the only Englishman aboard, the others were all Scotchmen and Scotchwomen. One of the men went about exhibiting specimens of giant-sized potatoes. "I heer 'twas a bad crop ye had in England," he repeated to passengers and "all the lightermen and watermen from the Nore to the bridge."

Still unable to eat porridge, thicker than ever, Keats noticed that even the ladies managed it, "with large awkward horn spoons into the bargain."

The tedious voyage ended on the seventeenth, at the London Docks, Keats free of throat soreness, a voyage toothache, and feeling after eight weeks he had been away as many months.

He rang the bell at Number One, Well Walk. Mrs. William Dilke came to the door. His appearance, she said, was shocking. Browned, shabby—his shoes about gone and his jacket bursting in the back—he wore his fur cap, shoulders stooped under the plaid and knapsack. "I cannot tell what he looked like!"

She drew him to a stuffed chair into which he sank gratefully and, at the look in Mrs. Dilke's eyes, quoted Shakespeare: " 'Bless thee, Bottom! Bless thee! Thou are translated!' "

. . . A glance at Tom, the swiftest glance, plunged his heart downward. He jested over the cause of his return—the sick boy was unfeignedly happy to have him home again—and got out for comfort and escape to see the Reynolds girls. Mrs. Dilke sat with Tom.

"Where is Charles Dilke?" Keats wondered.

"With his brother-in-law, Mr. Snook, Bedhampton. He himself is not well."

At the Reynoldses' his return was wholly overshadowed by the advent of Jane Cox. "You must see her!" bubbled Jane.

"And who is this Miss Cox?" he would know.

"Our cousin," at twenty-six, Jane led the conversation, interrupted on occasion by sprightly Mariane, five years her junior. "And she has fallen out, oh, most seriously, with her grandfather!"

"You are giving her asylum?"

"To so genteel and charming a girl, why not?" Mariane exclaimed.

"Most enchanting," Jane vowed. "You must see her," while Keats sat there all his nerves singing sadly of Tom's doom. He got back to his brother without meeting the lauded visitor.

Next time he called he saw Jane, already divested—through what feminine reasons he could fancy—of the charm

130

first ascribed. Jove! he thought, if not Cleopatra she is at least a Charmian. Her rich eastern look, fine eyes, fine manners, and her way of entering a room—all beguiled and entranced. He looked at the cousins, so oddly reticent; their eyes, he thought, glinted greenly. That night he lay awake, eyes and mind kept open by Jane Cox as they might have been by a tune of Mozart's.

"What do you think of her?" Mariane asked eagerly when he went the third time.

"She's well enough," he answered, thinking neither man nor woman should delight him, not while Tom lay suffering agony he was powerless to relieve.

"She's a horrible flirt," confided Mariane.

"So that's it," he watched Jane come into the room and, despite himself, was magnetized. The girls believed he did not like Jane Cox. Even at that moment he was cataloguing her: "A fine thing, in a worldly way; for there are two distinct tempers of mind in which we judge of things—the worldly, theatrical, and pantomimical; and the unearthly, spiritual, and ethereal."

Enlarging upon this thought to Georgiana, he continued, "In the former, Buonaparte, Lord Byron, and this Charmian hold the first place in our minds; in the latter, John Howard, Bishop Hooker rocking his child's cradle, and you my dear sister are the conquering feelings. As a man in the world, I love the rich talk of a Charmian; as an eternal being, I love the thought of you. I should like her to ruin me and I should like you to save me."

Was he willing to be ruined just now? Again no, not so long as Tom— Possibly, anyway, he appeared little and ridiculous in her sight. From the reviews of *Endymion*, he conceived she might think him so. Could she judge him by his poems? Out of the question! She was a fine animal, well-trained. . . . He "relapsed into poetry," escaped from "a

131

new strange, and threatening sorrow—and thankful for it."

When he looked in at 93 Fleet Street, Taylor warned him not to expect kindly reviews from either the *Quarterly* or *Blackwood.*

"It has been hinted to me that I might do well to call upon the Blackwoods," said Keats. "You will know whether I regarded that tacit bribe."

Taylor smiled ruefully. "I called to see Gifford, in the hope the *Quarterly* might be lenient in its review."

Keats's eyes widened. "That was kindly meant, but I doubt—"

"You have reason. I asked them to forget politics, that Leigh Hunt has been and is your friend, and that after all 'Endymion' is a poem, a work of art."

"Is the review yet out?" Keats had not seen the April number.

"Not as yet. Late. But I saw that Gifford had a review of the poem on his desk. He did not show it to me."

"Ah! Then we know what to expect."

"Meantime, *Blackwood's Edinburgh Magazine* is in the stalls. If you have not seen it, here is a copy. Don't let it bother you too much."

Keats took the copy and remarking, "Perhaps correctly labeled the Blackguard," went away. He would not read on the way home, but sank down on his favorite bench and opened the sheet at page 519. The Cockney School of Poetry, No. IV, ended on page 524 and was signed "Z."

"Subterfuge." La, la, why couldn't this snakelike letter give way to a full signature?

This "Z" had heard of Keats's first book of poems, "bad enough in its way." But it had not alarmed "Z" half so seriously as the "calm, settled, imperturbably drivelling idiocy of *Endymion.*" He affected to believe that the just celebrity of Joanna Baillie and Robert Burns had had "the melancholy effect of turning the heads of incapable men and women. . . . Our very footmen compose tragedies."

"Now where did 'Z' get this knowledge?" And Keats re-read: "His friends, we understand, destined him to the career of medicine, and he was bound apprentice some years ago to a worthy apothecary in town." But all had been undone by the malady: "He has caught the infection and that thoroughly." Johnny Keats and a few more city sparks were pleased to look upon themselves as so many future Shakespeares and Miltons.

"Z" attacked him personally: "From some verses addressed to various amiable individuals of the other sex, it appears that Johnny's affections are not confined to objects purely ethereal. Take, by way of specimen, the following prurient and vulgar lines"—the reader gasped—"evidently meant for some lady east of Temple Bar:

> *Add to the sweetness*
> *Of thy honied voice, the neatness*
> *Of thine ankle lightly turned, etc.*"

John Keats had not enough education, stated "Z." His land might as well be "old Tartary the fierce," as Greece.

"There be those who will say 'A hit, a very palpable hit,' " Keats straightened his shoulders there on the bench. "They are wrong."

"Only a boy of pretty abilities," "Z" called him, "which he has done everything in his power to spoil."

"It can do me no harm, this making me appear ridiculous," Keats considered. " 'Z' would respect me if I were in sight, whatever he may say when my back is turned."

He returned to the blackguardly page, lighted by a quotation of some thirty-five lines beginning, "A thing of beauty is a joy forever," and read in unfamiliar type, which contributed a self-detachment, his own poem, to the end of the quotation. "I thought it good," he said to himself; "and by the gods," he breathed defiance to "Z" and confidence in himself, saying aloud, "it *is* good." Almost cheerfully he read the final sneaking thrust of "Z." "We venture to make a small prophecy, that his bookseller will not a second time venture £50 upon anything he can write. It is a better and a wiser thing to be a starved apothecary than a starved poet; so back to the shop, Mr. John, back to plasters, pills, and ointment boxes, &c. But for Heaven's sakes, young Sangrado, be a little more sparing of extenuatives and soporifics in your practice than you have been in your poetry."

Again Keats asked himself, "Who told him of my apothecary-surgeon days? Would Bailey—up that way— Oh, no! Bailey would never talk of me or what I said to him in private conversation." No matter, after all, many persons knew he had studied medicine.

He folded the magazine, to be concealed from Tom. He would suffer too much, his brother would, in reading the filthy review. "Hunt is out of favor with these people," he told himself again. "Therefore, am I. These reviewers are petty, their jobs depend upon patronage of money-bags or authority; they truckle. . . . We are Liberals. What more need one ask for explanation?" Except when downhearted he was troubled no more by this review, nor did his friends speak of it.

Of others, he heard that Hazlitt was prosecuting *Blackwood's*, though at dinner at "Mistessey's" Hazlitt had been silent about this justifiable prosecution. *Blackwood's* had deemed it a duty to rip him in the same number that daggered himself. Jemmie Rice was in town but Keats had not seen him, writing Dilke, "nor shall I for some time as my throat has become worse after getting well." Reynolds also was away, happy with his sweetheart. "Gorge the honey of life," urged Keats. "I pity you as much that it cannot last forever, as I do myself now, drinking bitters. Give yourself up to it. I never was in love, yet the voice and shape of a woman has haunted me these two days." Jane Cox, Jane Cox, but he did not mention her name.

He could not leave his brother long enough to see Fanny at Walthamstow. Here was her letter of June 12, but lately received, yet she would wonder why he had not replied. He must tell her of Tom's being worse, always worse, and try to persuade Abbey to let her visit Hampstead. He would send her a copy of his new book and another of the first. "What else can I say to her? Her character, I have discovered, is yet unformed. Only a little girl. No wonder. Shut up with two old people." He could praise her letter: it was without fault. He could write with no pleasure, he told her, having a confounded toothache, and his throat troubled him. Oh, yes! She wanted a flageolet. "What for?" he asked. He would not advise her to play on it but would get her one if she told him why she wanted it so much. A day or two later he read a second request. "Persistent Fanny!" he laughed. "Seals and medals and now a wind instrument that will puff out her cheeks!"

He was in a continual fever. Tom's sickness pressed upon him all day; he would not escape it; he would suffer all the way with Tom—yet to be of service he must escape. In the presence of this awful decline he could not study and so plunged into "abstract images" to ease himself of Tom's "countenance, his voice, and feebleness." It seemed a crime to think of fame or poetry and yet he must think, or suffer more. He glanced at the unbidden image of Jane Cox; no, he would not repose his thoughts there. He read Ronsard. In the sonnet, "Nature ornant Cassandre," he found solace. "Love poured her beauty into my warm veins," he translated line twelve, and so ended.

To Dilke he wrote, "You have passed your romance, and

I never gave into it, or else I think this line a feast for one of your lovers." He laughed a little at a note from Haydon, visiting at the old home in Devon where his sister would not permit him to quote Shakespeare, lest he wake the children —Keats chuckled, knowing the power of that voice raised in Shakespeare—where illustrating something by a quotation at some gathering he heard one of the company say, "Lord, Mr. Haydon, you are full of *scraps!*"

At last Fanny was permitted to see her dying brother. John suffered from Tom's pain at parting and wondered, "Was it worth her coming?" He took her home by stage and returned at once. He got to the Hampstead-bound coach, he wrote, "half an hour before it set out, and counted the buns and tarts in a pastry-cook's window and was just beginning with the jellies." He was not sure she understood about Tom. . . . Better so.

2

The *Quarterly Review,* April, 1818, was published as late as September. The table of contents announced among other titles *Endymion: A Poetic Romance,* by John Keats, London, 1818. "I'll read it in a hurry—first," and, turning to page 204, Keats wrily gulped down the four-page dose. It left him shaken. Whether it was worse than the *Blackwood* potion or only so much additional nastiness he couldn't be sure. But returning to the first word, he swallowed a second draught of the unpalatable venom, drop by drop, commenting in silence as he absorbed it.

"Reviewers are often accused of not reading the works they profess to criticize, eh? And this one honestly confesses he has not read the book." He read slowly from the unsigned review, "Not that we have been wanting in our duty—far from it—indeed, we have made efforts almost as superhuman as the story itself appears to be, to get through it." Able to read only the first of the four Books, the reviewer would lament want of energy but for one consolation, "We are no better acquainted with the meaning of the Book through which we have so painfully toiled, than we are with that of the three which we have not looked into."

Keats smiled ferociously. "So I'm caviar to him and therefore to the general."

"It is not that Mr. Keats"—he read on—"(if that be his real name, for we almost doubt that any man in his senses would put his real name to such a rhapsody)"—

"Damn the beast!" he flung the *Quarterly* to the floor. "He knows who I am, knows my *Poems* of last year. This is not to be borne." Trembling, he strode up and down the room but could not keep away from the thing. Picking it up, an adder that might strike mortally, he read on: "It is not, we say, that the author has not powers of language, rays of fancy, and gleams of genius"—

"Thanks, nameless advocate, for these words"; he tasted bitter honey from this poison flower. "He has all these"— Keats read on—"but he is unhappily a disciple of the new school of what has been somewhere called Cockney poetry; which may be defined to consist of the most incongruous ideas in the most uncouth language." (He, Keats, a very priest of beauty, to be so rated by this pusillanimous, villain-critic pigmy, who dared not sign his name. "Who is this craven, hiding behind anonymity?")

The reviewer now proclaimed, "Mr. Leigh Hunt aspires to be the hierophant of this school." And Hunt was damned for recipes on the harmonious and sublime given in the Preface to "Rimini."

"This author is a copyist of Mr. Hunt—" Keats felt his cheeks afire. Peculiarly caught! He was, God knew, grateful to Hunt, always would be grateful. But also, God knew, he had broken away long ago from that influence. Nor could he forget what his friends had told of Hunt's intimating the role he had played in Keats's writing.

Here was an impasse. "But let us get on," and immediately he relearned that he was more unintelligible, almost as rugged, twice as diffuse, and ten times more tiresome and absurd than his prototype.

Drawn by a quotation from his own Preface, he formed an axiom: It is better not to apologize. For the reviewer quoted his words, "Knowing within myself the manner in which this poem has been produced, it is not without a feeling of regret that I make it public.—What manner I mean will be *quite clear* to the reader, who must soon perceive great inexperience, immaturity, and every other effort denoting a feverish attempt, rather than a deed accomplished." Now, he reflected, his discarded first Preface would have been even more vulnerable. His publishers and Reynolds had been wise.

But, the reviewer facetiously was begging his pardon, "This does not appear to us to be *quite so clear*—we really do not know what he means—but the next passage is more intelligible," and he resumed quoting: "The two first Books, and indeed the two last, I feel sensible, are not of such completion as to warrant their passing the press."

Again, Keats spoke miserably, "I am caught by my own undoing." He had told Taylor and Hessey—ah, but he had been glad they insisted upon publishing *Endymion,* notwithstanding what he, the author, had said.

"Thus 'the two first Books,' " continued the mordantly clever review, "are even in his own judgment unfit to appear, and 'the two last' are, it seems, in the same condition—and as two and two make four, and as that is the whole number of Books, we have a clear, and, we believe, a very just estimate of the entire work."

At that sally, Keats managed a rueful grin. "He makes me

damn my own more effectively—" He paused. True. More effectively than he had intended.

The reviewer, he understood, would have abstained from inflicting upon him any of the tortures of the "fierce hell of criticism" if he had not begged to be spared to write more; if the reviewer had not observed in him a certain degree of talent "which deserves to be put in the right way, or which at least ought to be warned of the wrong; and if, finally, he had not told us that he is of an age and temper which imperiously require mental discipline." Since the reviewer had been able to gather only that the work seemed to relate to the loves of Diana and Endymion, he must content himself with giving instances of diction and versification. "Whereat," Keats gathered, "he appears to be puzzled and perplexed."

According to the nameless one, he had written a line at random; then followed, not the thought excited by this line, but that suggested by the rhyme with which it concluded. "There is hardly a complete couplet enclosing a complete idea in the whole book." ("Eighteenth Century," pronounced Keats.) The poet wandered from one subject to another from association not of ideas but of sounds. (Keats grimaced, but noticed carefully the adduced examples and, generously, conceded that from a hostile point of view there was something to be said. "As there was for me in my tirades against Scotch and Irish," he recalled Brown's comment.)

Of the opening lines, for example:

> *Such the sun, the moon,*
> *Trees old, and young sprouting a shady boon*
> *For simple sheep—*

the critic remarked, "The word, and not the idea, moon, produces the simple sheep and their shady boon." That was funny, oh, yes!

He was amazed to read that "dooms . . . for the mighty

139

dead" would not have intruded themselves but for the preceding "fair musk-rose blooms." ("Now which did I first conceive?" he asked himself. Why, they had rushed along together. . . .) Other instances, the maliciously pointing finger emphasized and pulled askew from the context.

"Oh, I am sick!" Keats bent his head into his hands.

All but through the second reading, he came again upon the statement that he was adorning the language with new words. "As if language could be static and live!" Surely, the *Quarterly* contributor must be aware of this first principle of speech. But he was holding out for ridicule, this carper: "turtles *passion* their voices," "an arbor was *nested*," and so on, while to "supply the place of nouns thus verbalized, Mr. Keats with great fecundity spawns new ones, 'human *serpentry*,' 'wives prepare *needments*,'" and again so forth. "He has formed new verbs by the process of cutting off their natural tails, the adverbs, and affixing them to their foreheads." ("Sounds like the anthropophagi," Keats laughed without catharsis.) "Thus, 'the wine out-sparkled,' 'the multitude up-followed,' the 'wind up-blows.'

"But enough of Mr. Leigh Hunt and his simple neophyte." ("By heaven! As if it were not my book—mine—" he felt his hands clench. "Even so this gangrened devil who can drive a pen does not perceive the failure *I* perceive. Even my failure is beyond his compassing.") And so saying he was calmed.

Yet on bad days he read the hateful pages again and wondered more than ever whether he had any right to be a poet.

"Who wrote the article?" he asked his publishers. They did not know. None of his friends knew. It might be William Gifford or John Wilson Croker. It might even be Robert Southey.

"Let it not be Southey," agonized Keats. "Not the author of *Thalaba*. But it couldn't be. He is not like that."

Saturday, October 3, he read in the *Morning Chronicle* a letter from "J.S."—"In my defense. May be John Scott, may be James Smith." Thursday, the eighth, he read another letter over the signature, "R.B.," giving extracts from *Endymion* to prove the *Quarterly* critic "unreliable." Soothed, he was not healed.

3

"Reynolds is returned from Devon, Tom. Only a little while I'll be away." He closed the door softly on the invalid and Haslam, who had come to sit while Keats conferred with his friend in Fladgate's office.

"Yes, I read the dastardly unsigned attack in the *Quarterly* and both letters in the *Chronicle*"; he spoke calmly and in a manner to indicate, "What of them?"

"What shall I do, Jack?"

"My dear fellow! Publish your 'Isabella,' your 'Pot of Basil.' That would annul the attack."

"How—my Reynolds?"

" 'Isabella' will have too many friends who will not countenance such tomfoolery as these *Blackwood* and *Quarterly* critics have indulged." The newly articled man of law was harassed on his own account, but he threw a friendly arm around his friend's shoulders. They were not so erect as he was accustomed to see them. The dauntless falcon look was softened. A sober countenance kept company with the drooping figure.

"Men don't strain themselves over easy tasks." He could have said nothing more consoling. Keats stood straight and looked tall. Managing a happier expression, he drew from his pocket the fair copy of "Isabella." "Will you read it again?"

"For any small imperfections—yes."

"Do you regret your Muses?" Keats was thinking of the Valentine sonnet in which Reynolds had bidden them farewell.

"No, no. Not in the circumstances," he smiled, and Keats thought of the young woman who might become the "lovely wife" but who was yet a dream.

A bell in distant quarters was ringing. Reynolds got up. "How is Tom?"

"Only hanging on. Very ill." He returned to Well Walk, where Tom was asking for him. Haslam had gone and Mrs. Bentley was sitting by the bedside.

Next day he had a letter from Reynolds who found nothing to cavil at—perhaps one word might be altered. And the tale should be put forth, while interest was high. "I was most delighted at seeing you yesterday," he wrote, hardly knowing how to meet a friend so situated, and himself so confined. He had noticed what most raised his friend's spirits and repeated: "Men do not set their muscles, and strain their sinews to break a straw. I am confident," he went on, "that the 'Pot of Basil' hath that simplicity and quiet pathos, which are of sure sovereignty over all hearts."

Keats was cheered, and he faced himself again with better courage when he read: "Do you get *Fame*—and I shall have it in being your affectionate and steady friend." And Reynolds asked for copies of whatever he, Keats, might write. Good Caius!

Yet he would put out no poem—no poem so long as Tom—

The last week in October he heard from Dick Woodhouse, who had been at Bath and Weymouth for his health, about the "malicious, but weak and silly article on *Endymion*." Men of sense could see, with "J.S." of the *Chronicle*, "the criticism is *felo de se*." It was a self-condemning thing, "for the reviewer, in his undiscriminating stupidity, has laid his finger of contempt upon passages of such beauty, that no one with a spark of poetic feeling can read without a desire to know more of the poem."

A friend at Bath had asked, "if these are the worst passages, what must the best be?" He gathered from the daily papers that the review had roused indignation in a few who "do look with a jealous eye on the honor of English literature." But this was quite enough of such a "cobbling, carping, decasyllabic, finger-scanning criticaster."

In a conversation at Hessey's, Keats had spoken in Woodhouse's hearing about the riches of poetry being exhausted and his conclusion to write no more. The beauties of poetry were unexhausted and inexhaustible, Woodhouse averred, and he "deprecated" Keats's conclusion. The poet should not be dismayed at the yelpings of the tuneless, the envious, the malignant, or the undiscerning. . . . The entire letter Keats felt to be warm with admiration for his genius, fervid in hope for his work and belief in those who have a warm

> *affection for the cause*
> *Of stedfast genius toiling gallantly.*

"He quotes from my sonnet," and so recognizing Keats breathed more easily. "Now what shall I say to this friendly letter?"

He repeated, rather than first stated, two principal points about genius, achievements, and ambition. First, the poetical character, a thing per se and standing alone, has no self; it is everything and nothing. "It has no character—it enjoys light and shade; it lives in gusto, be it foul or fair, high or low, rich or poor, mean or elevated. . . . What shocks the virtuous philosopher delights the chameleon poet. It does no harm, from its relish of the dark side of things any more than from its taste for the bright one; because they both end in speculation."

143

"A poet is the most unpoetical thing in existence," he continued, "because he has no identity—he is continually . . . filling some other body.—The sun, the moon, the sea and men and women who are creatures of impulse are poetical and have about them an unchangeable attribute—the poet has none; no identity." He was being hard on poets! Nonetheless, he repeated, "He is certainly the most unpoetical of all God's creatures." The very instant he had declared he would write no more, he might have been cogitating on Saturn and Ops, with Hyperion in mind. In a room full of people he felt annihilated, whether among men or in a nursery.

Second, "I am ambitious of doing the world some good: if I should be spared, that may be the work of maturer years —in the interval I will assay to reach to as high a summit in poetry as the nerve bestowed upon me will suffer." He grinned at the source of this statement: climbing Nevis. Oh yes, there were limitations in aspiring to whatever heights. His one hope was not to lose interest in human affairs, that his indifference to applause, even from the finest spirits, would blunt no acuteness of what vision he might have. "I feel assured I should write from the mere yearning and fondness I have for the beautiful even if my night's labors should be burnt every morning, and no eye ever shine upon them."

After receiving from Hessey a copy of the *Chronicle* letter by "J.S.," he wrote: "I cannot but feel indebted to those gentlemen who have taken my part." Impelled to state a truth, which was no boast, that might reassure those friends, he wrote: "Praise or blame has but a momentary effect on the man whose love of beauty in the abstract makes him a severe critic of his own works. My own domestic criticism has given me pain without comparison beyond what *Blackwood* or the *Quarterly* could possibly inflict, and also when I feel I am right, no external praise can give me such a glow as my own

144

solitary reperception and ratification of what is fine. . . . I have written independently *without judgment*. I may write independently and *with judgment* hereafter. The genius of poetry must work out its own salvation in a man: it cannot be matured by law and precept, but by sensation and watchfulness in itself. . . . I was never afraid of failure; for I would sooner fail than not be among the greatest."

Now, as October waned toward November, he was almost constantly at his brother's call. Rarely did he leave the racked frame, stretched out, a skeleton but a suffering skeleton. One thing comforted both: George and Georgiana had landed safe in America.

IX. *Death of Tom. Fanny Brawne. Removal to Wentworth Place*

HOW could he tell George and Georgiana, without too much shock, about Tom? In a strange land they had troubles enough; he would spare them if he could. In mid-October, he wrote directly, compassionately: "I am grieved to say that I am not sorry you had not letters at Philadelphia; you could have had no good news of Tom and I have been withheld on his account from beginning these many days. I could not bring myself to say the truth, that he is not better but much worse." Was this sufficiently definite?

He tried again. "My dear brother and sister, take example from me and bear up against any calamity for my sake as I do for yours. . . . I have Fanny and I have you—three people whose happiness to me is sacred—and it does annul that selfish sorrow which I should otherwise fall into, living as I do with poor Tom, who looks upon me as his only comfort."

That last would give pain. He added: "The tears will come into your eyes—let them—and embrace each other—thank heaven for what happiness you have and after thinking a moment or two that you suffer in common with all mankind hold it not a sin to regain your cheerfulness."

Over there, somewhere in the vast wilds of America, they would be able partly to forget him and Tom . . . but he would not tell them so. He himself on the walking tour had all but forgotten—not Tom but Tom's illness.

How kind people were! Haslam, constantly helpful. Good old Mr. Lewis, letting scarcely a day pass without a visit— never a day without bringing or sending fruit of the nicest kind. Here he came now, with a little basket of grapes.

"Fine thing for a hot mouth," he ventured, and sat down beside Tom while Keats placed the blue-black clusters on a table near the bed.

"How is George?" Lewis asked on going.

Keats told him they had heard nothing further and, a moment later walking out a few steps, "I never feel like leaving him alone, but with you he revives a little." He waved toward Tom's room.

He went out occasionally to Dilke's, where they talked of the Bible and Shakespeare and Euclid—"different and indifferent matters." On the twenty-third of October, while Tom rested comfortably with Mr. Lewis beside him, Keats went again to Leigh Hunt's house in Lisson Grove. "My fate!" he silently exclaimed, when he found Ollier there. "He looks at me and talks to me," suspected Keats, "as if the reviewers were uppermost in his mind, and his own riddance of me a good thing." He shook off the feeling and talked about Tom, veiling his profound concern under the most cheerful face he could put on. He got away without opening his heart to Hunt or receiving any comfort. Only slightest signs of superficial interest in the dying boy.

Next day, in a street between Bedford Row and Lamb's Conduit, he met unexpectedly the lady he had seen at Hastings a year ago. He passed and turned back. She was, he thought, glad to see him and he walked on with her toward Islington, explaining that he was out only for air and one direction was as good as another. "But why to Islington?" he asked.

"I have a friend there who keeps a boarding school." They walked on.

During an exceedingly proper visit, in which she proved herself an enigma to Keats, he found himself wondering— he who thought he knew something of women! "She has been in a room with Reynolds and again with George, yet she is not one of the ladies 'east of Temple Bar'—as my enemy put it. What is she? A successor to the hetairae? Or *sui generis?*"

His thoughts were interrupted by the lady's saying good-by to her friend. Perhaps this boarding school is a genteel hint, thought Keats, and went out with her. Yes, he might see her home.

They walked in silence, sometimes through shabby, now through decent streets, and he was guessing what her apartment would be like, hardening himself to any surprise, when they turned in at a number in Gloucester Street, Queen Square. She invited him in. To his surprise, he found her quarters in excellent taste, or what his clique so regarded. She had books, pictures, a bronze of Napoleon, an Aeolian harp with sheet music lying about, a case of choice liqueurs. A parrot looked down solemnly from his perch, and a linnet hopped about in another cage.

"I should like us to be acquainted without any of our friends in common knowing it," she told him in response to an overture. "Here is my little storehouse," she opened a cupboard. "Your sick brother might like this grouse?" She selected one for Tom's dinner.

"I have kissed her," Keats was saying to himself, "and she rebuffs me. It seemed only living backward not to make some protestation!"

"You will please me now," said the lady, thoroughly in control, "if you will press my hand and go away." He went. After all, hers was the better taste. "And she has contrived to disappoint me in a way that makes me feel more pleasure than a simple kiss could give."

148

The grouse in a paper tucked under his arm, he passed out into the street, still puzzled. "Was she in a different disposition when I saw her before? Have I in fancy wronged her? I cannot tell." Perhaps women were, after all, mysterious beings for him, John Keats. He had no libidinous thoughts, he admitted, about this one. She and Georgiana were the only women near his own age whom he would be content to know for mind and friendship alone. He hoped for pleasant hours with her. "I may be of service to her in matters of taste."

Leaving the bird with Mrs. Bentley, he told Tom that the old Hastings acquaintance had provided their dinner.

He saw her several times. She sent other gifts to the invalid. But Tom's illness had routed Jane Cox, and already another young woman—appearing when Keats most needed some one to love—drove into oblivion the generous woman of Gloucester Street.

2

When Keats had set off for the North, he knew his friend's half of Wentworth Place was let for the time of his absence to Mrs. Samuel Brawne, a widow with three children. They were out by the time Brown returned, and now lived near by, on Downshire Hill. Their late landlord had been to see them in their new home but Keats, nursing his sick brother, had not accepted the casual invitation to come along.

One morning, out for a walk in the nipping air of autumn, he met a small young lady—Stylish, he thought at once—attended by a younger boy carrying a rake over his shoulder. The lady was in dark blue. As Keats passed them and the girl gave him a swift glance from under the cover of a fetching hat, he saw that her eyes were also blue, and her hair—or as much as was visible—was light golden-brown. Her cheeks

149

were rosy; they were walking fast, she and the rake-bearer. Keats turned a corner. He looked across and saw them turning in at Wentworth Place.

"Who was the Diana, or Venus, out for an airing with an attendant Cupid?" he asked Brown later, and explained.

"That would be Miss Fanny Brawne and her brother Sam," he was told. Sam had brought home a garden tool, either borrowed or carried off by mistake. Fanny Brawne liked to walk and was usually squired by her brother. Margaret, or "Toots," was only a little thing.

Whenever Keats thought of that meeting, he knew freshness and vigor had crossed his path.

Shortly afterward, when Brown was leaving Number One Well Walk after a call upon Tom, he told Keats of an invitation to the Dilkes'. "Mrs. Dilke says it will do you good to get out for a meal."

Keats looked toward his brother's room.

"I'll dig up a friend or send my maid to sit with him," Brown promised, and Keats said he would come but might not stay late.

Some days passed before Keats and Brown appeared together in the Dilke home, where Maria Dilke met them with a cheerful company air. "A surprise for you," she told them, "the Brawnes are coming." A moment of conversation, and the ting of the bell was succeeded by a general arrival. Young Charles bore the two youngsters away to some place of their own, and the ladies went to remove their wraps.

Keats, talking to Dilke about Tom, looked up as Mrs. Brawne entered. She greeted him kindly, asked about his brother, and spoke of his poems, which she had read and admired. While he was thanking her, he saw over Mrs. Brawne's shoulder the prettiest girl he had ever seen. She stood in the doorway, a dainty figure in white, soft white, down to her toes. About his height, he saw at once, now she

150

was hatless—for he also recognized at once the girl he had met on the road—and crowned by gold-brown hair that was the counterpart of his own. A blue ribbon, tangled up in her curls, enhanced the beauty of her eyes and the delicate coloring of her oval face. "My daughter," Mrs. Brawne was presently saying, and Keats was presented as the poet whose lines she had been reading.

Frank and unaffected, the girl held out her hand, and Keats felt the strength in her firm fingers. Here was a young woman vital, beautiful. And when he sat beside her at table, he was charmed into a spell by her pleasing intonations and trained voice, but still a seeming-natural voice; he was sensible she was not false or affected.

He remembered little of what was said at that dinner. He recalled saying his mother was Fanny, his sister was Fanny, and of breaking off in some confusion. She had rescued him by her bald statement, "And I am Fanny!"

From that time she held his thoughts, his imagination. Her mere existence made possible the contemplation of life without his brother. Not that he failed to give Tom all he was and had; but it was, he felt, the gift of a being enlarged, heightened, more than ever sensitive to all that wrought ecstasy. He did not mention her, except casually, to the sick boy; he did not talk of her to his friends. Only Brown, shrewd observer, suspected how it was with him. But, as yet, neither he nor Brown spoke of this consuming new interest.

He saw her as often as he could leave Tom and she would permit. He existed in memories of her beauty, trying to recapture the shifting phases of a personality none the less constant for manifold phases. She seemed pleased to be with him, in a companionable way. . . . Within a week he was convinced she was his mate, she and no other. He never wearied of watching the color flow and ebb under her delicate skin, the pure lines of her oval face, the inner self revealed

151

through her eyes—eyes he had early pronounced "peerless."

He who had let no woman possess his soul was humbled. If he felt worship for women in his young days, he had also felt that worship pine and die. In recent years, he had been fearfully distrustful of women. Mostly now he was sorry for them. In the hospital he had seen them dying of cancers, bearing children, suffering on the operating table. There were plenty of the sex, as a sex, "east of Temple Bar," and he recalled what he had written to Reynolds, "You are sensible no man can set down venery as a bestial or joyless thing until he is sick of it. . . ." Let that pass. Let all that side of his life go forever. . . . He got up to answer Tom's call.

The last day of October was his twenty-third birthday. He had written the Georges, "I hope I shall never marry. Though the most beautiful creature were waiting for me at the end of a journey or walk; though the carpet were of silk, the curtains of the morning clouds, the wine beyond claret; the window opening on Winandermere, I should not feel— or rather my happiness would not be so fine as my solitude is sublime. Then, instead of what I have described, there is sublimity to welcome me home. The roaring of the wind is my wife and the stars through the window-pane are my children. The mighty abstract idea I have of beauty in all things stifles the more divided and minute domestic happiness—an amiable wife and sweet children I contemplate as part of that beauty."

He lifted his watch lying before him and studied the miniature forming the back, the pearl-framed husband, wife, and two children. "But I must have a thousand of those beautiful particles to fill up my heart."

"How I would deceive myself!" He knew why, his imagination stronger, he was living not only on earth but in a thousand worlds. Knew why shapes of epic greatness stationed themselves about him, serving his spirit the office of a king's bodyguard. Why did he feel himself fighting with Achilles, shouting in the trenches? Why did he lead a pastoral life with Theocritus in the vales of Sicily? Or why, lost in memory of Troilus and Cressida, did he repeat, " 'I wander like a lost soul upon the Stygian banks, staying for waftage?' " How was it he could melt into thin air with a voluptuousness so delicate he was content to be alone?

His brain was creating Titans: Apollo in his mind was dethroning Hyperion, old god of the Sun; Neptune overthrowing Oceanus, Jupiter conquering Saturn. They were warring, these giants; the older gods that had wrought order from disorder out of chaos with the new gods who must succeed because the "first in beauty should be first in might." And, at times, he knew the epic conflict figured the war in his own soul.

He well knew to what he owed the mighty creative surge, now of all times when a dying brother would—because of his love for that brother—hold him infertile but for one young girl.

Was it possible love could do all this for a man? Now he doubted; but again he no longer had doubts of his poetic powers, or "I seldom have any," he wrote George and Georgiana. Again, he had no doubts of his passion for Fanny Brawne, no doubts she was the leaven that quickened all his being.

3

Fanny, Sister Fanny, was importunate. When she came in October he had taken her to the home of a friend and she had "let it out" to the Abbeys, who were firmer not to let her return. "It's difficult to advise her," he rubbed a perplexed brow and wound up by sending her a reminder that in childhood we may be associated with people "whose conduct forces us into duplicity and falsehood. . . . To the worst of people we should be open-hearted; but it is as well, as things are, to be prudent in making any communication to any one that may throw an impediment in the way of any little pleasures you may have. I do not recommend duplicity but prudence with such people."

"Will they read her mail?" Unthinkable! He folded and sealed the letter.

He went to see Abbey three times. "I cannot get his consent," he told Tom, "for her to come again soon. He says once between now and the Holy days will be sufficient."

To himself he said, "She will not see Tom again. Maybe—"

November drew the last ounce of strength from his exhausted body. Keats had not seen his mother die after the long illness she had endured while he was yet a little boy. His greatest sorrow had been that she was gone, and he had hidden from the world, his world, behind a desk at the Enfield school. Now he saw suffering he endured as his own, suffering that forecast his own end. Or would his end be the same? George and he had escaped so far. Yet again his throat was often sore—as Tom's had been, at first.

Absorbed in grief and worry, he was always getting into "painful trammels." He went to call on Rice who, he was told at the door, was engaged, and forthwith came away. Rice explained that a mistake had occurred and made an overture of what Keats termed *"un surcroit d'amitie."*

"I always take for granted the genuine heartedness of my friends," he assured Rice. Everybody was at times ambiguous in tongue or behavior, and he gave two instances of his own gaucherie.

Said a friend, "I shall go and see Severn this week."

"Ah," said Keats, "you want him to take your portrait!" The friend had flushed.

When the friend got up to go home, he asked, "Keats, when will you come to town again?" And he had replied, "I will let you have the manuscript next week." This time the friend looked angry.

"I am innocent," explained Keats, "but it seemed downright preintention!"

Occasional meetings with Fanny Brawne refreshed his soul, while he and Tom agonized toward the end of November.

The night of November 30 he did not close his eyes. All his medical knowledge and experience had told him this night would be the last. Early in the morning of December first, after fearful suffering Tom lay in seemingly painless quiet. Keats, watching, saw him make a slight movement, utter a faint sound, gently lifted him up and so held him until he died. . . . Keats closed his eyes, drew the sheet over the wasted body, straightened it neatly, and went to wake Brown in Wentworth Place. "Tom is no more," he said. Brown in silence took Keats's hand and so they remained a little while. Then Brown spoke, "Have nothing more to do with these lodgings, Keats. Alone, too. Had you not better live with me?"

Keats hesitated, then warmly pressing Brown's hand replied, "I think it would be better."

Friends were kind in helping with Tom's burial, at St. Stephen's, Coleman Street, on the seventh of December. Some of them went with him to see Sister Fanny or called at his and Brown's rooms. All made gestures of help from offers to remove him from the Bentleys' to telling cheerful stories that would make him smile a little. Bentley himself took over to Wentworth Place a basket of books. "I hope," said

Keats, "you and Mrs. Bentley will not be losers by my leaving—"

"No, oh, no!" Bentley assured him; "that is, we shall not soon find young gentlemen of whom we shall be so fond—" and Bentley got away with the empty basket.

Haslam brought thin paper for overseas letters. "Will you write to George, telling him—"

"I wish to do so," said Haslam and also would attend to any business near his father's place in Leadenhall Street.

Hunt invited Keats and Brown to the Novellos, where they were "devastated and excruciated with bad and repeated puns." Keats discerned anew that although Hunt was a pleasant fellow in the main, in reality he was vain, egotistical, and disgusting in taste and morals.

"He understands many a beautiful thing," reflected Keats, "but then, instead of giving other minds credit for the same degree of perception as he himself possesses—he begins an explanation in such a curious manner that our taste and self-love is offended continually." Hunt made fine things petty and beautiful things hateful.

With Brown, Keats saw *Brutus*, the new tragedy by John Howard Payne; it was poor, Kean was good. This was the first time, he remarked, that he had been to the theater since he and George went to the Lyceum, early in the year.

He renewed acquaintance with Lamb and Hazlitt, he and Hazlitt exchanging views on *Blackwood's*. An admirer sent him, anonymously, a check for £25. The author of *Scottish Chiefs*, Miss Jane Porter, had obliged—rather than flattered—in writing of his "true Parnassian fires."

All these details engaged him superficially. One thing gripped him vitally, completely. Held no longer by brotherly love and dearest duty, he lost himself in Fanny Brawne. He could not get rid of her; he did not wish to get rid of her. She had appeared, as at the wave of a magician,

156

when most needed. So deeply had she sunken into the depths of his being, she could be drawn to the surface with only most elaborate casualness. Keats hoped he was canny enough to seem casual. Mrs. Brawne, he wrote the Georges, was a very nice woman. Fanny, the older daughter, was beautiful, elegant, and graceful. ("This will never do: three adjectives glorifying her. I must dull the edge a trifle.") "Silly, fashionable, and strange," he added. ("Have I balanced the big compliment?") He spoke of their having a "tiff" now and then. ("Sounds like a lovers' spat, or will to Sister George."). "She behaves a little better, or I must have sheered off." Lest even so much might arouse keen-minded Georgiana's suspicions where a love affair possibly loomed, he plunged into deliberate nonsense about Miss Miller's birthday party. He might comply with the invitation to be there, that the party might not be destitute of dandies. He would appear in a complete dress of purple, hat and all. He would embroider a conquered list of beauties around his calves.

Brown's nephews were visiting their uncle, stirring up more or less pandemonium. At this point Brown came in, holding each by the hand, to announce, "We are going to the zoo, Keats, to see the lions."

Keats suppressed a "Thank God," and hoped they would enjoy the roars.

On the day now so quiet he tried to get on with "Hyperion" but, out of the vein, must take time to find it. Yet his mind had just been teeming with images, scenes of illimitable magnitude, and with highly appropriate phrases. Through his thoughts for the poem ran the bright thread of Fanny Brawne.

"Shall I give you Miss Brawne?" he resumed his letter. "She is about my height—with a fine style of countenance of the lengthen'd sort—" ("Aha!" Georgiana will say

157

knowingly.) "She manages to make her hair look well" (God forgive me, but this lack of enthusiasm will pass the American scrutiny). "Her nostrils are fine" ("Why should he be examining her nose?" Georgiana will ask.) "A little painful" (how is this to balance the scales, sister?). "Her mouth is good and bad" (she can't make much of this pro and con). "Her profile is better than her full face, which indeed is not full but pale and thin without showing any bone." (That will throw off Sister Georgiana. But to call that exquisite rose-leaf complexion "pale," Lord, forgive me.) He must make amends at once: "Her shape is very graceful and so are her movements" (now I am being too complimentary). "Her arms are good, her hands badish—her feet tolerable" (if this isn't a perfect balance, I know not what is), "and she is not seventeen." *

He sat back and regarded what he had written. Altogether showing minute interest on the part of John Keats. He continued: "But she is ignorant—monstrous in her behavior, flying out in all directions, calling people such names, that I was forced lately to make use of the term *Minx*—that is I think not from any innate vice but from a penchant she has for acting stylishly. I am, however, tired of such style" (O, am I?) "and shall decline any more of it." (There. Georgiana will think I'm through. And yet, would she?)

Why did he not wish to tell the two, so far away, of this amazing change in his life? Perhaps because nothing would come of it? Maybe. He might be fickle. Any hope he entertained might be doomed, anyway. But so it was. He held fast to his secret.

He wasn't through, however, with his gossip. Miss Brawne had had visiting her one Miss Caroline Robinson, whom they all "hated and smoked and baited," and perhaps had driven

---

* So he thought.

away. "Miss B— thinks her a paragon of fashion, and says she is the only woman she would change persons with. What a stupe! She is superior as a rose to a dandelion." (Make what you will of this opinion, Sister.)

"What an ugly old woman that Miss Robinson will make," Brown was getting into bed after an evening at the Brawnes'. Keats groaned aloud for some ten minutes.

He had not seen the "thing Kingston" again. The very thought of the gentleman whom Lamb had insulted at Haydon's dinner suggested a comedy, among the characters of which would be Hunt. For example, Scene: A little parlor. Enter Hunt, that man Gattie, Hazlitt, Mrs. Novello, Ollier.

> *Gattie—Ha, Hunt! Got into your new house. Ha! Mrs. Novello, seen "Altham and His Wife"?*
>
> *Mrs. Novello* (with a grin)—*It's Mr. Hunt's, isn't it?*
>
> *Gattie—Hunt's? No, ha! Mr. Ollier, I congratulate you upon the highest compliment I ever heard paid to the book. Mr. Hazlitt, I hope you are well.*
>
> *Hazlitt—Yes, sir; no, sir.*
>
> *Mr. Hunt* (at the music)—*"La Biondina," etc. Mr. Hazlitt, did you ever hear this? "La Biondina," etc.*
>
> *Mr. Hazlitt—Oh, no sir; I never—*
>
> *Ollier—Do, Hunt, give it us over again—divino—*
>
> *Gattie—Divino—Hunt, when does your Pocket Book come out?*
>
> *Hunt—What is this absorbs me quite? Oh, we are spinning on a little; we shall floridize soon, I hope. Such a thing was very much wanting. People think of nothing but money-getting. Now, for me, I am rather inclined to the liberal side of things—I am reckoned lax in my Christian principles, &c, &c, &c, &c.*

He had pretty thoroughly smoked the Hunt circle. He dropped the letter; he slept.

Sunday, the twenty-second, he dined with Haslam; Monday, the twenty-third, with Haydon. Monday morning he went to see his sister, to hear she was to be taken from school. "I shall strive all I can against her removal," he wrote George. Yet Abbey was her guardian. "There is really nothing I can do about it," he told himself.

With Dilke—who had gone with Mrs. Dilke into London for a short stay at the Christmas season—he had had a good day of shooting on the heath. Was that where he had got back his sore throat? But for it he would be with Brown in the country, at Chichester. If he could not keep well, what was to be the outcome of "Hyperion"? When not too concerned over his throat, he was turning to manners and customs long since past and to regions of the imagination. The present age appeared more and more inadequate. Mrs. Tighe's *Psyche* once had delighted him; Beattie's *Minstrel* had pleased him. Now he saw through them or saw only weakness, vapidity. Might a superior being look upon Shakespeare in the same light? Never!

This same inadequacy is discovered in women, he was thinking aloud to George and Georgiana, whether dressmaker, bluestocking, or the most charming sentimentalist. They differ but in a slight degree and are easily smokable. He admitted a few exceptions. (Fanny Brawne—was she so easily smoked? No.) Maybe he was sacrilegious. He had thought so little, perhaps he was certain of no truth "but from a clear perception of its beauty," and he was very young-minded even in that perceptive power. A year ago he had no perception for the cartoons of Raphael. Only by studying Guido's saints, painted in an opposite spirit, he began to read them a little. He would always have room left for the imagination. Fanny Brawne, now, gave room for wondering. He would never fathom her. If he did, it would be after a long time.

160

X. *Beginning of a Wonderful Year*

IN his best suit, with stiffened high collar and flowing tie, Keats sat down to New Year's Day dinner with Mrs. Brawne. Looking about the table at his comely hostess, vivacious small Margaret ("Toots"), the beautiful Fanny, and merry Mrs. Dilke, he resolved: "I shall go no more to Redhall's or Butler's or any squad where a fine feature cannot be mustered among the lot." Fanny talked of the latest dance and Maria Dilke twitted her pleasantly. Even Dilke's harping on his son's prowess was tolerable. "I feel this beginning of 1819 is auspicious," Keats told himself, and accepted another cake with white icing.

Back in his room, alone, he was miserable. He might come out of the dumps if he continued the letter to George and Georgiana. He told them of the dinner, at which "nothing particular passed." He picked up the paper, scanning it for what might interest: they might like to hear of the banquet given to Tom Moore in Dublin—and, then, despite resolution to keep a canny silence, reverted to his woe and his delight. "I never forget you except after seeing now and then some beautiful woman." That was a fever, he added, "whereas the thought of you both is a passion with me but for the most part a calm one." But he shied off; he could not speak of Fanny.

He sat there recalling her animated face, eloquent gestures, graceful attitudes. Did she know the meaning of love? How his throat ached. He should not have joined in the singing. . . .

161

He looked about for snuff, though he was giving up the habit. He had none. Why didn't Dilke appear? He'd promised to come and sit this evening. He began copying "Ever Let the Fancy Roam," in which he had insisted that pleasure is distant and evanescent:

> *At a touch sweet pleasure melteth*
> *Like to bubbles when rain pelteth.*

While copying twenty-five lines, beginning around the fortieth, he had a mental image of George reading and remembering: the foraging rooks of Hampstead Heath; all the flowers they had known when, as boys, they roamed the fields together, from the first hedgerow primrose to the daisy and the marigold. Freckled eggs of the robin: would George recall the hawthorn tree and the nest they had watched for fledglings? The swarming of bees nobody could forget! "Ring a bell! Draw them to that peachtree limb!" Nor would George forget the chief functionary, veiled, holding a smudge in thickly gloved hands. This poem would bring back to him all these joys and excitements of childhood.

But neither he nor little George would suspect the identity of the young lady who was source of the lines beginning:

> *Let then winged Fancy find*
> *Thee a mistress to thy mind.*
> *Dulcet-eyed as Ceres' daughter*
> *Ere the god of torment taught her*
> *How to frown and how to chide.*
>
> .   .   .
>
> *Never fulsome, ever new.*

Was it possible that for himself Fanny Brawne could be always new?

Balancing his poetry, he told them of Hazlitt's comment on Godwin, ending with lines that seemed quite correct: "The effect both in *Caleb Williams* and *St. Leon* is entirely

162

made out not by facts nor dates . . . but by intense and patient study of the human heart, and by the imagination projecting itself into certain situations, and capable of working up its imaginary feelings to the height of reality."

He told of other poems he had written. "Bards of Passion and of Mirth," which he would term "a sort of rondeau" [incorrectly so]; and the ten lines he had composed while Charlotte Reynolds played the piano to his listening. People might relish these things, he hazarded, "people who cannot bear the burden of a long poem."

Two days later Kirkman came to gossip with him. "I trust you have not been robbed and beaten again," Keats referred to Kirkman's recent adventure in Pond Street. He had not been, but in talking over relatives and their ways, he narrated a villainous trick his Uncle William had played. "He became our sole creditor," said he, "under pretence of serving Father, then put an execution on his own sister's goods. That is, my mother's."

"How could he?" asked Keats.

"Went into the family at Portsmouth, conversed with 'em; went out and sent in the sheriff's officer." Giving Keats no time for considering such unbrotherly action, he passed to another topic. "Have you heard of Archer's abominable behavior to Caroline Mathew?"

Keats murmured that he did not often see the Mathew family nowadays.

"Well, he's practically lived there nearly these two years; he's been amusing Caroline all this time—and now he writes Mrs. Mathew declaring he is unable to support a wife as he would wish, and so declining all thoughts of marriage."

"Mrs. Mathew doubtless had good reasons," suspected Keats, "for provoking him to such statement." In reporting the tidbit to the Georges, he added, "The worst is, Caroline is 27 years old."

163

Sitting there before his unfinished letter, he wondered whether it would be possible to obtain his inheritance and invest it through legal friends so as to bring a small competence. When Grandfather Jennings died, he had left more property than individual bequests amounted to. What would be best? "That is the question both Granny and Mother asked," he reflected, " 'What shall we do?' They were advised to let the estate be settled by the Chancery Court; and if they so agreed, my mother—who was now Mrs. Rawlings —and her husband, William Rawlings, must bring a friendly suit against Granny and Uncle Midgely, the executors. They brought the suit." He drew flowers on the back of a letter lying before him, but he saw not them so much as the result of that suit. "It has been hanging fire all these years. Doubtless it will end only with Fanny's coming of age. That will be, O Lord, six more long years." What, he wondered, absent-mindedly putting a leaf on a violet, would happen to his hopes? What to the promises made between him and Fanny Brawne?

"Let me be not downcast. 'Melancholy is the nurse of frenzy,' 'Of Cerberus and darkest Midnight born.' " He was not worse off, he ended, than when he told Fanny Brawne he loved her. Yet another voice urged, "Better give her up."

At that moment a sharp knock on the wall called him to tea. He smoothed his hair, pulled himself together and hurried into the adjoining house, where Mrs. Dilke had the service ready: bread and butter, celery, cakes, steaming tea and hot water. He and the lady always got on well together in a superficial way from the exchange of light persiflage to Gibbon's *History* or Wordsworth's *Sermons*.

"I still have qualms when recollecting that unsealed note of sham abuse I sent you"; John accepted his cup of India. "What if the servant had been able to read and you would see me no more?"

164

"But she could neither read nor write," Maria Dilke smiled. "As Charles said, 'Not even to her mother!'"

"Thank God!" Keats spoke over a buttered scone.

She inquired about his sister.

"Well enough, but missing her brothers. So long as the Abbey guardianship and the Chancery suit continue I can see her only now and then." He did not add that Abbey disapproved of Fanny's brothers and so kept her away from them as far as he possibly could.

His hostess indicated a face-screen, shading her cheeks from the heat of coals in the open fire, and lifted a work bag. "These are excellently done by a girl of her age."

"She wished to bring them, herself. Now that you have invited her I will do my best to arrange a visit."

Charles Dilke and his wife knew of that litigation and only Maria's knowledge of Keats's sensitive nature forbade her opening a discussion, though she believed it would help him to talk—and she felt she might have some wise counsel to offer. Instead, to divert him, she threw a celery stalk—playfully opening battle.

After the sham conflict, he returned to his room in better spirits. The violet on the back of the envelope reminded him of Fanny Brawne. "Give her up? I will not." He had never lacked, he thought, courage or determination; "If I may not have money, I will have Fame." He took from his desk drawer the script of "Hyperion," untouched for days.

"Deep in the shady sadness of a vale,"

he chanted, on past the "Goddess of the infant world," to the speech in Saturn's ear:

In solemn tenor and deep organ tone:
Some mourning words, which in our feeble tongue
Would come in these like accents; O how frail
To that large utterance of the early gods!

165

He felt uneasy. Something was wrong. He read the next line aloud:

"Saturn, look up!—Though wherefore, poor old King?

"The trouble with my 'Hyperion' is—I am tardy in see-ing—that my gigantic concepts are belittled by the introduc-tion of our human speech. Yet how get on with the story unless I employ words? Swath my characters in eternal silence? What then becomes of my drama? A pantomime!"

To be sure there were Milton's characters. *They* talk. "Ah, but," he answered himself, "though epic, they are—some of them—our presumable prototypes. It seems natural they should use our tongue. And where Jehovah speaks—" he smiled at memory of the speeches— "he is not entirely suc-cessful. A Van Dyke bearded ruler—Milton couldn't get rid of the image he knew in Charles—not the Great I Am, in-finite source of all that is or ever will be."

He turned the pages of unfinished "Hyperion," remem-bering his invocation of the Muse. The poem was to treat of the dethronement of Hyperion by Apollo, of Oceanus by Neptune, of Saturn by Jupiter. There had been Milton's tremendous "Battle of the Angels" for inspiration—

"But la! la! How is John Keats to surpass that?" and he spoke in deepest, most resonant tones:

"Michael bid sound
The archangel trumpet—"

with many lines thereafter. He recalled all the battle be-tween the fighting seraphim: Michael's sword that felled squadrons at once but met Satan's rocky, orbed shield of ten-fold adamant; the unspeakable fight between them, when at length the heavenly angel sheared at Satan's right side; when Uriel and Raphael armed in a rock of diamond were vanquished by Gabriel—through the long conflict until the mighty angels threw away their arms—

> *and to the hills*
> *Light as the lightning-glimpse they ran, they flew;*
> *From their foundations, loosening to and fro,*
> *They plucked the seated hills, with all their load,*
> *Rocks, waters, woods, and, by the shaggy tops*
> *Uplifting, bore them in their hands.*

Great God! Who was he, John Keats, to better that fight? How could he portray the war of giants for Saturn's return to his reign? He became hysterical thinking that if he could but have them hurling planets at one another. . . . "Even if I could, I'd probably get reviewed as showing a snow-ball squabble among Enfield babies."

He turned the pages of "Hyperion" to the point where he had tried to do without human words and voice:

> *There is a roaring in the bleak-grown pines*
> *When winter lifts his voice; there is a noise*
> *Among immortals when a god gives sign,*
> *With hushing finger, how he means to load*
> *His tongue with the full weight of utterless thought,*
> *With thunder, and with music, and with pomp:*
> *Such noise is like the roar of bleak-grown pines. . . .*

He paused, then read on to the line:

> *Leave the dinn'd air vibrating silverly.*

Keats's sense of poetic beauty was hurt by the human speech that followed: these mighty imaginings, these heroic figures must not speak the English tongue! "I can't go on." His mind flashed back to that evening when writing sonnets on the River Nile—he and Hunt and Shelley—he had read "Ozymandias."

167

Forever Young

Two vast and trunkless legs of stone
Stand in the desert—

and so on to

Look on my works, ye mighty, and despair!

"Those trunkless legs of stone must prefigure my poem, 'Hyperion.' A worthy concept, to be sure. Too worthy, my boy, and a Lost Cause.

"Has this resolution not to complete your poem anything to do with living or loving?" At this challenge to himself, he rebounded to the other problem: How can I love? How is it possible to ask a woman to marry me—"Little Keats," and not only "Little Keats"—that matters not—but a Keats without resources, in short, a pauper.

"My publishers might help again," he reminded himself. But the sense of "squareness and fairness" he had mentioned to them asked, "Will my works bring in money to repay them? I doubt they ever do."

"Then, again, are they worth anything?" whispered an imp.

"Past all doubting," he squared his shoulders. "Did Milton not receive five pounds for all of 'Paradise Lost'? And who doubts its worth?"

"Then write!"

"I will write. A thousand lines wait to be expressed. Short poems. Let them come short if not long."

He reverted to the idea that had haunted him since he first thought of it—a fancied situation becoming real . . . "Adam's Dream." He tucked it away and picked up the New Year's present Brown had given him: Burton's *Anatomy of Melancholy,* 612 pages, copy of an edition published five or six years ago. The book fascinated him; forgetting to sit down, he read and read, foot on chair round, before dropping from exhaustion into the chair. Reaching for his quill, he made notes along the margins. Here now, Part 2, Sec. 4, Memb. 1, Subs. 4: page 99: ". . . almost all jewels and precious stones have excellent vertues to pacify the affections of the mind." He laughed, and added this note: "Precious stones are certainly a remedy against Melancholy: a valuable diamond would effectually cure mine."

"And here in Part 3, Burton has much to say on arguments for marriage:

Hast thou meanes? thou hast one to keep and increase it.
Hast none? thou hast one to help get it.
Art in prosperity? thine happiness is doubled—

and so on for nine queries and favorable arguments. 'But how easy it is to answer these motives,' admits Burton, 'and to make antiparodia quite opposite unto it!' "

Burton offered: "Hast thou means? thou hast one to spend it," and Keats wrote firmly alongside the passage, "Aye—aye."

An "Ode on Melancholy" began to sing in his brain.

The dream poem had precedence. Now he remembered that a handsome Mrs. Jones met not long since had also suggested the subject. Adam and Eve: a girl and her lover. Ideas began rushing into place. He would call the girl Madeline, and himself—the lover—Lionel. (Might change that name—something supercilious and affected about Lionel.) Unaware of time, he conjured glorious visions, while his mind passed through the intensities of composition and decomposition that fed upon his soul and brain like fire. Place: a rich setting—holy scenes, or else faery-like; secondary characters—as foils—must be old; adornments, luxurious— These he created, rejected, and recreated, and before he slept knew that soon and suddenly he would bring them forth on a white page.

169

To Dick Woodhouse he had written briefly, savagely, before the holidays. Woodhouse had thought he might like an introduction to people of society, from whom he might derive advantage and gratification. "I must needs be flattered by making an impression on a set of ladies," Keats had said. "I should be content to do so in meretricious romance verse if they alone and not men were to judge." The fact was, he informed his friend, he must write and had no time for new acquaintances.

Worried over need for money, over himself and Fanny Brawne, and over a promised loan to Haydon, he went with some transient relief in early January to visit Dilke's father at Chichester and sister Mrs. Snook at Bedhampton. He needed to envision new scenes, and Charles Brown would be there for company.

After a few days with Dilke, Senior, whose entertainment consisted chiefly of dowager card parties, Keats and Brown moved along to Bedhampton, a walk of nine or ten miles, partly across the fields. They trudged easily, briskly, over icy ground on a crisp day, and Keats spoke of Haydon. "You know, Brown, when I wrote him that note saying somewhat about the feeling I had that would sacrifice all to his service, I must have had too much claret or for other cause been too —elevated." He knew in his heart he had been intoxicated with Fanny Brawne and her accepting him as a sweetheart. "But even so," he went on, "I begged him to make me his last mainstay, to try the long purses first. He said, you know, he would try every corner—and I hoped he would find a patron."

"He's had a number so far, hasn't he?" Brown's voice was sardonic.

"Most probably. So I borrowed £30 more from Taylor and Hessey, for myself." He added ruefully, "Then Haydon proposed getting his bond ready, with a two years' limit

for payment. I must do what I can when I get back to
London."

Cutting at the dead grasses with his walking stick, Brown
did not say what he thought: that a man ten years older than
Keats should be not only accepting—but begging—money
from him, a boy. "For everybody knows Haydon. He will
never repay it."

They walked on, talked on, Keats missing no detail of the
path and the road: frozen foliage, birds that seemed shiver-
ing, and tiny furred creatures scuttling away under faded
covers. In a pasture, there at the fence stood a flock of sheep
so still not even the bell of the wether tinkled. And under-
neath his observations, his remarks touching their recent
pastimes, a deeper stratum of his mind was busy with Fanny-
Madeline, John-Prospero and the setting. "Where was it we
saw the angels, Brown, with wings crossed on their breasts?"

"Lincluden," Charles told him.

A day or so after they were established in their guestrooms
at the Snook home, Keats sat before the wood fire, writing
on some of the thin paper Haslam had given him for letters
to America. The first draft of the "little poem" flowed off
easily; he believed it good. Brown praised "St. Agnes Eve."

While Brown tried to write to Dilke and Mrs. Dilke,
Keats's extraordinary spirits kept interrupting. "It may as
well be a joint composition, Brown," and Keats got in the last
line: "N.B. I beg leaf to withdraw all my puns—they are all
wash, an base uns." But before this atrocity on washing basins
he revealed that C.B. had shaved off his whiskers at the request of a lady, while he himself was wearing his shirt-collar
"up to eyes and ears."

He'd be fine if his throat would stop hurting.

Was he missing Fanny Brawne? Not while he could sub-
limate his longings in a poem called "St. Agnes Eve."

2

Back in Wentworth Place he wrote his sister, "I want you to teach me a few common dancing steps." He had sent her a volume of Goldsmith's *Poems* and now promised another book the first time he was in town in time to send it by the Walthamstow coach. "I am the only protector she has," and he had told her so. But what a difference in his feeling for her and the other Fanny! And what would she make of his sudden desire to dance?

Except when with Fanny Brawne he was sad or cynical. Was his throat making him see blue and green? "Conversation is not a search after knowledge, but an endeavor at effect," he said to Haydon, adducing Wordsworth and Hunt, otherwise opposites, as in this respect the same. "You know what, Haydon? I was about to approve something Wordsworth said that day I called but was restrained by Mrs. Wordsworth. She touched my arm, 'Mr. Wordsworth is never interrupted.' And, mind you, I was but agreeing with what he had remarked!"

3

In mid-February, he wrote the Georges he would send in the next packet his "Pot of Basil," "St. Agnes Eve," and if he should have finished it, a little thing called "The Eve of St. Mark." Fanny's Sunday frock he had reproduced in this last poem, but he was not telling them—or anybody else—so.

> "*From plaited lawn-frill, fine and thin,*
> *She lifted up her warm, sweet chin,*"

he repeated and continued not with the poem immediately but thought of his love, lost himself in his thoughts. How sweetly she bent her eyes on the object of her regard—when the object was himself. He did not like to see her face turned toward another. He went on with the picture of Bertha, "with bright drooping hair," and the story she read:

At length her constant eyelids come—

on to the end of the part written. Again, he dreamed of Fanny; and, dreaming, of that poem he wrote no more that day—or ever.

He would not go to Miss Miller's dance on the nineteenth of February; "a dance would injure my throat very much." Almost tired of men and things, he was seeing few persons, but Brown and Dilke had been kind and considerate. He had "had it out" with Abbey. "He knows he is the only man in England," Keats wrote his brother, "who dares say a thing to me I do not approve of without it being resented or at least noticed." He had written Abbey this conclusion and so made an alteration in his favor.

He was sorry to feel at odds with old Mr. Lewis, who had been so kind to Tom. Lewis had gone to town with Mrs. Brawne one morning this February and they had talked about himself, John Keats. "He is quite the little poet," said Lewis. Keats hooted. "You may as well say Buonaparte is quite the little soldier. You see what it is to be under six foot and not a lord." He was not at all pleased with that remark of the old man, particularly since it had been made to Mrs. Brawne.

Brown, who had been sitting opposite, got up, stretched himself, and went into the garden, where Dilke presently appeared. Keats paused in his letter-writing, looked at the Isle of Wight Shakespeare—adorned with the silk tassels Georgiana had affixed—and strolled to the window. Was spring in the air? There they stood talking, busily pointing out this or that, doubtless planning spring flowers—and cabbages.

Would Fanny go to Miss Miller's dance, even though he

could not be with her? He would not be selfish. She must be there. Yet those gold-braided young officers, reeking of glory from the Napoleonic wars, took a young woman's fancy. "But let her wear her pretty stylish clothes and be the most admired, most sought after—" He was torturing himself. As in a dream he sat down again, drew paper toward him, and wrote:

ODE TO FANNY

I

Physician Nature! let my spirit blood!
O ease my heart of verse and let me rest;
Throw me upon thy Tripod, till the flood
Of stifling numbers ebbs from my full breast.
A theme! a theme! great Nature, give a theme;
Let me begin my dream.
I come—I see thee as thou standest there,
Beckon me not into the wintry air.

II

Ah! dearest love, sweet home of all my fears,
And hopes, and joys, and panting miseries—
Tonight, if I may guess, thy beauty wears
A smile of such delight,
As brilliant and as bright,
As when with ravished, aching, vassal eyes,
Lost in soft amaze,
I gaze, I gaze!

III

Who now, with greedy looks, eats up my feast?
What stare outfaces now my silver moon!
Ah! keep that hand unravished at the least;
Let, let the amorous burn—
But, pr'ythee do not turn

174

Beginning of a Wonderful Year

The current of your heart from me so soon.
  O! save, in charity,
  The quickest pulse for me.

IV

Save it for me, sweet love! though music breathe
  Voluptuous visions into the warm air;
Though swimming through the dance's dangerous wreath;
    Be like an April day,
    Smiling and cold and gay,
A temperate lily, temperate as fair;
    Then, Heaven, there will be
    A warmer June for me.

V

Why, this—you'll say, my Fanny! is not true:
  Put your soft hand upon your snowy side,
Where the heart beats: confess—'tis nothing new—
    Must not a woman be
    A feather on the sea,
Sway'd to and fro by every wind and tide?
    Of as uncertain speed
    As blow-ball from the mead?

VI

I know it—and to know it is despair
  To one who loves you as I love, sweet Fanny!
Whose heart goes fluttering for you everywhere,
    Nor, when away you roam,
    Dare keep its wretched home,
Love, love alone, has pains severe and many:
    Then, loveliest! keep me free,
    From torturing jealousy.

VII

Ah! if you prize my subdued soul above
The poor, the fading, brief, pride of an hour;
Let none profane my Holy See of love.
  Or with a rude hand break
  The sacramental cake:
Let none else touch the just new-budded flower;
  If not—may my eyes close,
  Love! on their last repose.

Laying the sheets aside, he put on walking shoes, his hat, brushed himself a bit, and set out for a walk. Jealous? If suffering unendurable pain was to be jealous—yes! He turned a corner into an alley, on the run at the outraged cry of a kitten. There at the back door of a neighboring house, at which he was making a delivery, a heavy lout of a butcher's boy had fast hold of a little gray tail. "Drop it," said Keats quietly.

"Not for you," and the bully threatened the kitten with his free hand.

Keats threw off his coat and loosened his collar. "Will you drop that poor creature?" A louder meow from the kitten was the only reply. Keats dragged the hulk to his feet and began pummeling. He was certain of defeat, he said a little afterward to Brown, but the deliverer of beef was of no prowess, though he flailed away as well as his knowledge and code prompted. For a half hour they fought, tearing up the soft earth of the back alley, Keats getting a black eye, but at length coming off victor. The cat-torturer lay prone. Keats tucked in his shirt, drew on his coat and went home to have Brown put a piece of beef over his eye. It was black for a day or so.

I must be in fair condition, thought Keats. Damn it! I *will* go to that dance. After all, it was to be at his sister-in-law's cousin's home. Certainly, he should go for Mrs. Wylie's sake! He got over his black eye.

Dick Woodhouse looked in while he was retouching the "Ode to Fanny." He stuffed the incriminating sheets into a drawer and tried to look disinterested.

"Come out with me, Keats. Eat with me at my coffee-house."

Keats fussed with his collar and looked dubious.

"We should have a bottle of claret, you know."

Keats's palate responded to the word, the color, the conjured sensation. He put on his hat and took out a copy of "The Eve of St. Agnes." "Should you like to read my new poem? I've revised somewhat."

"You gratify my hopes," smiled Woodhouse. "We have all been wondering how you came on."

The luncheon, the claret, and the reception of his poem—which he read in the critic's rooms afterward—raised his spirit to the empyrean. He went back to Wentworth Place and wrote the Georges: "Now, I like claret; whenever I can have claret I must drink it—'tis the only palate affair that I am at all sensual in. How would it be to send some vine roots to America? If they could only make claret like this to drink on summer evenings in an arbor! It fills one's mouth with a gushing freshness," he declared, "then goes on down cool and feverless—then you do not feel it quarreling with your liver—no; it is rather a peace-maker and lies as quiet as it did in the grape. Then it is as fragrant as the Queen Bee; and the more ethereal part of it mounts into the brain, not assaulting the cerebral apartments like a bully in a bad house looking for his trull and hurrying from door to door bouncing against the wainscot; but rather walks like Aladdin about his enchanted palace so gently that you do not feel his step."

No other palate passion? Oh, Lord! He pleaded guilty

177

to "the breast of a partridge, the back of a hare, the backbone of a grouse, the wing and side of a pheasant, and a woodcock, passim." The lady of Hastings remet in town—without special interest—had made him many presents of such delicacies, which usually he handed on to others. She had just given him a pheasant that he had immediately presented to Mrs. Dilke. Shortly, the Dilkes, Rice, Reynolds, and he and Brown would dine off it next door.

Brown was "walking up and down the room a-breeding. Now at this moment he is being delivered of a couplet—and I daresay will be as well as can be expected. Gracious! He has twins."

He read the passage to Brown. "How do you like that now?"

"A physician's figure—and, as such, capital." Brown sat down at his side of the desk.

"How are you coming on, Brown?"

"Slowly. This old woman and devil business does not progress."

"No wonder. Fact is, Brown, you libel the devil, and as he is your Muse, how can you expect to write? Either you or the Muse must turn tail! Before you begin again, let's speak of Bailey. What do you think of his leaving Mariane Reynolds—you know I was sure of his devotion—for Miss Gleig?"

"She liked Bailey as a brother. He used to woo her," Brown's mouth puckered, "with the Bible and Jeremy Taylor under his arm." Keats remembered the picture of Taylor over Bailey's desk.

"They walked in no grove but Jeremy Taylor's," Brown emphasized and took up his crowquill.

Still lost in thoughts of Bailey, Keats said, "You know, while he was making impatient love to Mariane—as I understood—he was also cut up about a little jilt in the country

178

somewhere." He did not say she was Tamsine Leigh. He was seeing an idol, long toppling, crash.

"Perhaps he wishes to marry?" Brown smiled.

"That's the trouble. His so quickly taking to Miss Gleig can have no excuse except that of a ploughman who wants a wife."

"Keats! Keats! No other reason when there's a bishop in the family?" Brown knew any vicar or rector would have an eye open for preferments.

Keats opened wide eyes. He walked away from the empty pedestal.

"What does his friend—and your friend—James Rice think?"

"He has abandoned Bailey entirely," and Keats spoke from recent information. "The great thing to be considered is whether want of delicacy and principle, or want of knowledge and polite experience caused him so to behave with regard to women. There was even talk of a Miss Martin—"

"That was another Bailey," Brown laughed. "Don't take it to heart too much, Keats. Bailey is a parson; he has been, I doubt not, a continent fellow. His heart is correspondingly susceptible. You must know that, and should make allowances."

But Keats could not be sorry that Bailey had lost all his connections in town.

4

The "Ode on Melancholy" refused to shape itself in the mood of luxurious tenderness he had conceived. To save himself, he could not help beginning:

Though you should build a bark of dead men's bones,
And rear a phantom gibbet for a mast

> *Stitch creeds together for a sail, with groans*
> *To fill it out, blood-stained and aghast;*
> *Although your rudder be a dragon's tail*
> *Long sever'd, yet still hard with agony,*
> *Your cordage large uprootings from the skull*
> *Of bald Medusa, certes you would fail*
> *To find the Melancholy—whether she*
> *Dreameth in any isle of Lethe dull.*

"Ghastly as a charnel-house. It won't do, won't do." He pushed aside the page and went out into the garden. Fanny Brawne presently came out to sit with him under the mulberry tree. Gradually, his thoughts and feelings veered in the direction he had charted. When he took up the ode again he began his second stanza:

> *No, no, go not to Lethe, neither twist*
> *Wolf's bane, tight-rooted, for its poisonous wine;*
> *Nor suffer thy pale forehead to be kiss'd*
> *By nightshade, ruby grape of Proserpine;*
> *Make not your rosary of yew-berries,*
> *Nor let the beetle, nor the death-moth be*
> *Your mournful Psyche, nor the downy owl*
> *A partner in your sorrow's mysteries;*
> *For shade to shade to shade will come too drowsily,*
> *And drown the wakeful anguish of the soul.*

Yet he needed something for contrast! Something lively. An angry mood of Fanny he recalled, and went on with the third stanza:

> *But when the melancholy fit shall fall*
> *Sudden from heaven like a weeping cloud,*
> *That fosters the droop-headed flowers all,*
> *And hides the green hill in an April shroud;*

180

Then glut thy sorrow on a morning rose,
  Or on the rainbow of the salt sand-wave,
Or on the wealth of globed peonies;
  Or if thy mistress some rich anger shows,
Emprison her soft hand and let her rave,
  And feed deep, deep upon her peerless eyes.

But he must return to the dominant mood, and write the final stanza:

She dwells with Beauty—Beauty that must die;
  And Joy, whose hand is ever at his lips
Bidding adieu; and aching pleasure nigh,
  Turning to poison while the bee-mouth sips:
Ay, in the very temple of Delight
  Veil'd Melancholy has her sovran shrine,
Though seen of none save him whose strenuous tongue
  Can burst Joy's grape against his palate fine;
His soul shall taste the sadness of her might,
  And be among her cloudy trophies hung.

Many times he reworked the stanzas before attaining this form, and still he was not satisfied. "The first stanza must be left off," and so wrote out a fair copy, beginning, "No, no, go not to Lethe. . . ." At last, he knew the poem too self-revelatory, but he would publish it.

5

"I am resolved," he told Haydon, March 8, "never to write for the sake of writing or making a poem but from running over with any little knowledge or experience which many years of reflection may perhaps give me; otherwise, I will be dumb." Nor would he write for his livelihood, as he had thought of doing, for he "would not run with that most vulgar of all crowds, the literary." Every three or four days or so, he must be at Abbey's or the lawyer's. But before he got the money for Haydon, he opened another importunate note: "Before the 20th if you could help me it would be nectar and manna and all the blessings of gratified thirst."

On that same March 8, Keats with Severn "took a turn round" the British Museum, where for the first time he saw the Sphinx "of a giant size and most voluptuous Egyptian expression." In the evening he and Brown had Severn "with the book-seller and print-virtuoso, Cawthorn," to dinner.

"Have you heard of our Hampstead parson's latest?" Brown referred to the vicar, the Reverend Samuel White, D.D. Keats knew Brown's casualness portended something luscious or laughable. All egged Brown to let them have it.

"When black cloth was being put up for the Queen's mourning, he asked the workmen to hang it wrong side out."

"Why?" somebody cautiously asked, fearing a "sell."

"Why, indeed! It's his perquisite." But nobody smiled.

"It will be all the better when taken down," their host explained, and they knew he had not been jesting.

Brown was keeping his table one of good fellowship. "What do you think of my latest palindrome?" He waited for the last ejaculation over the vicar's "closeness" and spoke slowly, "Evil is a name of foeman, as I live." Somebody took out a pencil and Brown, to save the linen tablecloth, provided a slip of paper.

"Right. Same backward as forward." And Brown said he felt pretty sure somebody had invented it long before. It was too obvious. "But have you heard my anagram on 'John Keats'?"

Nobody had, for he had not divulged it. " 'Thanks, Joe,' " he told them.

For a moment all were silent, rearranging the letters of Keats's name, and Cawthorn, who had used the slip of paper, first spoke, "Correct. But why," he teased, " 'Thanks, Joe'? What does it signify."

"Oh, nothing!" Brown laughed inconsequentially. But Keats smiled at Joseph Severn, who half-rose and bowed.

Soon, Severn went home to paint; the other three climbed a coach for Covent Garden. Keats damned the play, Sheil's *Evadne*, "bad even in comparison with 1818, the Augustan age of the drama."

He was tired when he lay down that night. Was he junketing about too much? burning up too much brain tissue? thinking too much of Fanny Brawne?

XI. *Turmoil, in a Year Still Admirable*

AMONG the beads about his cup of life this March, 1819, Keats mentioned an appropriate letter from Hazlitt to Gifford, part of which he copied. "It begins thus," he told the Georges: " 'Sir, you have an ugly trick of saying what is not true of any one you do not like; and it will be the object of this letter to cure you of it.' " They would understand that Hazlitt was doing a good turn for Keats and other suffering writers in so striking out for himself.

Fanny Brawne walked with him on the heath, enticing his spirits out of the melancholy wherein they persisted. She thought he could, in little things, make his sister's life happier. "Tell her what you do; ask her what she would like from you." Fanny Brawne had a healthy wonder, succeeded by lively indignation, over Fanny's being kept from her brother, whose visits to her were either denied or received grudgingly by her guardian.

When he wrote Fanny, he told of going to Miss Miller's dance—she was acquainted with at least the names of the Wylie relations—and inquired whether she would like some Tassie seals, a book, pencils, or drawing paper—anything but live stock. Then remembering his own fondness for birds and fishes, he weakened, considering a goldfish bowl. One that would hold ten pails of water and be kept fresh with pipes to let water flow in and out. "I would put it before a painted window," he was thinking how he would have it for himself, "and shade it all around with myrtles and japonicas. I should like the window to open onto the Lake of Ge-

184

neva—and there I'd sit and read all day like the picture of somebody reading."

Fanny wanted to know the name of the gentleman who had called with him the last time he came. It was Haslam, who had succeeded to his father's post with Frampton and Sons, and of whom Keats had been mindful after the elder Haslam's recent death. She also wished to know the answers to some questions about her confirmation. He presented her with a Catechism, at the same time undertaking replies to her numbered queries. That letter of March 31 he ended, "Your affectionate Parson John."

But before that time he had gone again to see Abbey. His need for cash was acute. In Pancras Lane he found the man still harping on trades.

"I advise you to become a hatter, John. It's a good business." The smug merchant had no eye for the proud poetic figure; no feeling for the expressive hazel eyes, waving bright mane, or sensitive face.

Keats, for his part, was measuring Abbey, "I believe all this is self-interest on his side." On being told the chancery suit was *in statu quo*, he walked out.

Desperate, he wondered, "Shall I go to Edinburgh and continue my studies in medicine?" He would hate taking fees, though to do that was no worse than writing poems and have them fly-blown by reviewers. "I must earn a living—if I have *her*." So, perplexed, uneasy, he turned in at 93 Fleet Street.

A clerk came forward. "Mr. Taylor has just set out to dine with you," he exclaimed, "and with the artist, Mr. Hilton."

Keats overtook them and later returned cityward with them as far as Camden Town. The thing uppermost now was Taylor's urging him to get ready the new book of poems; "We are eager to bring out your volume." How to exist, how

185

to get along without Edinburgh and hatmaking—all forgotten in the renewed assurance that his poetry was desired. He would write, write. And Hilton was to paint his portrait! He walked, a winged Mercury, back to Wentworth Place, "smoking a segar," in fine feather with himself and all who counted. His head teemed with verses he must get out of it this very spring. He would write, he would be with Fanny, nearer than ever, for Dilke was moving to Westminster and the Brawnes were again in the semidetached house, but in the other half from that they had first occupied.

Severn would also paint a miniature of himself, Keats. He hoped Fanny Brawne would wish it as a gift—after Severn had quite ended with its exhibition, if exhibit he must.

"I am fit. The kitten-teaser proved that for me. But I do need more exercise." Out with a cricket bat, almost immediately he received a white ball full on his eye. Though inflammation had died down by the next morning, he was discouraged: his eyes meant too much—and this was his second black eye of the year!

Simultaneously, after floating in the ether, intoxicated over being wanted by Taylor and Hessey and by Fanny Brawne's loving sympathy, he plunged into black despair, a reaction from the heights, and from despair into a mood of negation. A dead level after extreme ups and downs. All capacity for feeling exhausted, he wrote: "Neither poetry, nor ambition, nor love have any alertness of countenance as they pass by me. They seem rather like three figures on a Greek vase— a man and two women whom no one but myself could distinguish in their disguisement."

Did the only happiness lie in complete indolence? Now there's an idea. I shall most certainly write an "Ode on Indolence"! Already he was again moving upward, even while approving the flats.

Yet he indulged bitterness over selfishness and self-interest. Everywhere! If the hawk wants a mate, so does man. "They set about it and procure one in the same manner." So with nests and food—in the same manner. In their leisures, man smokes a pipe, while the hawk balances about the clouds. A stoat or a fieldmouse "peeping out of the withered grass— the creature hath a purpose and its eyes are bright with it. I go amongst the buildings of a city and I see a man hurrying along—to what? The creature has a purpose and his eyes are bright with it."

He had no doubt that thousands of people unheard of had hearts completely disinterested. "I can remember but two—Socrates and Jesus—their histories evince it." It was lamentable that "the history of the latter was written and revised by men interested in the pious frauds of religion. Yet through this I see his splendor." Linking one thought to another, he arrived at another truth, "Nothing ever becomes real till it is experienced." He had not meant to send his brother and sister the sonnet "Why did I laugh tonight?" but after writing them in a vein which should assure them he would bear well the buffets of the world, he set it down:

Why did I laugh tonight? No voice will tell:
  No god, no demon of severe response
Deigns to reply from heaven or from hell.—
  Then to my human heart I turn at once—
Heart! thou and I are here sad and alone;
  Say, wherefore did I laugh? O mortal pain!
O darkness! darkness! ever must I moan
  To question heaven and hell and heart in vain!
Why did I laugh? I know this being's lease,
  My fancy to its utmost blisses spreads;
Yet could I on this very midnight cease,
  And the world's gaudy ensigns see in shreds.
Verse, fame and beauty are intense indeed
But death intenser—Death is Life's high meed.

187

"My case is hopeless," he told himself, and told himself again.

"When you are vital enough to write such a sonnet?" another self jeered.

"I can do nothing *except* write poems," the dominant self retorted. "I dream poems. But poetry, such as I write, receives no pounds, shillings, and but few pence. Unless my publishers give it to me," he added. "Suppose I should be willing to study medicine? How should I find money to get through at Edinburgh? Consult George? Ah, I did that too often in old days. He has cares—too many—in America." Lost in his own arguments, he wound up, "Death is the end of life. Why not early as well as later? But O, Fanny, Fanny!"

2

Of late he had been occupied with attitudes. Was a poetic variation introducing itself? Or was his preoccupation a result of Brown's proposing they write a drama together? He had written of sitting by a window and reading like the picture of somebody reading. "The candles are burnt out," he wrote in the long letter to George and Georgiana, "and I am using the last taper—which has a long snuff on it. The fire is at its last click—I am sitting with my back to it, with one foot rather askew upon the rug and the other with the heel a little elevated from the carpet. I am writing this on the *Maid's Tragedy*, which I have read since tea with great pleasure." Besides the Beaumont and Fletcher volume, on the table lay two volumes of Chaucer, and Tom Moore's new book, *Tom Cribb's Memorial to Congress*. Trifles, admitted. But he would like nothing better than that they would give like descriptions of themselves.

"What if we had pictures of Shakespeare showing him at

188

this or that? What if we knew in what position he wrote when he began, 'To be or not to be!' "

Beset by attitudes, postures, he thought again of Grecian urns. One he had examined flashed what prefigured an allegory of himself and Fanny Brawne. Or did it? He went to see it once more—the lovely vase that pictured players of pipe and timbrel, a heifer lowing at the skies, a fair youth and his bride. Art and life were different, he reflected, placing the urn back on its pedestal. But the compensation of art lay in the unchanging character of the artist's work. The youth and maiden fixed in the marble thousands of years ago by a Greek artist would be forever young, while he and Fanny—he thought a moment of the unsatisfactory "Ode on Melancholy" before returning to the difference and the likeness between art and life. They are both true and both beautiful. "Why beauty *is* truth, truth *is* beauty!" He wrote the first draft of the "Ode on a Grecian Urn," and so eased the pain about his heart. It came easily, almost perfectly, at first composition.

I

Thou still unravished bride of quietness,
Thou foster-child of silence and slow time,
Sylvan historian, who canst thus express
A flowery tale more sweetly than our rhyme:
What leaf-fringed legend haunts about thy shape
Of deities or of mortals or of both
In Tempe or the dales of Arcady?
What men or gods are these? What maidens loth?
What mad pursuit? What struggle to escape?
What pipes and timbrels? What wild ecstasy?

II

Heard melodies are sweet, but those unheard
Are sweeter; therefore, ye soft pipes, play on;

Forever Young

Not to the sensual ear, but, more endear'd,
Pipe to the spirit ditties of no tone:
Fair youth, beneath the trees, thou canst not leave
Thy song, nor ever can those trees be bare;
Bold lover, never, never, canst thou kiss,
Though winning near the goal—yet, do not grieve;
She cannot fade, though thou hast not thy bliss,
For ever wilt thou love and she be fair!

III

Ah, happy boughs! that cannot shed
Your leaves, nor ever bid the spring adieu;
And happy melodist, unwearied,
For ever piping songs for ever new;
More happy love! more happy, happy love!
For ever warm, and still to be enjoy'd,
For ever panting, and for ever young;
All breathing human passion far above,
That leaves a heart high-sorrowful and cloy'd
A burning forehead, and a parching tongue.

IV

Who are these coming to the sacrifice?
To what green altar, O mysterious priest,
Lead'st thou that heifer lowing at the skies,
And all her silken flanks with garlands drest?
What little town by river or sea shore,
Or mountain-built with peaceful citadel,
Is emptied of this folk, this pious morn?
And, little town, thy streets for evermore
Will silent be; and not a soul to tell
Why thou art desolate, can e'er return.

V

O Attic shape! Fair attitude! with brede
Of marble men and maidens overwrought,

190

With forest branches and the trodden weed;
  Thou, silent form, dost tease us out of thought
As doth eternity: Cold pastoral!
  When old age shall this generation waste,
  Thou shalt remain in midst of other woe
Than ours, a friend to man, to whom thou say'st,
  "Beauty is truth, truth beauty—that is all
Ye know on earth, and all ye need to know."

After a little, he reverted to the "Ode on Melancholy" and the third stanza, which progressed a step in another direction from that in the ode on the urn.

And what of the "Ode on Indolence"? Other ideas were pushing it aside: he knew he would complete at least one more full volume from a wealth of ideas and burning of thought. It would be his best, so far.

3

"Will you dine with me, Sunday, the fourth of April?" he asked Georgiana's brothers. They would be there.

"Will you come to dinner, Sunday the fourth?" invited Mrs. Brawne. He would be there. But a few days afterwards he remembered the boys and would have excused himself. "Bring them along," she commanded. So all dined at the Brawnes'; then came Davenport, the merchant, and Hunt to eat with him and Brown. Talk, talk, talk, bore, bore, from Davenport, who "from a sense of weakness thought it incumbent upon him to show off." Keats was completely fagged. Brown grew melancholy. Hunt, snatching a backhanded sort of compliment in Davenport's behavior, was the most cheerful of the four. Brown grumbled for two or three days.

"Have you been," asked Hunt, "to Sir John Leicester's Gallery?"

Keats confessed to remissness in that particular.

"Then come along, my dear fellow, do, with me," and together they saw Northcote, Hilton, Bewick, "and many more of great and little note." Haydon's big painting was not progressing and he had not yet made a sketch of Keats's head.

Now came a hilarious bit of work by Reynolds. Hearing that Daddy Wordsworth would publish a poem entitled "Peter Bell," he forestalled the original, using as motto, "I am the real Simon Pure." Later in the month, Keats and Brown were again hosts, to Taylor, Woodhouse, and Reynolds—all of whom came early. They began to play cards about nine "and the night continuing dark and rainy, they could not think of returning to town." So they played till very daylight, and Keats was not worth a sixpence all day. But he was cheerful because Woodhouse praised all the poems he had seen of recent weeks.

"Junkets," said Reynolds in the talk after dinner, "give Hunt a hint to take notice of my 'Peter Bell,' in the *Examiner*."

"I'll write a little notice, myself, Jack." It came out Sunday, April 25, and was reprinted in next day's issue. "You will call it a little politic," Keats wrote George, "seeing I keep clear of all parties."

"Have you seen the new Covent Garden Opera?" Taylor asked.

"*Heart of Midlothian?* Yes," spoke Reynolds.

"Shortly after the opening," said Keats, "dull and half-damn'd."

After they had got well into April, Keats could go out at night and went to Dr. Sawrey's, where things were pleasant in the home of Tom's doctor, for he had squired Fanny Brawne, and Reynolds was there.

On the eleventh, walking alone towards Highgate, in the lane winding alongside Lord Mansfield's Park, he recognized one of two figures he was about to meet as that of Green, demonstrator at Guy's Hospital. In speaking to his old acquaintance he was presented to "Mr. Coleridge." He fell in with them and plodded on at the great man's "alderman after-dinner pace" for nearly two miles. In the hour or less he was with the two, he was amazed at the number of things Coleridge broached: "Nightingales, Poetry—on Poetical Sensation—Metaphysics—Different genera and species of dreams—Nightmare—a dream accompanied by a sense of touch—single and double touch—a dream related—First and Second Consciousness—the difference explained between Will and Volition—so many metaphysicians from a want of smoking the second consciousness—Monsters—the Kraken—Mermaids—Southey believes in them—Southey's belief too much diluted—A ghost story—Good morning—I heard his voice as he came towards me—I heard it as he moved away—I had heard it all the interval—if it may be called so. He was civil enough to ask me to call on him at Highgate."

Unsettled, again, in the spring weather he got from Haydon an accusing letter, charging he had held out delusive hopes in every letter on slight foundations; "and now when I find it is out of your power to do what your heart led you to offer—I am plunged into all my old difficulties." He had probably not tried the long purses first, Keats suspected. Haydon was sensible of the trouble taken but could not help complaining because the result was so totally unexpected and sudden.

A wretched business, and he was to blame in promising too much. "My dear Haydon," he began, "when I offered you assistance I thought I had it in my hand; I thought I had nothing to do but to do. The difficulties I met with arose from the alertness and suspicion of Abbey; and especially from the affairs being still in a lawyer's hand—who has

193

been draining our property for the last six years of every charge he could make."

Ten times more harassed than if he alone had been concerned in such a gain or loss, he had told Haydon all the particulars as well and as literally as possible; only by degrees he had found out the obstacles.

He censured himself in feeling that his own imprudence and neglect had left accounts entirely in Abbey's power. In short, he had much less than he had hoped for and even if all were in hand, all he could do would be to subtract a modest two years' subsistence and lend Haydon the rest, "but I cannot say how soon I could become possessed of it." He was humble enough to confess that he had parted from time to time with little sums, totaling nearly £200, with which he might have formed gradually a library to his taste. His chances, indeed, of being paid at even a distant period were slight. "I am doubly hurt at the slightly reproachful tone of your note and at the occasion of it . . . now you have maimed me again. . . . I dread as much as the plague the idle fever of two months more without any fruit."

Finally, Haydon must understand his plight when he urged the artist's going to the city to see Abbey, "for I am persuaded that to me alone he will not concede a jot." Ultimately, he was able to advance Haydon £30.

While this Haydon affair, seemingly small as it was, ran its slow length from a beginning some time back, "maiming" his poetry, he was aware that his inner preoccupations were of three levels, not rigidly divided but shading one into the other. On top, floated the timely or daily details of so little moment as to cause no interference with his writing; below that level, increasing cares of varied nature perturbed his thoughts, drawing him from poesy—whether he studied or wrote. In the deepest layer reigned Fanny Brawne. No, the figure was scarcely true: she was at the bottom, to be sure,

194

but also on the top and in the middle and throughout. In a word, she absorbed him, and yet there were the other layers: daily visits and talks and simple duties went on, and though he complained at being interrupted, maimed, he was writing with zest and spirit unequaled for so long a period.

When in the first April warmth, he was able to do more physical labor, he finished the ordeal of going through Tom's possessions, all this time at the Bentleys'. When he came across letters signed "Amena," his fists doubled. He had learned that Charles Wells had pretended to be a lady who wrote love letters to a dying man—Tom. He paused in his clearing up to read the full correspondence and concluded the fellow must have had an accomplice. He thought "Amena's" letters were in a man's hand imitating a woman's; surely, they were in a man's language—without even the art of imitation there. As he had read, sitting there by his brother's sad belongings, he thought death not too bad for the villain who out of vanity and love of intrigue would so cruelly deceive a sanguine temperament with show of friendship. By the gods, he would be revengeful; he would be a half-suspended sword over Wells's head! The rat should have rat's bane for his vanity. "Let us leave him to his misery alone, except when we can throw in a little more."

He himself had once received "some roses" from this Wells, in propitiation for some wrong real or fancied. He recalled what he had written and published by way of thanks —in his first volume—

Soft voices had they, that with tender plea
Whisper'd of peace and truth, and friendliness unquell'd . . .

So had he written of the roses. He'd like to tear the pages from the book!

4

No wonder he felt he was at a stand in versifying, he thought on running over his several maimings, and so wrote the Georges in the letter to which he turned now and then. Yet he enclosed a slight thing, "When they were come unto the Faery's Court," in which nobody would guess he saw Fanny Brawne's face in her glass when he wrote:

—then she took
Her pocket mirror and began to look
First at herself and then at him and then
She smil'd at her own beauteous face again.

In this same letter he told them of the claret drinking the other day when Dilke, Reynolds, Brown, Skynner, and he were on hand. He had dreamed afterward of being in that circle of hell where Dante placed Paola and Francesca; he felt himself floating about the whirling atmosphere with a beautiful figure to whose lips his were joined as for an age; even in the midst of cold and darkness he was warm; sometimes on flowery treetops suddenly springing up they rested with the lightness of a cloud until the wind blew them away again. Oh, that he could dream it every night! He wrote, as soon as he woke, a sonnet on the dream: "As Hermes once took to his feathers light," in which he slightly limned Fanny:

Pale were the sweet lips I saw,
Pale were the lips I kissed and fair the form
I floated with about that melancholy storm.

Then falling into a junkets mood, he wrote four or five hundred words of sheer nonsense to Georgiana. "Put a hedgehog into George's hat," he advised. "Pour a little water into his rifle. Soak his boots in a pail of water. Cut his

jacket round into shreds like a Roman kilt or the back of my
grandmother's stays. Sew *off* his buttons."

This April, Brown's again-visiting nephews had afflicted
him like so many wasps, with their voices—piercing and
shrill. "Sometimes am I all wound with Browns," he paro-
died, recalling the adders of Caliban in the *Tempest*, "who
with cloven tongues do hiss me into madness." But, praise
be, the servant had come this morning to take them away.
Now he could repay Brown for Spenserian stanzas directed
against himself and Fanny Brawne.

Considering Charles's gay disposition, *embonpoint*, bald-
ness, and lush-growing beard constantly demanding a razor,
he wrote:

> *He is to weet a melancholy Carle,*
> *Thin in the waist with bushy head of hair—*
> *As hath the seeded thistle when in parle*
> *It holds the zephyr ere it sendeth fair*
> *Its light balloons into the summer air.—*
> *Thereto his beard had not began to bloom,*
> *No brush had touched his chin or a razor sheer,*
> *No care had touch'd his cheek with mortal doom,*
> *But new he was and bright as scarf from Persian loom.*

"What else? He loves wine, fish, flesh, fowl, rich sauces, and
exceedingly democratic company—to put it mildly," and he
went on:

> *Ne cared he for wine, or half and half,*
> *Ne cared he for fish or flesh or fowl,*
> *And sauces held he worthless as the chaff,*
> *He's deign'd the swineherd at the wassail bowl,*
> *Ne with lewd ribbalds sat he cheek by jowl*
> *Ne with sly lemans in the scorner's chair;*
> *But after water brooks this Pilgrim's soul*

Panted, and all his food was woodland air—
Though he would ofttimes feast on gilliflowers rare.

"I need one more stanza, and so his skill in low idioms and his knowledge of purlieus frequented by the ungodly, I will fashion thus":

The slang of cities in no wise he knew;
Tipping the wink *to him was heathen Greek;*
He sipp'd no olden Tom or ruin blue,
Or nantz or cherry brandy, drank full meek
By many a damsel hoarse and rouge of cheek;
Nor did he know each aged watchman's beat—
Nor in obscured purlieus would he seek
For curled Jewesses with ankles neat,
Who as they walk abroad make tinkling with their feet.

"This business has raised my spirits," and he laid aside the verses, saying, "This character would insure Brown a situation in the establishment of Patient Griselda."

His junketish mood persisted in a note to his sister. "O there is nothing like fine weather, and health and books, and a fine country, and a contented mind, and diligent habit of reading and thinking, and an amulet against the ennui—and, please heaven, a little claret-wine cool out of a cellar a mile deep—with a few or a good many ratafia cakes—a rocky basin to bathe in, a strawberry bed to say your prayers to Flora in, a pad nag to go you ten miles or so; two or three sensible people to chat with; two or three spiteful folks to spar with; two or three odd fishes to laugh at and two or three numskulls to argue with—instead of using dumb bells on a rainy day—

Two or three posies
With two or three simples
Two or three noses

198

> *With two or three pimples;*
> *Two or three wise men,*
> *And two or three ninnys;*
> *Two or three purses*
> *And two or three guineas;*
> *Two or three raps,*
> *At two or three doors,*
> *Two or three naps*
> *Of two or three hours—*
> *Two or three cats*
> *And two or three mice,*
> *Two or three sprats*
> *At a very great price—*
> *Two or three sandies*
> *And two or three tabbies*
> *Two or three dandies—*
> *And two Mrs.———(Mum!)"*

and so to the end of the jingle, after which he dramatized his departure: "Good bye, I've an appointment—can't stop—pon word—good bye—now don't get up—open the door myself—go-o-od bye—see ye Monday. J— K—"

Reading over this *jeu d'esprit*, he recalled that Fanny Brawne had said something like this: "My dear Keats, don't you suppose that Mrs. Abbey reads Fanny's letters before Fanny herself sees them?"

"I'll chance it." Would she think of the rhyme for "tabbies," in any event?

The door opened and Brown poked his head in. "Keats, you here? I want to tip you the wink—" and wondered why Keats laughed until he read the characterization of himself. He took it in good part, "with the dry grins," since he had been quite humorously malicious in his stanzas against Keats and Miss Brawne.

The month wore on, dropping days to the twenty-fifth, when the short comment on Reynolds' "Peter Bell" appeared in print. He was at Taylor's with Woodhouse and got the bolstering his soul needed. Later a panorama of ships at the North Pole, unfolded in a hall of Leicester Square, affected him eerily, uncannily, and the impression—which he said was impossible to describe—joined to Woodhouse's praise, prompted "La Belle Dame sans Merci."

"This will be a ballad." The first stanza wrote itself under flying fingers:

> *O what can ail thee, knight-at-arms,*
> *Alone and palely loitering?*
> *The sedge has wither'd from the lake,*
> *And no birds sing.*

The second, the third, and on. I shall call it after that Alan Chartier thing in "Chaucerian" translation, he thought, as he wrote.

At once he sent a copy to the Georges. When he came to copying the stanza:

> *She took me to her elfin grot,*
> *And there she sigh'd and wept full sore,*
> *And there I shut her wild, wild eyes,*
> *With kisses four,*

he explained humorously:

" 'Why four kisses?' you will say. Why four because I wish to restrain the headlong impetuosity of my Muse—she would fain have said 'score' without hurting the rhyme—but we must temper the Imagination, as the critics say, with judgment. I was obliged to choose an even number that both eyes might have fair play: and to speak truly I think two apiece quite sufficient."

At that he grinned and said to himself, "My tongue is in

my cheek, as they will know well," and finished: "Suppose I had said seven; there would have been three and a half apiece—a very awkward affair—and well got out of on my side."

Those icebergs continued to haunt him. The cold desolation of the Leicester Square Panorama set him to thinking of the four elements. Of fire, air, earth, and water, there were but two in those Polar regions. Only air and water—and the water frozen! What about a chorus of four faeries? Salamander, Zephyr, Dusketha, Breama. The song followed swiftly on "La Belle Dame," its origin the same. To be sure a contributory source was the sum of a hundred pounds or so from Abbey. Much as he needed money, glad as he was to get so much, he believed he should have had a greater balance.

Woodhouse had urged him to continue. "Your friends will not let you suffer for necessities."

Ah, but Dick knew nothing of Fanny Brawne, nothing of his absorption in her beauty, in herself, nothing of his torments and despairs.

To stimulate his imagination, he began to read again old Robertson, the historian, who had done him so fine a service toward the Chapman's Homer sonnet. With it he read, alternately, Voltaire's *Siècle de Louis XIV*, impressed by the truth that in each book the great body of people were in lamentable case—the earlier peoples bearing mortal pains if not the bailiffs, debts, and poverties of the later. Man, as King Lear had said, was but a "poor, bare, forked animal," destined to hardships and disquietude.

If man improved by degrees his physical accommodations, there were still waiting—witness Voltaire's study—fresh annoyances, "and there is still a heaven with its stars above his head." In a philosophic mood, Keats concluded, "The point at which man may arrive is as far as the parallel state in in-

201

animate nature, and no further. For instance, suppose a rose
to have sensation; it blooms . . . but there comes a cold
wind, a hot sun . . . it cannot destroy its annoyances—they
are as native to the world as itself . . . no man can be
happy. . . . Call the world . . . the vale of soul-making.
Then you will find out the use of the world."

Further, "I will call the world a school instituted for the
purpose of teaching little children to read—I will call the
human heart the hornbook used in that school; and I will call
the *child able to read* the soul made from that *school* and its
hornbook." So, he conceived God made individual beings,
souls, identical souls, from the sparks of his own essence. This
system of soul-making, he suspected, might have been the
parent of all the more palpable and personal schemes of
redemption, among the Zoroastrians, the Christians, and the
Hindoos.

But what forms man? The answer, he saw, is circumstance. Circumstances are touchstones of the heart, touchstones are provings of the heart, and these provings are but
fortifiers or alterers of his nature. He believed there was a
soul before it came into the world. Before it came, however,
it was but an intelligence without an identity, and the identity
must somehow be established. Again, he saw the heart as the
medium for establishing such identity, a medium possible
only in a world of circumstance.

How had it been with himself, John Keats? His heart had
been proved through his own family, as all men's are altered.
How much more proved and altered since he had met
Fanny! Six or seven months ago? An eon ago. Whatever his
state of mind, into however many levels his thoughts arranged themselves, however many light affairs consumed his
time, however wholly Fanny absorbed him, he felt growth,
expansion in poetic power.

He would write, nor question an atom of the future, even

his own survival or marriage with Fanny. After thinking out to his own satisfaction the process of soul-making, he wrote two sonnets on Fame. "In the first," he decreed, "I will take up some of my ruminations of this moment." In an assumed gayer mood he wrote the second.

While he wrote, Brown came in to rummage about and discover some of Keats's "old sins, sonnets so to say." Brown no less than Woodhouse kept him at work and heartened. Startled by Brown's whistle and exclamation, "When did you, Keats, write this poem 'To Sleep'?" he looked up. "A few days back. Is it good?"

"Superb, and a new rhyme scheme." He began *a,b,b,a*-ing, and Keats got up to look at the sheet with him.

"Yes," he said. "The scheme is *a-b-b-a, c-d-c-d, b-c-d, e-d-e*. You chanted it correctly. I think the legitimate sonnet stanza does not suit the English language too well. The lines pounce. The other kind appears too elegiac. So I've experimented—in what you have here. In another sonnet I've tried to describe it."

Brown read aloud:

"TO SLEEP

> O soft embalmer of the still midnight,
>   Shutting with careful fingers and benign
> Our gloom-pleas'd eyes, embower'd from the light
>   Enshaded in forgetfulness divine—
> O soothest sleep, if so it please thee, close
>   In midst of this thine hymn my willing eyes,
> Or wait the amen, ere thy poppy throws
>   Around my bed its dewy charities—
> Then save me or the passed day will shine
>   Upon my pillow breeding many woes;
> Save me from curious conscience that still lords
>   Its strength for darkness, burrowing like a mole—

Forever Young

Turn the key deftly in the oiled wards
And seal the hushed casket of my soul."

Repeating the final line, he laid down the sheet. Sternly looking at the gratified face and beaming eyes across the table, he punningly remarked: "What you need is a guardian, not an Abbey, my lad," and began putting together pages or parts of pages found behind books, thrust into books, or lying loose in the medley of the desk drawer, even on top of the desk.

Impishly delighted, Keats read the sonnet-description of his new form, playing yet further with the rhyme scheme: "If by dull rhymes our English must be chain'd," and on to the end. "How does this compare with Wordsworth's 'scanty plot of ground'?" he asked in high spirits.

"Humph," Brown read it for himself. "She will be bound with garlands of her own," he finished, and took off his glasses. "I should say, Keats, that so long as Daddy Wordsworth lives, his will be considered better. But there will be other generations. You will be known and you will be loved better than the Rydal man."

For some days thereafter, Keats felt—from cogitations on soul-making, his recent sonnets, and Brown's approval— somewhat eased of the "burthen of the mystery." Steadier in mind and heart, he picked up his Greek and Latin authors quickly to find a theme that set his imagination burning, his fancy winging.

This he learned: Psyche was not embodied as a goddess until after the Augustan Age, in the time of Apuleius, and so was never worshiped with the ancient fervor.

"I am more orthodox, I hope," he wrote, "than to let a heathen goddess be so neglected." How could he not write an "Ode to Psyche," after his recent meditations on the soul? To the

204

Turmoil, in a Year Still Admirable

latest born and loveliest vision far
Of all Olympus' faded hierarchy,

he wrote; to her who had no altar heaped with flowers—

No voice, no lute, no pipe, no incense sweet
From chain-swung censer teeming,
No shrine, no grove, no oracle, no heat
Of pale-mouth'd prophet dreaming—

he would be all these things.

Yes, I will be thy priest and build a fane
In some untrodden region of my mind,
Where branched thoughts new grown with pleasant pain
Instead of pines shall murmur in the wind.
Far, far around shall those dark cluster'd trees
Fledge the wild-ridged mountains steep by steep,
And there by Zephyrs' streams and birds and bees
The moss-lain Dryads shall be lull'd to sleep.
And in the midst of this wide quietness
A rosy sanctuary will I dress
With the wreath'd trellis of a working brain;
With buds and bells and stars without a name;
With all the gardener fancy e'er could feign
Who breeding flowers will never breed the same—
And there shall be for thee all soft delight
That shadowy thought can win;
A bright torch and a casement ope at night
To let the warm love in.

Brown told him it was incomparable. On the third of May
he copied it for the Georges. A happy season: "everything is
in delightful forwardness; the violets are not withered before
the peeping of the first rose."

"This poem," he declared, "is the first and only one with

which I have taken even moderate pains." Brown sardonically told him to unspare a few more pains.

He knocked on the Brawnes' door, the ode in hand, to urge Fanny out for a walk. He read the poem and wondered whether she captured all the meaning, though her comments and questions were charmingly apt.

5

He tingled with excitement roused by a letter from America. After a "great deal of fatigue and harass," the Georges were settled tolerably in comfort at Louisville, Kentucky. It appeared this Kentucky was one of the United States, admitted to the Union in 1792. He dashed to Mrs. Wylie's house with the letter. "Read it and after your boys have seen it send it to Haslam—if you will."

To Haslam he wrote, "Send it to me like lightning that I may take it to Walthamstow." Fanny would be on tenterhooks to read it. A week later he was having to tell her all he could remember; the letter had been returned, torn in a thousand pieces. Some misadventure. . . .

His thoughts were again on making money, now he was relieved over George, and he was told he might go as surgeon on an East India ship. His doctor approved the plan and, besides, the post would be sufficiently lucrative. The alternative, a choice of two poisons—he wrote Miss Jeffrey at Teignmouth—"is leading a fevrous life alone with poetry. This latter will suit me best; for I cannot resolve to give up my studies."

He would rather conquer his indolence and strain his nerves at some grand poem than be in a "dunderheaded Indiaman." Having to choose between energy and despair, he would choose to be energetic, but the world had taken on a Quakerish look:

Turmoil, in a Year Still Admirable

Nothing can bring back the hour
Of splendor in the grass and glory in the flower.

Once he had thought this a melancholist's dream. . . . But surgeon on a ship trading to the East Indies? Not yet.

In response to his request of Miss Jeffrey or her mother for a possible lodging, "commodious for its cheapness," she proposed Bradley. The situation struck him favorably; he might go there in the course of the summer. It was now, he reflected, getting on for the middle of June, and he could not go at once because he had promised Rice, who was not well, to go with him to the Isle of Wight. No, he did not think an Indiaman would destroy the energies of his mind. "To be thrown among people who care not for you, with whom you have no sympathies, forces the mind upon its own resources. . . . An Indiaman is a little world." One of the great reasons, he affirmed, that the English have produced the finest writers is that the English world has ill-treated them during their lives and fostered them after their deaths. The face of Shakespeare, topping the bust above his inkwell, gave him pause. "No. They didn't value even you."

He smiled a *sardonicus risus* at the thought: Where is the English poet who has ever given a magnificent entertainment at the christening of one of his hero's horses, as Boyardo did? "He was a noble poet of romance; not a miserable and mighty poet of the human heart." The middle age of Shakespeare was all clouded over; his days were not more happy than his own Hamlet's; Ben Jonson was a common soldier in the low countries. . . . But for all that, he repeated, he would not yet go aboard an Indiaman. Just now he was very idle, averse to writing "both from the overpowering idea of our dead poets and from abatement of my love of fame." And Milton's lines flashed before him, lines once not accepted:

Fame is the spur that the clear spirit doth raise,
That last infirmity of noble mind. . . .

207

It was no longer his infirmity. "Have I not just written an 'Ode on Indolence'?" He saw again the three figures "with bowed necks, and joined hands, side-faced, in placid sandals and in white robes . . ." passing like figures on a marble urn, and returning with the shifting of the vase. Love, ambition, and poesy—he knew the three, and ached for wings to follow them. The figures faded, and he had no wings:

> *O, folly! What is love and where is it?*
> *And for that poor ambition—it springs*
> *From a man's little heart's short fever-fit;*
> *For poesy!—no—she has not a joy—*
> *At least for me—so sweet as drowsy noons,*
> *And evenings steep'd in honied indolence.*

Once more, he saw the figures pass:

> *. . . adieu! Ye cannot raise*
> *My head cool-bedded in the flowery grass;*
> *For I would not be dieted with praise,*
> *A pet lamb in a sentimental farce!*
> *Fade softly from my eyes, and be once more*
> *In masque-like figures on the dreamy urn;*
> *Farewell! I yet have visions for the night,*
> *And for the day faint visions there is store;*
> *Vanish, ye phantoms from my idle spright,*
> *Into the clouds, and never more return!*

"I have enjoyed writing this Ode," he declared, "more than anything else in 1819." Here was Brown sitting opposite, narrating a scandalous "Life of David," to succeed the story of the Old Woman and the Devil. "He reads me passages as he writes them, stuffing my infidel mouth as though I were a young rook. Infidel rooks do not provender with Elisha's ravens."

208

XII. *The Good Year Continues—*

NOW, this May of 1819, a nightingale had built her nest among the thorns of a plum tree at Wentworth Place, and her mate had begun to sing. One evening Keats laid down his pen and listened; Brown listened, eyes on the rapt face of his young friend, and said to himself, "He never tires of the bird's song."

Next morning, he saw Keats take up his chair from the breakfast table, but said nothing while he watched the journey end at a grass plot near the plum tree. Keats took some scraps of paper from a book under his arm, and sat down.

After two or three hours he entered the study, where Brown was already at work, and carelessly thrust the fragments behind some books on the shelf. He turned to face inquiring eyes. "I've been composing an 'Ode to the Nightingale,' Brown," and did not object when the scraps were removed.

"Less legible than usual," Brown tried to arrange the stanzas, "high speed!" After a few moments he spoke again, "I think you have done something rather remarkable—if we can bring order out of chaos."

Together they fitted the stanzas, and Keats read them aloud. Brown was silent, having no words for this amazingly perfect thing, this great poem. That it was magnificent he had no doubt. He looked about for more verses, "Literally fugitive, Keats. Do take care of your scripts."

"You may," said Keats magnanimously, "copy any verses I write."

209

Brown thrust his still unfinished story into the drawer. "See here, Keats. Surely, you will wish to show this poem to—" he motioned to the other side of the house— "one or two others."

Keats looked up, innocent-eyed. Brown stood by or walked about until the stanzas were copied, and Keats went out.

Sheets in hand, he knocked at Fanny's door. "Come out into the garden," he begged.

While she read, in the voice always to him alluring, he followed her progress, more interested in her than in his ode.

" 'My heart aches,' " she began, and he thought, Not as it ached last night.

> ". . . *and a drowsy numbness pains*
> *My sense, as though of hemlock I had drunk,*
> *Or opened some dull opiate to the drains*
> *One minute past, and Lethewards had sunk:*"

Fanny looked up as if to comment but, at the unfathomable sadness in his eyes, turned back to the script.

> " *'Tis not through envy of thy happy lot,*
> *But being too happy in thine happiness,—*
> *That thou, light-winged Dryad of the trees,*
> *In some melodious plot*
> *Of beechen green and shadows numberless,*
> *Singest of summer in full-throated ease.*

" 'Melodious plot'!" she repeated. "Beautiful whether you mean full of song or from harmony of greens." Over "full-throated ease," her eyes filled at thought of his own often painful throat. But he could not know why—and kissed her bright hair.

> "*O, for a draught of vintage! that hath been*
> *Cool'd a long age in the deep-delved earth,*

210

Tasting of Flora and the country green,
  Dance, and Provençal song, and sunburnt mirth!

"Your claret?" her eyes were merry—eyes, which Keats observed as she looked up, might just have lodged in her head from the sky above the trees.

"Yes," he emphasized, "I would I had a cellar a mile deep."

" 'Sunburnt mirth,' " she quoted. "How apt! Country dancers, sun-tanned, but nobody except you, my dear, ever would have thought of 'sunburnt mirth.' "

"It covers a good many details," Keats admitted unblushingly.

She resumed her reading, while Keats took her free hand. So absorbed was the owner she did not withdraw it.

" 'O, for a beaker full of the warm South,' " again she paused but only to say to herself, "This also covers many details."

"Full of the true, the blushful Hippocrene,' " she read on. "Hippocrene?"

"Fount of the muses, my sweet. Waters good for inspiration. But I prefer the wine, you know."

"With beaded bubbles winking at the brim,
  And purple-stainéd mouth;
That I might drink, and leave the world unseen,
  And with thee fade away into the forest dim:

" 'Beaded bubbles'!" she exclaimed. "Why, that's the way wine behaves."

"Oh, yes! I think so," said the poet complacently.

"Fade far away, dissolve, and quite forget
  What thou amongst the leaves hast never known,
The weariness, the fever, and the fret
  Here, where men sit and hear each other groan;

> *Where palsy shakes a few, sad, last gray hairs,*
>   *Where youth grows pale and spectre-thin and dies;"*

She knew of whom he had been thinking in that last line and for a moment held his hand—that still held her own—to her cheek.

> *"Where but to think is to be full of sorrow*
>   *And leaden-eyed despairs,*
> *Where beauty cannot keep her lustrous eyes,*
>   *Or new love pine at them beyond tomorrow."*

Sometimes he frightened her, not seeing her for days and then calmly talking of going away. Would she, for him, lose her lustrous eyes? Would he forget them, forget herself?

Holding back a sigh, she continued, but Keats sat in a dream; he had not thought of the way this passage might affect her. And yet—had she not inspired them?

> *"Away, away! for I will fly to thee,*
>   *Not charioted by Bacchus and his pards—*

"Pards?" but quickly she answered herself, "Leopards!" Keats agreed. "Not room enough for the whole animal."

" 'But on the viewless wings of poesy,' " she read, and felt her heart expanding more and more at the indescribable genius of the poem. "Ineffable!" but she did not speak aloud.

> *"Though the dull brain perplexes and retards:*
> *Already with thee! Tender is the night,*
>   *And haply the Queen-Moon is on her throne,*
> *Cluster'd around by all her starry Fays;*
>   *But here there is no light,*
> *Save what from heaven is with the breezes blown*
>   *Through verdurous glooms and winding mossy ways.*

"A dark wood—no light except through the branches," she said, to hold the picture, and went on:

212

"I cannot see what flowers are at my feet,
Nor what soft incense hangs upon the boughs—

" 'Soft incense,' " again she was enchanted by the peculiar aptness. It was as if she brushed with her fingertips the plum-tree blossoms, now in full and fragrant flower.

"But in embalmed darkness, guess each sweet
Wherewith the seasonable month endows
The grass, the thicket, and the fruit-tree wild;
White hawthorn, and the pastoral eglantine;
Fast-fading violets cover'd up in leaves;
And mid-May's eldest child,
The coming musk-rose, full of dewy wine,
The murmurous haunt of flies on summer eves."

She laid down the tablet. "The only way violets ever faded," she affirmed, "but never before have I read the description." She repeated the final lines of the stanza. "I'm drunk," she smiled, "but not sure I like the flies."

"But, dear Fanny, you know I could not say 'bees'!" He studied her expressive face and felt her thoughts as she made the mental transfer and asked, "Now, could I?"

"N-o," she said in a small voice, and took up the ode.

"Darkling I listen; and for many a time
I have been half in love with easeful Death,"

No, oh, no! But she did not lift her eyes from the page, did not bring the words to her lips, and of her expression he caught nothing.

"How do you mean 'darkling'?" she wanted to know.

"What do you think?" he countered.

"It might be *you* feeling dark, or the forest being dark—or—"

"What about 'little dark thing'?" he laughed.

213

"I like that. But the word can mean—I think—all of these."

"If you like"; again he was generous.

> *"Call'd him soft names in many a mused rhyme,*
> *To take into the air my quiet breath;*
> *Now more than ever seems it rich to die,*
> *To cease upon the midnight with no pain,*
> *While thou are pouring forth thy soul abroad*
> *In such an ecstasy!"*

How he had caught the passion of the bird's song . . . These lines were throbbing, bursting with it!

> *"Still wouldst thou sing, and I have ears in vain—*
> *To thy high requiem become a sod."*

She lifted a sad face. Her Keats a sod. "God forbid!" she spoke to her heart alone.

" 'Thou wast not born for death, immortal Bird,' " she read with a slight emphasis on 'death.'

Keats stirred. "A little more stress on 'Thou,' dear Fanny!"

She reread the line, " '*Thou* wast not born for death,' " and he told her that was what he meant. A contrast—

> *"No hungry generations tread thee down;*
> *The voice I hear this passing night was heard*
> *In ancient days by emperor and clown:*
> *Perhaps the self-same song that found a path*
> *Through the sad heart of Ruth, when, sick for home,*
> *She stood in tears amid the alien corn;"*

Her own tears rushed. This beauty was not bearable . . . but she read on not quite so firmly, a film over her eyes:

> *"The same that oft-times hath*
> *Charmed magic casements, opening on the foam*
> *Of perilous seas, in faery lands forlorn."*

214

The film grew insupportable, falling in two drops down her cheeks. She turned her face to wipe them away. They mustn't stain this page. "Those," she said brokenly, "are the most marvelous three lines I've ever read."

"Why, Fanny, dear—" Keats knew not what to say. Never had one of his poems so moved her.

Now she was on the final stanza:

"Folorn!" She saw that he had mispelled the word—but what did mere spelling matter!

"Folorn! the word is like a bell—"

"And so it is, my Keats!" She repeated in a bell-like chime, "Fo'lorn, fo'lorn, fo'lorn," Yes, she thought, more like a bell without that *r*!

> "*To toll thee back from thee to my sole self!*
>   *Adieu!—*"

"No, darling"—for she had pronounced "adieu" in her best French—"the English way."

> "*Adieu! The fancy cannot cheat so well*
>   *As she is fam'd to do, deceiving elf.*
>   *Adieu, adieu! thy plaintive anthem fades*
>   *Past the near meadows, over the still stream,*
>   *Up the hill-side; and now 'tis buried deep*
>   *In the next valley glades:*
>   *Was it a vision, or a waking dream?*
>   *Fled is that music:—Do I wake or sleep?*"

"Now I must reread it, at once!" And Keats had no objection so long as he might sit and read *her* poetry.

Her second rendering was better than the first. Keats himself felt something not felt when writing. She was an excellently trained reader, his Fanny.

The poem, perfect for her, rose in his own judgment. He

215

must send it to Haydon, right away. But Fanny wished to read it again, and Mother must see it.

"My only fair copy," he murmured.

"I would lose it," she assured him, "for nothing on earth."

Back in the study, Keats found that Brown had written to James Elmes, Editor of *Annals of the Fine Arts,* suggesting that Keats had a new poem for publication before it appeared in a volume. Elmes asked him to send it on.

"But it's at Mrs. Brawne's," said Keats.

"Get it," commanded Brown, unusually stern. "You are not to give up your writing."

Keats retrieved it, after Fanny had made the copy for herself, and in July read the printed version.

2

So it was, he said to himself, he was brought round again to fix himself in poesy. "I cannot resolve to give up my favorite studies," he wrote his sister, "so I purpose to retire into the country and set my mind at work once more." The fact was that one necessity for getting away consisted of vacant beds he and Brown owned. Friends, continually dropping in to stay overnight, interrupted both.

Gay-mooded, he poked good-natured fun at the Abbeys. If the man retired from business "he would live a long time upon his fat and be none the worse for a good long Lent." So Mrs. Abbey had been serving Lisbon wine! Had she drained the gooseberry? "Truly," he ended in a burst she would recognize as drawn from life, "I cannot delay making another visit—asked to take lunch—whether I will have ale, wine, take sugar—objection to green—like cream—thin bread and butter—another cup—agreeable—enough sugar— little more cream—too weak—12 shillin &c, &c, &c. Lord! I must come again."

216

When he "came again," June 16, he told her he was going to the back of the Isle of Wight, with a Mr. Rice, a friend in ill-health. He could not send her the head of himself that Mr. Severn had painted because it was "now too dear," but he gave her "a very capital profile" done by Mr. Brown.

He put off asking Haydon, last of all, for money lent. He had received at the Abbeys a letter from his aunt's solicitor with the information she was about to file a bill in chancery against the Keats children. "More law suits!" groaned Keats. Brown had lent him money, saying, "You must never give up your poetry," but if his venture should fail again, " 'Ye hear no more of me,' as Chaucer says."

He did not send Haydon the ode. He had got back his copy on the twelfth of June, and on the fourteenth sent it to Elmes.

"A fellow, one Benjamin, will rent my house for the summer." Brown was helping him get ready for the Isle of Wight.

"Then you will come along?" Keats hoped.

"I daresay." In fact, Brown meant to join him. The poet must be kept at work, and he could not work without a friend near at hand.

The last day of June, he said good-by to Fanny Brawne. "I will never return to London, my love, if my fate does not turn up Pam or at least a court-card."

"You will return," prophesied Fanny.

3

Early in July, Keats sat at the window of Eglantine Villa, in Shanklin, looking out over the housetops on a "beautiful hilly country with a glimpse of the sea." What were those white wings? Weathercocks? No, only sails flying past cottage chimneys between him and the ocean. His crowquill was in his hand, and he began, "My dearest Lady," before telling her all that was in his heart. He had written Tuesday evening, but that letter was too much in the strain of finesse and sentiment of ladies and gentlemen in Rousseau's day. He was glad he had had no opportunity of sending that letter! Morning was the time for him to write, anyway, for in the sepulchral night-loneliness of his room, he gave way to rhapsodies at which he had often laughed in another man.

Rice had gone out. He himself would be free as a stag this fine morning, wandering about the coast, if remembrance of her did not weigh so heavily upon him. "I have never known any unalloy'd happiness for many days together: the death or sickness of some one has always spoilt my hours—and now when none such troubles oppress me, it is, you must confess, very hard that another sort of pain should haunt me. Ask yourself, my love, whether you are not very cruel to have so entrammeled me, so destroyed my freedom."

He paused to look out upon the hills and glimpses of the sea, and asked himself whether he wished to be free. He thought not. But still he asked her to confess her cruelty and to console him all she could in a letter as rich as a draught of poppies. "Write the softest words and kiss them, that I may at least touch my lips where yours have been.

"For myself, I know not how to express my devotion to so fair a form: I want a brighter word than bright, a fairer word than fair."

A flutter of yellow wings, a whirlwind of yellow wings, drew his eyes to the lawn. "I almost wish we were butterflies and lived but three summer days—three such days with you I could fill with more delight than fifty common years could ever attain." Yet, he assured her, he could never act selfishly, however selfishly he might feel. He could center all his happiness in her, but could not expect to possess her heart so entirely; indeed, "if I thought you felt as much for me as

218

I do for you at this moment, I do not think I could restrain myself from seeing you again tomorrow."

Upon him fell a sense of doom, of which he could not but suggest something in his close: "In case of the worst that can happen," though he might live meanwhile upon hope and chance, "I shall still love you. But what hatred shall I have for another!" He sent greetings to all her family.

Rice came back, shortly after he had sealed the letter. "What is that great bundle, Jemmie?"

"A ham," and Rice laid it down on the table at which Keats was still sitting.

"Why?"

"I think a ham is not a wrong thing to have in a house," he took it up to put away on the kitchen shelf.

From Newport, where Keats rode to post his letter, he returned in a heavy rain, damp, coughing, hungry. It *was* good to have a ham in the house. Still he coughed and his throat continued to hurt. He had not got over the cold acquired some ten days ago from going to Portsmouth, "by water," he punned, referring to his seat on top of the coach in a steady downpour. He had walked with the other fellows, moreover, up hills to relieve the horses.

Some of these things he told his sister. And knowing she would like the picture of pretty Bonchurch, he told her of the romantic cottages, "covered with creepers and honey-suckles, with roses and eglantines peeping in at the windows." He expected to amuse her by saying if he could play upon a guitar he might make a fortune with an old song—she had seen London street singers—and get two blessings at once—a lady's heart and the rheumatism. For he conceived these pretty cottages to hold romantic old maids, fond of novels, or soldiers' widows with pretty jointures. "But I am almost afraid to peep at those little windows—for a pretty window should show a pretty face, and as the world goes chances are

219

against me." It was too bad, he thought, as he told her Rice was a very good fellow, indeed, that the noble and wise and generous should suffer from miserable health.

To himself he confessed that Fanny Brawne's being so far away was making him wretched. He wrote her that once he had been afraid of such love as his for her, fearing it would burn him up. But if she would love him fully, the fire would not be more than they could bear.

"Do the remarks of certain horrid people," she had inquired, "mean it depends upon them whether you see me again?" And she would not have him praise her beauty!

He knew, he wrote back, to whom she referred: "Do understand me, my love, in this. I have so much of you in my heart that I must turn mentor when I see a chance of harm befalling you. I would never see anything but pleasure in your eyes, love on your lips, and happiness in your steps. . . . Why may I not speak of your beauty, since without that I never could have loved you? I cannot conceive any beginning of such love as I have for you but beauty. There may be a sort of love for which, without the least sneer at it, I have the highest respect and can admire it in others: but it has not the richness, the bloom, the full form, the enchantment of love after my own heart. So let me speak of your beauty, though to my own endangering. . . ."

Despite Fanny and his constant feeling for her, he was using time well on the Isle. He had discovered another story, the engrossing tale of Lamia, and had begun a longish poem on the snake-lady before leaving Wentworth Place. He worked at it diligently, after finishing the first act of his and Brown's drama, "Otho the Great"; and he was, besides, reading Burton on *Love*. He had finished (Part 3) Love's Beginning, Object, Definition, Division, pages 159 to 166 of his copy, when his feelings burst forth on the margin: "Here is the old plague spot; the pestilence, the raw scrofula. I mean that there is nothing disgraces me in my own eyes so much as being one of a race of eyes, nose, and mouth beings in a planet called the earth who, all, from Plato to Wesley have always mingled goatish, whinnyish, lustful love with the abstract adoration of the Deity. I don't understand Greek—is the love of God and the love of women expressed by the same word in Greek? I hope my little mind is wrong—if not I could— Has Plato separated these loves? Ha! I see how they endeavor to divide—but there appears to be a horrid relationship."

Fanny Brawne had written him she had dreamed and, possibly ominous, had seen a comet in the early days of July. Yes, he had seen it, too, and hoped it was a sign poor Rice would soon be better. Send the dream, that he might interpret it.

Working on "Otho" and "Lamia," he marveled on his changed mind and heart: once he had wings; now he had lost them, reversing the change from chrysalis to butterfly. Did this human love change every man to a practical fellow? "If so, I would not have it otherwise if only practicality prove a stage on the way to possessing Fanny." And he hoped, he wrote Reynolds, "to have a pair of patient sublunary legs."

Absence from Fanny, sympathy with Rice, and his own sad prophesyings threw him into an irritable state of health. He fancied omens: even the chance obliteration of Fanny's name from the sealing wax on her letter startled him. He was in much the frame of nerves he had suffered when after Tom's death he fancied a white rabbit in the garden incarnated his brother's spirit. The rabbit had been killed and served up for dinner; but at his horror-stricken cry and rush from the table, nobody could even taste it. . . .

Yet in writing to his love he checked himself from speaking too much of his depression and told her the "Histoire de la Corbeille," from the *New Oriental Stories* of the Comte

221

de Caylus. How glad he was she was in the same world as himself and not separated, as was the lady in Paradise from the melancholy men who had suffered her enchantments.

"When will your volume be ready?" she had asked.

He tried not to be annoyed, but questions about the forwardness of his books always vexed him. She could not see his frown as he replied, "I cannot say . . . I have three or four stories half done, but as I cannot write for the mere sake of the press, I am obliged to let them progress or lie still as my fancy chooses. . . . 'Twill be no matter, for poems are as common as newspapers, and I do not see why it is a greater crime in me than in another to let the verses of a half-fledged brain tumble into the reading-rooms and drawing-room windows."

Before he knew it he was plump in the middle of July! He must take a day off and spy at the parties who came looking at the "very great Lion," Shanklin Chine. "I wish I had as many guineas as there have been spy-glasses in it," he told Fanny. He took his candle and went to his lonely room at night, feeling that an eternity would pass before he saw her. But "I will say a month," and having once kissed her would rather be alone at his tasks in Shanklin "than in the bustle and hateful literary chit-chat . . . your letters keep me alive. My sweet girl, I cannot speak my love for you. Good night! and/Ever Yours/John Keats."

4

Rice advanced in misery. They were doing each other no good. The chief drawback was their location: hills screened their house from the sea, except on the southeast. Fogs and mist rolled in from that direction, enveloping them in dampness as enervating as the smoke of London.

"This is not the place for me, Keats. I'm going back," Rice

222

announced his intention to return to London and possibly to go on to Dublin. "You must stay, of course," he added. "Brown will soon be along. You two must finish your tragedy and score a success with it."

"You'll stay, Jemmie, until he comes?"

"By all means," and with that promise Keats waited for Brown.

In a day or two here he came, accompanied by Martin the publisher, and for several days the four did nothing but play cards in one small room, night and morning. "I cannot even obey her request to write tonight," Keats told himself on the twenty-fourth of July. Brown had found a moment for telling him Miss Brawne was not looking well, so confirming her own report of ill-health. Thank God, Rice and Martin would go tomorrow and he would be at liberty.

Sunday night, then, he wrote: "You cannot conceive how I ache to be with you: how I would die for one hour—for what is in the world?" She must pardon him if he wandered in his writing for all day he had been occupied upon an abstract poem and, besides, he was deep in love with her. "You were an age in feeling that love," she had mocked him. Far from it. "The very first week I knew you"—he might have said the first time he got a good look at her—"I wrote myself your vassal; but burnt the letter as the very next time I saw you I thought you manifested some dislike to me. If you should ever feel for man at the first sight what I did for you, I am lost. Yet I should not quarrel with you, but hate myself if such a thing were to happen—only I should burst if the thing were not as fine a man as you are a woman."

He picked up her letter, lying there before him, and read again: "You must be satisfied in knowing that I admired you much more than your friend."

He wrote on: "My dear love, I cannot believe there ever was or ever could be anything to admire in me especially as

223

far as sight goes—I cannot be admired, I am not a thing to be admired. You are, I love you; all I can bring you is a swooning admiration of your beauty." Yes, she absorbed him. He had no pleasure in being what the world calls "settled," in domestic cares; yet for her he would meet those cares. "Though," he added, "if it would leave you happier, I would rather die than do so."

Thinking of her gay hair, heavenly eyes, and divine face, he wrote further: "I have two luxuries to brood over in my walks, your loveliness and the hour of my death. O, that I could have possession of them both in the same minute." Because it battered the wings of his self-will, he hated the world; he could take sweet poison from her lips, from no other's, to send him out of it.

Thinking to make him a present, she had asked about his seal. "It is marked like a family tablecloth," he explained, "with my mother's initial *F* for Fanny: put between my father's initials."

5

Next morning, Monday, Brown sat down, as at home, on the other side of the table and continued his story of Otho; for he was providing the plot to Keats's lines. "Now, what we have for the second act is this," and he unfolded the action as he had conceived it.

"I understand," said Keats, and at once began to write. Finishing each sheet, he passed it on to Brown, who approved. After a few pages, and after walking about the room, "breeding," as Keats said, Brown passed a hand over his hot brow. "Tell you what," he paused until the writer lifted his face, "we need an elephant in this play."

"Are you jesting?" Keats was used to the comic thoughts behind his friend's card-player countenance.

"No, oh no! Good stage property. But I'm not sure," he hesitated, "whether Otho's menagerie included one—and everything must be of the historic."

Considering devices to match Brown's, Keats made Otho threaten "cold pig" for the newly married couple. "The emperor must have a spice of drollery, you know."

"Good Lord, Keats. You say that this fellow lies three days on his back for love?"

"I say," said Keats gnomishly and waited for criticism.

"Spoils the unity of time," said the critic.

"But it's in harmony with Ludolph's character," argued the author.

"I consent," and they got along.

Later, Brown read lines narrating the princess's blowing-up of her hairdresser, for smearing her cheek with pomade, and spoiling her rouge. "Oh, I say, this won't do."

"Why not? It's natural," Keats grinned.

"So are many things. Best omit this passage." So they got on to the end of the fourth act. Two days, while Keats wrote, Brown gadded around the Isle with his old knapsack. In one of the rest periods he drew Keats out to Shanklin church, which he began sketching. Keats ragged him and challenged him to a trial of skill. Pleased at the raillery from high spirits, Brown lent him a crayon.

"We'll keep the sketches to contend for a prize at the gallery," said Keats.

Reynolds, though now a solicitor, had written a successful one-act musical entertainment, *One, Two, Three, Four, Five: by Advertisement*. Perhaps Brown's old luck would return: perhaps they would have a greatly successful play in "Otho."

"But we need a library." Keats was hampered for lack of reference works.

"We might find one at Winchester." Thoughtfully, and rather surprisingly, Brown added, "I might go to Bedhamp-

225

ton, to Snook's, while you work there." His mind was on a private matter he would keep to himself.

Keats's thoughts, also, were his own. "And while he is away, I will make the short trip to London, to see *her.*" Aloud, he remarked, "The voice of the old lady over the way is, forsooth, getting to be a plague."

A few minutes later, while Brown poured out tea, he exclaimed, "Thank God, the knob of the teapot was knocked off—it seemed as unalterable as the face of our fisherman!" At the prospect of getting away, he began hating this quietude, the very posts in the yard. . . .

"You enjoyed the races at Cowes, though?" Brown twinkled.

"Never have I seen"—Keats recalled the tacking yachts and boats, full sailed—"anything so beautiful in the way of motion."

He wrote Fanny of the projected move and of hard work on the tragedy. "I am not idle enough for proper downright love-letters—I leave this minute a scene in our tragedy and see you (think it not blasphemy) through the mist of plots, speeches, counterplots, and counterspeeches. The lover is madder than I am—I am nothing to him—" he lied gallantly: tortured Ludolph was drawn from his own being and torture. He was glad she wished to see him and would hold him to his promise to come to her shortly. He would keep that promise with as much sorrow as gladness, "for I am not one of the Paladins of old who lived upon water, grass, and smiles for years together."

Reminding himself and her that he would receive her letters more quickly at Winchester, he fell to musing on the exchange of cliffs, woods, hills, sands, and rocks for the cathedral. But he would like Swiss scenery, he told her. "We might spend a pleasant year at Berne or Zurich—if it should please Venus to hear my 'Beseech thee to hear us, O Goddess.' And if she should hear, God forbid we should . . . turn into a pond, a stagnant Lethe—a vile crescent, row or buildings. Better be imprudent movables than prudent fixtures. . . . Go out and winter at teaparties, freeze at dinners; bake at dances; simmer at routs. . . . You ask after my health, not telling me whether you are better. I am quite well. Your going out is no proof that you are: how is it? Late hours will do you great harm."

August 13, they left Shanklin. Passing to Southampton they saw from the deck of their little vessel, a still smaller craft, well-manned, two naval officers at the stern. "Looks like a collision," said Brown calmly. "Hold fast."

"We are tacking about," said Keats, but both braced themselves for a shock. The bowlines of their own vessel caught the masts of the naval ship and snapped them off close by the planks. The passenger boat shivered, but moved on and, looking back, the two saw the officer's shell plunging and righting itself.

"Look at our crew," said Brown.

"Neither officers nor men moving a muscle. Admirable!"

They took the stage up to Winchester.

XIII. –And Ends

"SMELL the air from those Downs!" They had settled in Colebrook Street and were surrounded by a "fresh-looking country."

"Worth sixpence a pint," said Keats. "Let's walk."

From their back gate they crossed a street into the cathedral yard, passed under trees along a paved path in front of the building, and turned left under a stone doorway. They were now at the other side of the pile, which they left behind in strolling through two college-like squares that appeared to be dwelling-places of deans and other churchmen, all "garnished with grass and shaded with trees." Through one of the old city gates they walked through a college street, crossing some meadows at the end, at length arriving at "a country alley of gardens." They were now at the foundation of St. Cross, interesting for its gothic tower and alms-square, whence they passed over the St. Cross meadows to a beautifully clear river. This was the first mile of the walk Keats took almost every day for an hour before dinner. Sometimes he went farther afield.

Old ambitions and new had him by the neck and were shaking him hard. What if he might revolutionize modern dramatic writing as Kean had revolutionized acting? What if he might upset the "drawling of the blue-stocking literary world"? If he might do these things in a few years, he would die content, "and my friends should drink a dozen of claret on my tomb." He was more and more convinced that a "fine writer"—possibly excepting the human friend philosopher—

228

was the most genuine being in the world. Shakespeare and Milton became greater and greater wonders.

Something of these thoughts he wrote Bailey who, he had learned, had at last got married to Miss Gleig and was living at St. Andrews. He would never again feel the same regard for Bailey; but, after all, Bailey had befriended him and he could not be too critical.

He bent his energies to the last act of "Otho," an act Brown left entirely to him. With return of health and serenity, a friend at hand or near at hand, he felt the surge of creation, as well as the hard necessity of inventing details—

> *Clamped to the work*
> *Serpent in an eagle's claws!*

Much of the time he wrote against the fiddle-sawing of his landlady's son. The sounds bored his ears like gimlets.

What of Fanny Brawne? He confessed she seemed remote, far away. "I see you through a mist: as I dare say you do me by this time." Let her remain in the mist; let her be shrouded from his vision, that the pain of loving might be less fierce— so his high aims would conquer.

"You have changed," she wrote him in effect. "What must I believe?"

"Believe in the first letters I wrote you," he replied. "I assure you I felt as I wrote—I could not write so now." The visions in his brain, his uneasy spirits—though now more easy—and his unguessed fate all spread out as a veil between him and Fanny.

Was he being selfish now? He had told her, more than once, he could not be selfish where she was concerned. So he would temper his seeming lack of ardor: "Remember, I have had no idle leisure to brood over you—'tis well perhaps I have not. I could not have endured the throngs of jealousies

229

that used to haunt me before I had plunged so deeply into imaginary interests."

Would she understand that, even so, she was at the core of his life, the basis of his creation? "I am in complete cue," he went on—"in the fever; and shall in these four months do an immense deal."

Well, then, he couldn't help it if he was ungallant and unloverlike—"I am no officer in yawning quarters" (with an eye to some of her old escorts) "and no parson-Romeo," his thought slanting toward Bailey. What would William of Wykeham think of him—that William whose "Manners makyth man" dominated education here in Winchester after all the years!

His mind, heaped to the full, was stuffed like a cricket-ball; if he tried to fill it more, it would burst! Most women would hate him for so writing . . . hate him for having so hard a mind as to forget them; forget the brightest realities for the dull imaginations of the brain. But she would see through any attempt at artificial passion. " 'Tis harsh, harsh, I know it— My heart seems now made of iron—I could not write a proper answer to an invitation to Idalia."

"You promised you would come to me soon," she half-reproached him. "You did not come, and I urged you."

"You are trying to make me keep my promise," he wrote back.

From the tone of her next letter, she was most likely offended; but she asked if he were.

He was only playful, he assured her; but he would beg her pardon. It was just that her pride should be alarmed—seriously. But he could not do as he pleased: his cash resources had been stopped; everything he spent increased his debts. "Though of my own money I should be careless, of my friends' I must be spare." He could not quite bring himself to say that Brown was his mainstay just now. He knew, moreover, that Brown expected repayment, with interest. That was but fair: Brown hadn't much money.

Unable to write a loving masterpiece, he told Fanny of Winchester, of Cowes and the races there, of the accident in crossing the Solent. Yet, as he wrote and thought of her, it seemed that a few more moments would uncrystallize and dissolve him. "I must not give way to it—but turn to my writing again—if I fail, I shall die hard." Meantime, he must forget her. He would be working.

He knew she would try to understand even before she wrote him of exercising all her patience.

Only a little later, he stared at a sentence in a letter he had written Taylor: "I equally dislike the favor of the public with the love of a woman—they are both a cloying treacle to the wings of independence." "What manner of man am I?" he asked himself. The occasion of the letter was a request for another advance. Brown, "not at all flush," had proposed to stand with himself responsibility for any money borrowed in this manner.

He fancied Taylor saying, "How a solitary life engenders pride and egotism!" For again he was reading from a less ardent mood, "I shall ever consider people as debtors to me for verses, not myself to them for admiration."

And what could he say to Taylor's supposed comment on the solitary life? "True, I know it does—but this pride and egotism will enable me to write finer things than anybody else can write—so I will indulge it." The good word and favor of the public were, to him, no more than a drummer boy holding out his hand familiarly to a field-marshal. He would not put further words into Taylor's mouth, but could not resist hearing one final imagined statement from his publisher: "Poor Keats! The articles in the *Quarterly* and *Blackwood's* are still rankling."

He turned his letter over to Brown, who added in his own

231

note details that would help: The Chancery suit would not be injurious, probably, to Keats's prospects. Others owed him 230 pounds; Brown, himself, though depending upon quarterly and half-yearly driblets from his property, yet had ample means to warrant his signing Keats's note; and he, Brown, knew that Keats had no other name to offer.

They had come, Keats observed as he wrote the date, to the twenty-third of August. They waited. No reply. They were down to a few shillings. "We must write to friends." Only a dead silence. They talked of landing in Winchester jail.

"We have piped and no one hath danced," said Keats. "Come, let us unpack our hearts with curses!" They had read Godwin's seventeenth-century story in which Mandeville tells of his association with Lisle, at Oxford.

"So! We may relieve our feelings," Brown agreed. And as Lisle and Mandeville discharged invectives "with solemnity, fervor, eloquence, richness of style and imagination," they two began to feel they were discharging a duty, and their hearts "attained a higher degree of complacency."

"Go on with 'Lamia,'" laughed Brown, "even if we are taken up here in Winchester."

And Keats wrote, demon-inspired by the straits through which they moved. Brown, meantime, went to Bedhampton and Chichester, knowing the friends there would help. He returned with thirty pounds and so, on the last day of August, they were able to pay the landlady. Five days later, Keats got from Hessey a thirty-pound bank post bill, and heard at the same time that a sum (for which he had been waiting three weeks) had been sent by mistake to Chichester.

Now they were wealthy. "Between us we have £60, besides what is waiting in the Chichester post office," joyfully Keats wrote Hessey. "To be a complete Midas I suppose some one will send me a pair of Ass's ears by the wagon."

232

The delay had occurred because Taylor, ill, had gone to the country and the partners had communicated before deciding to advance another thirty pounds. Luxuriating in his new wealth, affluence to a man recently all but starving, Keats wrote gratefully to each publisher. Loquacious, in new independence, he hoped Taylor had found a dry, elevated country, open to currents of air; he had himself suffered by going first to Shanklin. He felt like making, and did make, a long disquisition on agriculture and city work in connection with health—all in favor of cities—and apologized for writing in "fiery phrase" in his first letter. He would not have done so had he known Taylor was ill. He confided that "Otho" was finished and Brown liked it very much. "But he is not a fit judge as I have only acted as midwife to his plot, and of course he will be fond of his child."

"You are still a surgeon, Keats," said Brown looking over this letter. "Do you know how often you refer to signs and symbols and actualities of your old profession?"

" 'Tis natural," Keats returned. "I was understudy to a doctor, and a hospital walker longer by far than I have been a poet." He beamed upon Brown. "Ain't it so?" More seriously, he went on, "Everything may be made subservient to your main cause. When I was a surgeon that was not so. Knowledge was divided into provinces. Now I know all branches of knowledge are but parts of one whole."

Brown read on. "I have finished 'Lamia,' and am now occupied in revising 'St. Agnes Eve' and studying Italian." And after a note on Ariosto and Spenser he saw that Keats had crossed the letter with lines from "Lamia"—some sixty, beginning, "A haunting music, sole perhaps and lone," and ending, "Then makes his shiny mouth a napkin for his thumb."

For these verses Brown did not pause. He had read them, and he awaited publication of the best volume his friend had so far assembled. He was about to leave for Bedhampton and Chichester—and elsewhere—visiting for three weeks. In fact, the time had come when he thought he must be married to that husky servant girl, Abbie, whose strong body combined with his worthy brains he had hoped would produce a marvelous child. He expected to meet Abbie in Ireland; but of this plan he said nothing to Keats. He indicated that now was the time for a poet to be alone with his studies and writing. "You are well, composed in spirit and—" he broke off. Though he said no more, he suspected Keats was far less absorbed in Miss Fanny Brawne.

"If any letters come for me," he said on leaving, "do not forward them, but open them and give me the marrow in a few words." That request could arouse no suspicion, he knew, that he was going where he wished no letters following him up.

In a few days, in which no letters had arrived, Keats was inspired to do a little clowning. "Chas. Brown," he wrote in effect, "Sir, By drinking your damn'd tank water, I have got the gravel. What reparation can you make to me and my family?" Signed "Nathan Benjamin."

"Now, how did I know that chap's name was Nathan?" he wondered. For so it was, and to him at Wentworth Place, Brown wrote: "Sir, I cannot offer you any remuneration until your gravel shall have formed itself into a stone, when I will cut you with pleasure."

"If he had not sent the letter to Benjamin," argued the perpetrator of the jest, "I should think from his punning he had smoked me out. But he did send it." The "reply" from Brown drew from Nathan Benjamin an insistent request for explanation of the "singular circumstance."

"When I read your letter and his following, I roared," Brown wrote from Bedhampton, "and in came Mr. Snook,

234

who on reading them seem'd likely to burst the hoops of his fat sides—so the joke has told well."

2

Keats laid down a letter from George urging his presence at Abbey's place of business, to discover what he could about the chancery suit that was inevitable if Aunt Jennings could not be dissuaded from going into court. He lost no time, stepping into the late coach, September 10.

Reflecting for the nth time that he had always left business details to George, he should be glad if his brother must now rely upon him. He knew Abbey was actually withholding money expected by George, as one consequence of this chancery threat. Yet it was hard that just as he had engaged himself in study more intense, writing more mature than he had yet achieved, he must stop to do what he could with Abbey and Aunt Jennings. He was going chiefly to learn now what he could do—if anything—and to plan accordingly.

In the long twilight, he was aware of sights and smells and sounds of autumn. The fields were stubble now; farmers had cut oats and wheat, and with them most of the scarlet poppies, of late flaming in thousands around Winchester. Beech trees were pure yellow, not gold, just flaming yellow, right yellow, bright yellow. No woman's hair could show the burnished sheen of that tall round giant there by the roadside. Fanny? What of Fanny? When was it he loved a girl named Fanny? He had lived in other lands, other times, since he loved her—the time of Otho, the time of ancient Corinth.

"Do I not love her now? Have I not in Act V, Scene 5, of 'Otho' pictured her:

So perfect so divine, that our poor eyes
Are dazzled with the sweet proportioning?"

235

He was inclined to discount that portrait. . . . Honestly, he didn't know whether he loved her. He did know he was at peace, and the air held a fine, "temperate sharpness." Yet over there to west and south lazy blue mists rose warmly; here, by the inn, at which they were changing teams, a pear tree doubly welcomed the travelers who alighted under its plump fragrance. Farther on, against a red brick wall espaliered peaches shone, gold and red, in the last light of day. He tasted in fancy those peaches; he must eat peaches soon; he was hungry.

Here was a field where the worker had laid down his scythe and gone to enjoy his simple fare. Autumn was abroad: every house, every tree, every field proclaimed his presence. What if one could *see* autumn? What would he be like? What of an ode to autumn, season of mists and mellow fruitfulness? The pictures he had unrolled so far on this journey melted into others. A bee buzzed its humming way across his vision. Over there under a dimly seen thatched house, a vine was heavy with grapes. In the garden at the rear he just glimpsed a beehive or two as he turned his thoughts to London.

"What a ride!" He got down joyously—London was home and he loved home best—but sobered at the prospect of meeting Abbey.

In the Counting House, Pancras Lane, Abbey behaved "extremely well" to him, appointing Monday evening at seven at his residence to discuss the business. This was Saturday. Time to see Fanny Brawne. Did he wish to see her? "I only know I cannot resolve to mix any pleasure with my days." At the moment, he was enjoying "a half-comfortable sullenness in downright perplexities." But there were Woodhouse and others.

At 93 Fleet Street he found the literary adviser. After stating the reason for his being in town he remarked, "I also have with me half of 'Lamia,' copied fair. The rest is rough. I'd like to read you what I have here."

The critic would be overjoyed. "But, my dear Keats, I'm going away tomorrow, and I'm busy this afternoon. Could you have breakfast with me?"

Delighted, and he would see Hessey, in Taylor's absence.

"Can you publish—immediately—'Lamia' and 'The Eve of St. Agnes'?"

Hessey, always deferring to Taylor, played with his inkwell only a moment before saying he thought it could not answer to do so just then.

By nine o'clock next morning, Keats was at Woodhouse's place and there remained until the vacation-bent friend left for Weymouth at three o'clock.

"I wondered that you said nothing of 'Isabella,' Keats, when you were asking about immediate publication—"

Keats looked awkward. "I cannot bear 'Isabella' now."

"But why?" Woodhouse paused in packing a bag.

"It appears to me mawkish." Keats looked obstinate.

"This certainly is not so," Woodhouse assured him.

"There is another matter," and now he hesitated, "I wish an alteration in 'The Eve of St. Agnes.' "

"It's perfect, man!" Woodhouse spoke more amazedly than before.

"No." Keats took out a copy and turned to Stanza XXXVI:

Beyond a mortal man impassion'd far
At these voluptuous accents he arose,
Ethereal, flush'd, and like a throbbing star
Seen mid the sapphire heaven's deep repose
Into her dream he melted, as the rose
Blendeth its odour with the violet—
Solution sweet.—

237

Woodhouse waited. What was coming?

"You will recall perhaps that Porphyro sets himself to persuade Madeline to go away with him, 'For o'er the Dartmoor black I have a home for thee.' I shall say, 'For o'er the southern moor—' "

Woodhouse waved away the change, relieved. "A small alteration."

Keats was not through. "In the version as it stands they go to be married. Hear my change." And in the revision, Woodhouse heard, to his horror, that "as soon as Madeline confessed her love, Porphyro winds by degrees his arms about her, presses breast to breast and acts all the acts of a bona fide husband, while she fancies she is only playing the part of a wife in a dream!"

Keats stopped reading, to see his critic, petrified, aghast.

"There are no improper expressions," insisted Keats. "All is left to inference, and the reader's imagination is heightened—"

"Indeed!" agreed Woodhouse. "Yet your alteration of some three stanzas will render the poem unfit for ladies, and scarcely to be mentioned by them among 'things that are.' "

"I do not wish ladies to read my poetry," Keats's lower jaw moved forward. "I write for men. If in the former version there was opening for a doubt what took place, it was my fault for not writing clearly and comprehensibly."

Woodhouse continued to stare.

"I should despise a man," Keats went on, "who would be such a eunuch in sentiment as to leave a maid, with that character about her, in such a situation, and should despise myself to write about it—"

"My dear Keats—"

"Despise myself," and he continued with what Woodhouse called "Keats-like rhodomontade."

"Let Taylor see your revision," the critic brought him up.

238

Whereupon Keats drew out the half-finished "Lamia" and composed himself to begin:

Upon a time before the faery broods
Drove nymph and satyr from the prosperous woods—

while Woodhouse reflected, "How wretchedly he reads this supreme verse!" He recognized in himself a slowness in catching even the sense of poetry hearing it read—by a best reader—for the first time. "And Keats's must be studied to be appreciated properly," he added to himself.

Yet, as he sat and listened, the poetry came now and then upon him and made him, the listener, "start, as though a sea-nymph quired." When the last line lay quivering on the air, Woodhouse exclaimed over his pleasure and the anticipation of reading all the story. He looked at his watch.

Keats got up, thrusting the sheets inside his coat. "Why do you never write to me?" he asked, Woodhouse rushing at bag, coat, and stick.

"I shall amend, dear boy, but stipulate that all the reciprocity, as Paddy says, 'must not be on one side.'" He led the way out and just caught the coach.

Keats shook his hand and promised to drop a line to Bath —Woodhouse would continue to that spa from Weymouth— "and if it should be in verse, I daresay you will forgive me!"

Woodhouse had to himself the inside of the coach, where he was amused to sum up all that had happened in the six hours as well as to remember what part he must report to Taylor. He covered the essentials in a letter from Weymouth on the twentieth of September and five days later Taylor replied from Bakewell. Woodhouse read that Taylor thought this particular folly of Keats was the most stupid of which he could conceive. "He does not bear the ill opinion of the world calmly, yet he will not allow it to form a good opinion of him and his writings." And he recalled Keats's repentance of his conduct when *Endymion* was published, his expressions of mortification and disgust showing he had met with a result different from that anticipated. Yet here Keats was again challenging the world!

"I do not know how the meaning of the new stanzas is wrapped up, but I will not be accessory (I can answer also for Hessey, I think) towards publishing that which is read only by men." If Keats, further, knew truly the worth of woman's society and suffrage, he would never have thought of depriving himself of them. "So far as he is unconsciously silly in this proceeding, I am sorry for him, but for the rest I cannot but confess to you that it excites in me the strongest sentiments of disapprobation. Therefore, my dear Richard, if he will not so far concede to my wishes as to leave the passage as it originally stood, I must be content to admire his poems with some other imprint, and in so being I can reap as much delight from the perusal of them as if they were our own property, without having the disgusting consideration attached to them of our approving by the 'Imprimatur' those parts which are unfit for publication."

Still, if Woodhouse thought him too severe, he would suspend judgment till he saw or heard more. Woodhouse later spoke to Keats, using all his tact, he felt, in urging the first version.

3

That evening in Henrietta Street, Keats dined with Mrs. Wylie, Henry, and Charles. All greeted him warmly, even to young Charles—home but a few days from a visit in Paris —and Keats would not disturb their peace by mentioning the cause of his trip to London. Yet portions of George's letter were entertaining after a sadly dramatic fashion. Audubon, the artist-naturalist, George reported, had sold him a boat

240

laden with merchandise which, at the time of the sale, he averred Audubon knew had been sunk in the Mississippi River.

"I don't believe George is fit to deal with the American world," Keats had about concluded. But he did not say so to the Wylies.

"You're a greater blade than ever, Henry," he was taking in the handsome coat, waistcoat, and buff trousers. "And you've lost some of your Spanish brown."

Henry passed a complacent hand over his smooth face, and bowed.

Standing at the window with Charles, who was too aptly "quizzing the passengers," Keats saw that his beard had begun to curl, little twists down the side of his face, "getting properly thickish on the angles of the visage."

"You young son-of-a-gun, you will have a notable pair of whiskers!"

Charles grinned and led 'John' back to the ladies. "How shiny your gown is in front, Mother!"

"Can't you see it's an apron?" Henry challenged. Indeed, his mother had covered the front of her dress with the slick material used for lining the purple stuff.

"It's the first day I've worn the apron, Charles," but Keats observed in astute silence it was the first time for the whole costume.

"A fine cook you have, Mrs. Wylie"; ladies liked to be complimented on their dinners.

"Only a trifle lame," said the lady deprecatingly.

"That improves her, makes her go more swimmingly. By the way, when I came tonight and asked, 'Is Mrs. Wylie within?' she gave such a large five-and-thirty year old smile, I looked around from the stairway—"

"Oh, you foolish young men!" Mrs. Wylie smiled and asked Charles to draw the curtains. "My cook was merely entranced at the thought of admitting a poet," she said to Keats.

"You must hear some of Georgiana's letter to me," and walking to a cabinet, she drew out an envelope, obviously ready for reference. "I'll read the description of the baby," and she quoted the exact measurements, with the young mother's comments on the delicate nails of hands and feet.

Span-long elf, thought Keats but he only thanked Mrs. Wylie for letting him know the baby's dimensions. He would write to Georgiana his appreciation. . . .

Next day he visited his sister at Walthamstow. Finding her well, he talked briefly and went on to see other friends. He felt strange as he walked the streets—Reynolds in the country, Dilke's family all in the country, Taylor at Nottingham, Haslam much occupied with "love and business." Keats studied his lady's picture, done by Severn. Too cunning for Haslam, he thought but did not say. After all, it was Haslam's affair. With Rice, however, he had a fine talk, "There is no one I like to pass a day with better."

Immediately before setting out for Walthamstow, he wrote Fanny Brawne from Fleet Street, where he had dropped in again. He told her he had come up from Winchester Friday—and had not yet been to Hampstead. Knowing well his life must be spent in fatigue and trouble, he had endeavored to wean himself from her. "For to myself alone, what can be much of a misery?" For himself he could despise all events but he could not cease to love her. He would return to Winchester next day—though he put off going to Wednesday—and she would hear from him in a few days. "I am a coward; I cannot bear the pain of being happy; 'tis out of the question: I must admit no thought of it."

A trifle before seven he stood at Abbey's door, as he had stood that morning in calling on his sister. After tea, Keats

242

passed over the note George had enclosed to Abbey and also the pertinent part of George's letter to himself.

"I'm anxious about this affair, John, I confess." Abbey crossed a plump white-stockinged leg over the other.

"What can you do, sir?" Keats asked after a pause in which his host had sat smoothing the white stockings.

"I will forward his money as soon as possible." And Abbey rambled on about applying to Mrs. Midgely Jennings' Attorney, Gliddon, and trying to be expeditious in getting rid of the claim. Other comments showed he had apparently advanced the business; but Keats craved certainty.

"How long—how soon?" he hazarded.

"That is hard to say. I will write you as soon as I can bring matters to bear." He made as if to drop the subject, and picking up a magazine face down on the table at his elbow exclaimed, "What a fellow is this Lord Byron!"

Wants to draw me out, thought Keats.

After reading laboriously and aloud some extracts from "Don Juan," "Ugh!" he grunted and began blowing up the author.

"It is a flash poem," said Keats. He left shortly, with a deeper sense of being in a low estate than he had known for some time. Nor was George better off. Here he was, of sound mind and brain—he hoped—still unable to raise any sum by the promise of any poem, "No, not by the mortgage of my intellect." He brightened in thinking of "Otho." Surely, they would accept it at either Drury Lane or Covent Garden.

He must earn money. There were no books at Winchester, as he had hoped. He would write Dilke and find out what chances he might have on the auction block of intellect for sale. If any, he would move to a cheap lodging in Westminster, doing without pleasures if need be until he had a competence.

So thinking, he woke to the familiar sights and sounds of

Cheapside, having forgotten to mail some letters. Returning to put them in the post office, he met Abbey by chance in Bucklersbury. They walked together through the Poultry as far as the hatter's shop, in which Abbey said he had an interest.

"I need a good assistant," he eyed Keats.

Keats's face was innocent but he was thinking, I do believe if I could be a hatter, I might be one.

Wednesday, he set out, beside the coachman, for Winchester. If his friends thought he did not eat when traveling, they should see him this day! He liked the look of the signs, and the coachman's face said "Eat, eat, eat." And he, John Keats, probably ate to persuade himself he was somebody, for he never felt more contemptible than when sitting by the side of so good-looking a driver. The coachman only nibbled. He had had, he confessed, a religious "call."

"A Hercules Methodist!" exclaimed Keats to himself, and wished he had so sweet a breath to sing as had that fellow. "I'd give a penny for his whistle and bow to all the girls on the road." All along, as in coming to London, he sniffed and felt and heard autumn.

4

Four days later, Sunday the nineteenth of September, in this 1819, he walked his favorite mile and struck for the fields. He passed a hazel thicket and smelled perfume from apples in the cider-press near the orchard and barns. Sad, for autumn preluded winter, he remembered the spring and the summer. Yet, he reflected, autumn had its own peculiar beauty. He stood watching the sunset under bars of clouds, then turned to his room near the cathedral. The light breeze rose and fell; lambs bleated from the hills, and humble insects buzzed above the shallows or among the hedges. He

244

entered his doorway to the twittering of swallows, as in a trance passed in, threw off his hat, drew paper toward him, and wrote:

TO AUTUMN

I

Season of mists and mellow fruitfulness,
Close bosom-friend of the maturing sun;
Conspiring with him how to load and bless
With fruit the vines that round the thatch-eves run;
To bend with apples the moss'd cottage-trees,
And fill all fruit with ripeness to the core;
To swell the gourd, and plump the hazel shells
With a sweet kernel; to set budding more,
And still more, later flowers for the bees,
Until they think warm days will never cease,
For summer has o'er-brimmed their clammy cells.

II

Who hath not seen thee oft amid thy store?
Sometimes whoever seeks abroad may find
Thee sitting careless on a granary floor,
Thy hair soft-lifted by the winnowing wind;
Or on a half-reap'd furrow sound asleep,
Drows'd with the fume of poppies, while thy hook
Spares the next swath and all its twined flowers:
And sometimes like a gleaner thou dost keep
Steady thy laden head against a brook;
Or by a cyder-press, with patient look,
Thou watchest the last oozings hours by hours.

III

Where are the songs of Spring? Ay, where are they?
Think not of them, thou hast thy music too—

Forever Young

While barred clouds bloom the soft-dying day,
And touch the stubble plains with rosy hue;
Then in a wailful choir the small gnats mourn
Among the river shallows borne aloft
Or sinking as the light wind lives or dies;
And full-grown lambs loud bleat from hilly bourn;
Hedge-crickets sing; and now with treble soft
The red-breast whistles from a garden croft;
And gathering swallows twitter in the skies.

"I never lik'd stubble-fields so much as now," he wrote Reynolds the following Tuesday. "Aye, better than the chilly green of the Spring. Somehow a stubble plain looks warm—in the same way that some pictures look warm—This struck me so much in my Sunday's walk that I composed upon it."

But he had been intoxicated with the wine of autumn since climbing the coach for London.

XIV. *Perturbéd Spirit*

"KEPEN in solitarinesse," he wrote more letters for substitute to Brown's companionship. Woodhouse had said, "I count on seeing Reynolds at Bath," and to 8 Duke Street he sent on September 21 the hope they would pass some pleasant time together: he would add to their pleasure by a brace of letters. Should he tell of the street disturbance the night he and Brown arrived? Of yesterday, when a Mayor was elected? Of the excessively maiden-like streets of Winchester —"door-steps always fresh from the flannel?" Or of his Sunday walk? All this to Reynolds, whom he also told of giving up "Hyperion."

Sure that Woodhouse could not keep from Reynolds a certain change desired in "The Eve of St. Agnes," he requested a "third opinion in the first discussion" between the two. "You know I will not give up my argument: In my walk today I stooped under a rail that lay across my path, and asked myself, 'Why did I not get over?' 'Because,' answered I, 'no one wanted to force you under.' I would give a guinea to be a good reasonable man—good sound sense—a says what he thinks, and does what he says man—and did not take snuff."

For Woodhouse he copied "To Autumn," and junketishly remarked: "My poetry will never be fit for anything. It doesn't cover the ground well. You see she is off her guard and doesn't move a peg. . . . Now a blow in the spondee will finish her." As he wrote "doesn't cover the ground," he saw file before him a number of his poems he so judged. The

247

latest was this brevity on the present season. Then that "Ode on Melancholy." . . . He had written that grim, that Dantesque first stanza, whereas he had meant to suggest tenderness, "beauty that must die," and had surrendered that beginning. Three stanzas left, surely not covering the ground. And what would anybody make of the beginning: "No, no! go not to Lethe. . . ."

He shóok his head over incapacities and spoke of other writers. Would Dick tell Jack of the fairy tale, *Undine?* Out in London over a year ago, it had fallen only of late under his eyes. Also he would know whether Reynolds had read any of the American Charles Brockden Brown's novels. "I have read *Wieland*—very powerful—something like Godwin. Between Schiller and Godwin. . . . More clever in plot and incident than Godwin. . . . Powerful genius—accomplished horrors."

How quiet this town! "The knockers are dieted to three raps per diem."

Weary, he went to bed, "revolving certain circumstances chiefly connected with a late American letter." Though they were young, he and his brother were in a parlous situation. He would work and share what he had with George—at least, until age made him more selfish. He drifted into troubled slumber.

Throughout his ten-day continued letter to George and Georgiana, he repeated that he would help them. He could bear real ills better than imaginary ones, was becoming accustomed to privations of pleasures of sense. "Whenever I find myself growing vaporish, I rouse myself, wash and put on a clean shirt, brush my hair and clothes, tie my shoestrings neatly and in fact adonize as I were going out—then, all clean and comfortable, I sit down to write."

This "adonizing" brought vividly back the days he had made himself presentable for Fanny Brawne. "I feel I can bear anything—any misery, even imprisonment—so long as I have neither wife nor child." They might take this amiss. He added, "Perhaps you will say yours are your only comfort—they must be." He was not quite clear how they could be to George—in Georgiana's opinion—if not to himself; but let it pass. It would pass if he diverted attention to the baby —and he wrote: "Let her have only delicate nails on hands and feet and teeth as small as a May-fly's—who will live you his life on a square inch of oak-leaf." This idea roused a ready contrast: Nails that child must have quite different from those of the market women in Winchester, "who plough into the butter and make a quarter-pound taste of it." He knew. Did he not buy butter for the rolls "just ris," as the bakers' wives said?

On the financial problem again he advised George to manage the next year as well as possible—"the next month, I mean, for I trust you will soon receive Abbey's remittance. What he can send you will not be a sufficient capital to ensure you any command in America." He confessed that what Abbey held of his own was "nearly anticipated" by debts. But, again, he would live in hope of being able to increase it for George and Georgiana. He could bear real ills, he insisted: he had not had the blue devils once since receiving George's latest letter.

George would be agog to hear his political views, and he spoke of the three great changes in social history, as he saw them, concluding (of the present conflict in England), "This is no contest between Whig and Tory, but between right and wrong. There is scarcely a grain of party spirit. . . . Right and Wrong considered by each man abstractedly is the fashion." He cited the cases of Carlile, the bookseller, who had been jailed for circulating pamphlets, "The Deist"; and Henry Hunt's triumphal entry into London. Carlile had found bail to many thousands of pounds: "They are afraid to prosecute: they are afraid of his defence." He thought the trial would light a flame not easily extinguished. Here were two experiments in real liberty.

Of things literary, he had read a passage in the *Anatomy of Melancholy* he would have given his favorite leg to have written as a speech in a play. He copied for the Georges the 350 words beginning, "Every lover adores his mistress though she be very deformed of herself," etc. This passage would amuse them more than so much poetry. But later he copied the fragment, "The Eve of St. Mark," which he thought they would like because it would give the sensation of walking about an old country town on a coolish evening.

Copying the poem, he felt as often he had felt, "Writing has this disadvantage of speaking—one cannot write a wink or a nod, or a grin or a purse of the lips, or a *smile*— O law! One cannot put one's finger to one's nose or yerk ye in the ribs, or lay hold of your button in writing—but in all the most lively and titterly parts of my letter you must not fail to imagine me, as the epic poets say, now here, now there, now with one foot pointed at the ceiling, now with another —now with my pen on my ear, now with my elbow in my mouth. O my friends, you lose the action—and attitude is everything (O, those dramatists! he yearned), as Fuseli said when he took up his leg like a musket to shoot a swallow just darting behind his shoulder. And yet, does not the word mum! go for one's finger beside the nose. I hope it does." In a best junkets-spirit he thought and acted and spoke for them in a scene with their baby. . . .

By the morning of the twenty-first of September he had not heard from Brown. He had written Brown two letters. Had he become an object of suspicion and were his letters being opened? He would rage against the ceiling but was in a lodginghouse and, moreover, "a little cowardly." The Major in the next room would run him through the body!

250

To Woodhouse he suggested hiring a show-wagon, himself the occupant, a trumpeter preceding the display, "Here's the wonderful man whose letters won't go."

In that same letter to Woodhouse, he felt he should explain his dislike to "Isabella." "It is what I should call, were I a reviewer, 'a weak-sided poem' with an amusing sober-sadness about it. . . . If I may say so, in my dramatic capacity, I enter fully into the feeling; but in propria persona, I should be apt to quiz it, myself." Oh, this business of writing a play caused you to see many things differently! He thought there was no objection to "Lamia" such as to "Isabella," or on the same grounds; but certainly to "St. Agnes Eve"— "only not so glaring."

Concerned with story and action, he amused himself and he hoped Woodhouse by continuing, auctorially, Smollett's *Humphry Clinker*. Only for a few lines.

His promises to George put him on the trail for work. To Dilke, in the Navy Pay Office, he wrote of his resolution to attempt acquiring money by "temporary writing in periodical works. . . . I will traffic. Anything but mortgage my brain to Blackwood." It occurred to him that Dilke might think he wanted tact. That was easy to achieve. "You may be up to the slang of a cock-pit in three battles." He had learned better than to speak his mind on every subject with utmost simplicity as he had done a year or two ago. He was confident he could shine up an article on any subject without much knowledge of it, "aye, like an orange." More seriously, he declared, "I would willingly have recourse to other means. I cannot; I am fit for nothing but literature."

He forestalled, also, Dilke's possible advice to wait for the issue of the tragedy, "Otho the Great." "No; there cannot be greater uncertainties east, west, north, and south than concerning dramatic composition." As for poetry, he had no trust in it, and only marveled that people read so much.

He selected a nectarine from a basket of the fruit—fresh, ripe, golden-red. He held it to his mouth with one hand while writing with the other. "Good God, how fine! It went down soft, pulpy, slushy, oozy—all its delicious embonpoint melted down my throat like a large beatified strawberry. I shall certainly breed." But his hands must be washed, and, while he paused, he had the conviction that he must take lodgings away from Brown. Not really from Brown, but from Fanny Brawne. He feared the result, a relapse, if he saw her too constantly. So, would Dilke look about for a room or rooms in Marsham or.Romney Street? Near Dilke and also near Mrs. Wylie in Henrietta—though he would not be influenced by the lady's proximity—"rooms like the gallants' legs in Massinger's time, 'as good as the times allow, sir.'"

Those articles in the *Examiner* sent by Dilke had put him into spirits: "Notwithstanding my aristocratic temper, I cannot help being very much pleased with the present public proceedings. I hope sincerely I shall be able to put a mite of help to the Liberal side of the question before I die."

In all his worries over money, he was filled with a growing sense of what Brown was doing for him. Here he was, able, strong— Oh, a little trifle of a sore throat now and then when he had been imprudent—and he was, in a way of speaking, Brown's dependent. Good Brown, who knew he would not lose a shilling—but then others knew the same. Were they like Brown? Decidedly no.

On the twenty-third of September, then, he confessed to Brown who he believed was at Bedhampton, "I am getting into an idle-minded vicious way of life, almost too content to live upon others. In no period of my life have I acted with any self-will but in throwing up the apothecary profession. That I do not repent of." He told Brown of his plans to live in cheap lodgings and to get "the theatricals of some paper," while he composed when he could his deliberate poems.

"Good God! What a short while you have known me! . . . You have been living for others more than any man I know. This is a vexation to me, because it has been depriving you, in the very prime of your life, of pleasures which it was your duty to procure." He had got into the way of looking to Brown as a help in all difficulties. He must break the neck of that habit; at the end of another year Brown should applaud him not for verses but conduct.

Brown might wonder why he was leaving the comfortable quarters at Wentworth Place. "If you live at Hampstead next winter—I like ***** and I cannot help it. On that account I had better not live there." Meantime, they must meet in London, around the middle of October, and "set at" the theaters with "Otho."

His letter crossed one posted at Bedhampton. "I feel from Brown's letter he may believe me unhappy," and he wrote reassuringly, saying again that imaginary grievances had always tormented him more than real ones. . . . "Real grievances are displacers of passion. The imaginary nail a man down for a sufferer as on a cross; the real spur him up into an agent." He would like to tell Brown how he felt, but would—if possible—avoid sentimentality. "I wish at one view you would see my heart towards you," he finally set down. " 'Tis only from a high tone of feeling that I can put that word upon paper—out of poetry."

Before posting his letter to America he recalled that Georgiana had asked for one large sheet, all to herself. She had tried to quiz him about getting a sore throat by promenading in the rain with a red-haired girl. Had she been hearing gossip of Fanny and himself? He would not admit to her any understanding of her drift. "A catch in the rain occasioned my last sore throat," he told her, "but as for red-

253

haired girls—upon my word, I do not recollect ever having seen one. Are you quizzing me or Miss Waldegrave when you talk of promenading?" His sister-in-law was exceedingly fond of puns: he displayed some ingenuity in playing on "pound" and "pun." And, she would surely be interested in the latest story about Charles Lamb. A child in arms was passing by his chair when he took hold of the long clothes, saying, "Where, God bless me, where does it leave off?" He recounted his several little jokes, and saw her laughing over an inadvertent visit he had paid to the Major's wife next door.

Brown came back. He had not heard from Keats because he had been at Chichester while Keats still directed his letters to Bedhampton. When Brown told this tale to his friend, who received it without question, he might have said what Keats had once said to Severn, "You are the most astonishingly suggestive innocent I ever met." The lost letters—well, they might still be crossing between Bedhampton and Ireland.

Brown heard Keats's arguments for moving to Westminster and concurred. At once, October first, Keats definitely asked Dilke to engage a sitting room and bedroom, "for myself alone," and to consider the essentials of quiet and cheapness. Two days later, he quite as definitely asked Haydon to procure him a ticket to the British Museum. "I will make a better use of it than I did in the first instance."

"Let's go up to London, Friday, the eighth," he suggested.

"Our week will be up then," agreed Brown. "That will be the best day."

2

"Dilke has taken two rooms for me at 25 College Street"; Keats passed over the letter to Brown.

"That's just off his own, Great Smith," Brown was localizing aloud, "and across from the College Yard. You'll have the Abbey, the Houses of Parliament, and the river all within your scope of vision."

"Sounds well enough," and yet it did not sound well. He was feeling what it would be like away from the "melancholy Carle."

Brown knew Keats could never live alone.

"Brown—I must come to see you often. And you will visit me?"

Brown assured him of both events, so far as he was concerned, and Saturday each went his way. Keats scattered impedimenta over the two rooms in College Street, called to see Dilke, and looked up other friends.

Sunday he was drawn back to Wentworth Place. He would pay a call upon Fanny Brawne and try to have an understanding. . . . And all the summer months he had been absent from her were as if they had never been. All the stirring of his energies to hard work, all the resolution to deny love were as nothing. "O, God," he told himself, "I had not thought it would be like this. I hoped I was free. The time away has only grappled my soul to hers with hoops of steel."

Alone in his rooms, he recalled her light brilliance, "There is nothing in the world so bright and delicate." She had dazzled him yesterday. Was she trying to charm him, to bring him to his knees? Nonsense! She had only been herself, Fanny, giving him those evidences of affection he had known before he went away, evidences all coated over with his studies, forgotten through financial puzzles, and—be it admitted—deliberately forgotten.

They had not been alone all of yesterday: Brown was there, Mrs. Brawne was there. Now, he lived again all he

255

had lived yesterday. In these months out of London, he had not lived—except in imagination.

"When shall we pass a day alone?" he asked. "I have had a thousand kisses, for which with my whole soul I thank love —but if you should deny me the thousand and first—'twould put me to the proof of how great a misery I could live through." By way of pretended retaliation, she had made a very pretty threat. He knew she could not mean it, but, "If you should ever carry [it] into execution—believe me, 'tis not my pride, my vanity or any petty passion would torment me—really 'twould break my heart—I could not bear it." Mrs. Dilke was accepting Mrs. Brawne's invitation and would be going with him any fine day to Wentworth Place.

This College Street abode he could not endure. His loneliness was multiplied a thousandfold. Oh, to be back with Brown, in his old quarters! He did not set up his shelves of books. He used his rooms only for sleeping and writing— but could scarcely make fair copies of verses already composed. His soul cried out without ceasing for Fanny Brawne; he saw not the page but her blue, blue eyes, warm throat, and angelic complexion. Two days later he had advanced his copying not at all. "I must write to her again!" and was sending her another letter before she had replied to his first. While he wrote, hers came. Would he not be happier away from her? And, again, she playfully threatened: she had not punished him, she said, for his seemingly neglectful behavior.

Abject, oh, he was abject. But love made him proud in his abjectness.

25 College Street

My dearest girl

 This moment I have set myself to copy some verses out fair. I cannot proceed with any degree of content. I must write you a line or two and see if that will assist in dismissing you from my mind for ever so short a time. Upon my soul, I can think of nothing else. The time is passed when I had power to advise and warn you against the unpromising morning of my life. My love has made me selfish. I cannot exist without you. I am forgetful of everything but seeing you again—my life seems to stop there—I see no further. You have absorb'd me. I have a sensation at the present moment as though I was dissolving—I should be exquisitely miserable without the hope of soon seeing you. I should be afraid to separate myself far from you. My sweet Fanny, will your heart never change? My love, will it? I have no limit now to my love— Your note came in just here—I cannot be happier away from you. 'Tis richer than an argosy of pearls. Do not threat me even in jest. I have been astonished that men could die martyrs for religion—I have shudder'd at it. I shudder no more— Love is my religion—I could die for that. I could die for you. My creed is love and you are its tenet. You have ravish'd me away by a power I cannot resist; and yet I could resist till I saw you; and even since I have seen you I have endeavored often 'to reason against the reasons of my love.' I can do that no more. The pain would be too great. My love is selfish. I cannot breathe without you.

Yours for ever

John Keats.

He sealed the letter and sat a moment, weighing whether he should mail it or write another. "It's the way I feel, God help me," and walked to the post office. "How will she take it?" he asked himself after it was irrevocably out of his hands.

When Brown invited him to visit a few days, he was off at once. Poetry, his new volume for which he was making fair copies, all forgotten. He was following his heart.

Part of the time he was in the semidetached house next

door. Sharing meals with Fanny, watching her flit about the house, his being one great throb over the grace of her movements, while he never tired of her delicate color, deepening or paling, always enhanced by the white-lawn frills.

Invited to return on the old footing, he accepted instantly Brown's suggestion that he move back. One trip sufficed to bring his little heap of worldly possessions. He came back, he now wrote his sister, "induced by the habit I have acquired of this room I am now in and also from the pleasure of being free from paying any attentions to a diminutive house-keeping." He would not permit himself to grow melancholy over the indebtedness he was in to Brown. They paid half and half toward their common expenses—but he was behind. "Mr. Brown has been my great friend for some time—without him I should have been in, perhaps, personal distress. As I know you love me though I do not deserve it, I am sure you will take pleasure in being a friend to Mr. Brown even before you know him." He did not forget to tell her he had a "couple of shells" for her—that she would call pretty—and to say he had left off animal food.

After he had surrendered his rooms in College Street, he went back for a few days to be with the Dilkes. All were astonished at his idleness and thoughtfulness, whereas the truth was he was miserable away from Fanny.

"I should like to cast the die for love or death," he wrote. "I have no patience with anything else—if you ever intend to be cruel to me—as you say in jest now, but perhaps sometime may be in earnest—be so now—and I will—my mind is in a tremble, I cannot tell what I am writing. Ever my love, yours."

Back at Wentworth Place he was as near his heart's desire as possible unless they had been married and in a home of their own. He faced reasons against marriage: it could not be —yet. While he sat rewriting "Hyperion" in the form of a vision, he could look out upon the garden through which she passed. From the second floor he saw her light form flash by the window—if he happened to be near the casement, and often he stood there—and he was familiar with her hours in the garden. There they met for walks up and down the paths, in the sun; there they sat on the rustic bench if the day was warm, or from it walked to the mulberry tree for its shade.

Again he was unhappy to the depths when she went to dances or routs, to those crowded rooms in which his sore throat forbade his presence—even with her. Would he selfishly deny her the gayety of those halls and homes? No, and yes. If in fancy he could see her without attendant beaux, those men encircling her in the measures of the languorous waltz, he would say, "Go, enjoy yourself, my Fanny," and could mean it. But a man must be less than mortal or more than superman to see her so surrender herself—if she loved him.

To counter her pleasures, though he might not admit to himself this reason, he resumed the lectures delivered by Hazlitt, now talking at the Surrey Institution about the dramatists of the Elizabethan Age. Heaven knew, he told himself, if he ever succeeded in his hopes of dramatic composition, he could do with what so high an authority might say.

To Severn, who begged him to see "The Cave of Despair," he wrote that he would after the picture was hung in a good light. Meantime, let the artist come and chat all day, except for nine hours of sleep in his "little crib." Shortly after Severn received the gold medal, Keats dined with Hilton and three other artists at the home of Hilton's brother-in-law. The subject of conversation was this award.

"The first gold medal given in twelve years!" one exclaimed.

259

"And a very inferior painting," proclaimed a scornful *ex cathedra* judge.

"Then how—why?—" Keats began.

"Oh, the artist is an old fellow, who has competed frequently for the prize," said one who did not know Keats was aware of Severn's age. "The Council gave the medal out of pity; not for any merit."

Keats looked from face to face of the four artists, all of whom knew the statement false, expecting "a flat contradiction."

Nobody said, "On the contrary, he is not quite twenty-six."

Keats spoke then, his face warm, his voice deep. "I have seen the painting and recognized its merits, as well as its origin in Spenser. You know well he is a young man, and you know also that this painting is his first attempt for a prize of any kind. I will not longer sit at the same table with such traducers and snobs." He rapidly left the party.

3

Old dissatisfactions prompted him to write Taylor, "I have come to a determination not to publish anything I have now already written." He thought he would do well to untether Fancy and let her roam amid marvels, for the marvelous was most enticing and the surest guarantee of harmonious numbers. Yet he was at odds with himself about the marvelous: "Wonders are no wonders to me." However badly his small dramatic skill might serve dramatic composition he thought it would be sufficient for a poem. The coloring of "The Eve of St. Agnes" he wished to diffuse throughout a poem in which character and sentiment would be figures to such drapery. If he could write two or three such in the next six years, he would be nerved up by them to the writing of a

few fine plays—"my greatest ambition when I do feel ambitious." Even then he was reading Holinshed's "Elizabeth,"
and considering the Earl of Leicester as a promising subject.
Taylor had talked to him about this topic and promised books
bearing on it. His low-spirited Muse would be encouraged if
Taylor would send these and any others of service—"or
rather by letting me know when our errand cart man shall
call with my little box."

He was not sorry to be brought about face when Woodhouse told him, "We cannot let you off the projected volume. We are bringing out your poems in the Spring of
1820." Now it was the middle of November: soon he would
be reading proof.

From a call upon Taylor, he walked on to see Abbey. The
merchant had remitted to George's agent, he said, much
smaller sums than he had expected to send.

"Why?" Keats asked with lively interest and sinking
spirits.

"First, the stocks are very low; second, I am unwilling to
venture more till this business of Mrs. Midgely Jennings is
at rest."

"But you promised to do all in your power to advance it?"
He spoke against hope. Had he not seen this delay protracted
already beyond George's endurance?

"You may rely upon me, John," Abbey's reply was pom-
pous. "I also hope by the day of settlement she will make no
claim."

"What is the present status?" Keats expected more circum-
locution.

"She has not withdrawn her claim but she has not instituted action against you heirs."

Clear enough, Keats thought. Aloud he put another question: "Who must pay the expenses of the suit if she sues?"

"You, even if she loses," Abbey's expressionless face suggested neither sympathy nor any other emotion.

"Could you not advance money to George?" Keats tried to infuse the notion of this being the logical thing.

"No." The tea-and-coffee dealer was firm. "Though the risk be small, I am persuaded George would lose it in America."

"What of the stocks recovering?" What would George be doing now—if he were here, Keats wondered.

"They may recover, possibly. If so, they may be sold at not too great disadvantage."

"I know that not much of my money can remain, Mr. Abbey," Keats spoke casually enough, despite the difficult speech. "But I have had none from you for ten months. How do you suppose I pay my bills?"

"Too bad the circumstances are what they are"; Abbey must have had a twinge of conscience. "I will advance you a few pounds on my own responsibility." He reached for a banking account book.

While Keats waited, Abbey looked up—"I say, John," and presently laid down his quill, "why don't you become a bookseller? You are a book fancier."

His face burning, while he knew he was staring most rudely, Keats exclaimed, "A—a bookseller?"

Obviously seeing not the slightest difference between a poet and one who sold poetry, Abbey repeated, "You like books, don't you?"

Keats thought of the Commissioner of Stamps, John Kingston, at Haydon's dinner. Here was a worthy match. "First, he wanted me to be a surgeon and apprenticed me to Hammond. Next, he wanted me to be a hatter. Now a bookseller. What hereafter? What was it he compared my first poems to? A Quaker's horse. Damn him!"

"I hear your friend Hunt was arrested the other day. . . ."

Abbey handed over the order for pounds, shilling, pence—on which the ink was now dry.

"He is dating his letters from home," parried John. "Thank you," and walked out.

He sauntered along the well-known streets, wondering what he must do if Elliston of Drury Lane rejected "Otho." How many weeks ago was it, anyway, since Brown had made and submitted a fair copy? Three, at least. Brown was sanguine. But he, Keats, how could he be hopeful about anything? Hope was left out of his nature.

The wind caught him at the throat; he drew up his collar and debated whether he should try to see his sister. "I can do nothing for George, and I am in no mood or state to call upon her—I can scarcely credit the fact that I have not seen her since I came back—five, six weeks ago."

Disjoined thoughts and worries vexing his brain, he returned to Wentworth Place. How he needed encouragement to write anything worth while—if it were not soon granted—Just a little better fortune for George, happier news from George—even so much would free him halfway.

He was not to find encouragement. On his desk lay a letter from a stockbroker in Throgmorton, to whom he had ventured to write about his and his brother's affairs. "A most abusive letter," he wrote George, "committing you and myself to destruction without reprieve." Scarcely able to summon a smile in reverse, he thought, I must tell Severn he'd best put me into his "Cave of Despair."

When Brown came in, lugubrious enough, he inquired mechanically, "No luck?"

"Elliston has not rejected 'Otho,'" Brown replied, "but wishes to put it off till next season."

"That is, he'll find an excuse not to stage it, at all?"

"Probably," Brown spoke so swiftly, Keats knew he had

been thinking the same thing. "We might withdraw it," he added, "and try it at Covent Garden."

" 'Twould do my heart good to see Macready as Ludolph." Keats felt warmed by the roseate vision.

"We'll think it over. Meanwhile, I've heard a good yarn. A bit on the off-side but, well, pathological. I think 'Dr.' Keats could bear it."

"You would not merely 'think' could you see the sights I've seen, Brown."

"Very well, then. It seems there was a man and his wife had to go a long journey on foot. In the course of their travels they came to a river, which rolled knee-deep over the pebbles—"

Keats heard it all: "I'll pass it on to the Georges," but he was not in a fun-finding mood.

Brown walked around behind Keats and ran his hand over sleeve and shoulder. "Tearing out in the shoulder-seam."

"I'll tell Rice," said the bursting one, "I've got to have the coat you left there."

Though patched up presently, he was told by his doctor, "Your clothing is not sufficiently heavy. Have a warm greatcoat made. Get some thick shoes." Keats ruefully looked at his neat footgear. He had paid over three pounds for those boots—he liked his feet to be trim.

"I feel warm," he protested.

"Yes," agreed the doctor, knowing the deceptive symptoms, "and your throat suffers with every change of the weather. Be advised."

But even after he bought the coat and shoes he coughed and his throat was one constant ache. What could he do to be well! Might death not be best? Would not eternal negation put an end to all his poor mundane perplexities? How long ago it seemed since he had written, "I have been half in love

264

with easeful Death?" Was this the way the latter end of man's life approached? His eyes rounded at the idea.

He was not enthusiastic over the delivery of all his poems to Taylor, but enjoyed a transient gleam of humor after telling Abbey of the spring publication.

"Why don't you try tea-brokerage, John?" Abbey asked inconsequentially.

Perhaps he will offer me a commission for his House, thought John cannily. "It would be little trouble, God knows, and would give me a handsome profit." He hoped none of this thought was in his voice when he said, "I should have no objection to the broker's trade." Perhaps he might soon make over the business to George. Whereat his eyes must have brightened. For the moment he showed so much willingness, Abbey made out a case of what must be done in such work, rather retreating from his proposal. He's coy, thought John, and said to the merchant, "but I fear it might not suit my abilities."

Abbey looked relieved, he thought, rather than further concerned about his ex-ward, or a tea-brokerage for John Keats. "Apothecary, surgeon, hatter, bookseller, broker— Oh, Lord! Rich man, poor man, beggarman, thief—" and he felt himself grinning all of a hundred yards out of Abbey's office. A passing acquaintance might have thought him the happiest of men.

"Why not come to hear the boys speechify on breaking-up day?" wrote Charles Cowden Clarke from Enfield.

" 'Twould bring back old times," he considered, as well as interrupt his and Brown's dogtrot of breakfast, dinner—not tea, for they had left off that meal—supper, sleep, confab, stirring the fire, and reading.

"I'll lay you a pocket-piece"—he wrote his sister he would go for the speaking— "we shall have 'My name is Norval.' "

When he read "The Eve of St. Agnes" to Clarke, he stopped at the line, in Stanza XXIX:

"The hall door shuts again, and all the noise is gone."

Clarke raised inquiring eyes. Back through the years he heard young Edward Holmes scuffling away from the door, when he, Clarke, stopped playing the piano. Dawn appeared in his eyes, and Keats said, "I remembered how I used to listen in bed to your music at school."

"Poor Keats," he could not help thinking, "in these days of Bible-Crown-and-Constitution, you might better have been a robber."

Soon came a letter in George's best script for him to deliver to Mrs. Wylie. If the letter contained bad news, never could it have been addressed in so unnervous and healthy a fashion. "Our sister is also well, or George would have made strange work with K's and W's. The little baby is well, or he would have formed precious vowels and consonants."

This excellent logic did not, however, prepare him for the news of the letter: George was coming to England.

Now, truly was he happy and buoyant. George would settle his affairs, and they would see something of each other.

George followed close on the heels of his letter.

XV. End of Junkets: Last Year for Keats

GEORGE was stouter, more mature; hardier, Keats thought. Was his hair receding?

"What of Georgiana, and little Georgiana Emily?" Once again he was looking up at his big younger brother.

"She dislikes America, John." John did not marvel at that dislike. Hers had been hard experience in a new land. "As for our daughter," paterfamilias spoke, "there is no child like her—original—pretty—"

"Would needs be, having that mother"; whereat George bowed, meeting the implication, and recounted her abilities in a number of small incidents.

They were all at Mrs. Wylie's, and that lady consumed his words or, if he was silent, yet watched him as though beholding a traveler from another planet, wiping her eyes when George mentioned or implied something to him no longer a hardship but "exceedingly primitive" from her metropolitan experience.

Keats felt himself a man of family, as he had felt eighteen months ago, and not sorry George was getting affairs straightened out. He might have suspected his own incapability had brought this brother back were it not that not one of his three latest letters had got to Louisville before George left for England. The first of those letters had been mailed in May, 1819, eight months back. No wonder—

While a stream of narrative rushed from the "settler's" mouth, Keats was thinking he could please Georgiana by writing a long letter to be sent by her husband, who could remain only a fortnight or so.

"Why not longer?" Two weeks only. . . .

"My dear John, think of the long time required to come and return. Two months will be a short time."

Of course. And there was Georgiana, alone without him— all that made the country endurable. When he began the letter he said the most comforting thing he could invent out of his sympathy: "You have a heart that will take hold of your children. Even George's absence will make things better —his return will banish what must be your greatest sorrow and at the same time minor ones with it." And he referred to Robinson Crusoe who, in danger of perishing on the waters, looked back to his island as a haven and having regained it was content with solitude. As for Georgiana Emily, "I have a lively faith that yours is the very gem of all children. Ain't I its uncle?"

He told her what her husband was doing that very day, Thursday, January 13. After dinner he had gone to Deptford, to see Haslam's betrothed. He himself could not bring himself to meet the "innamorata." Like a magnet with a repelling end, by the time he got to Greenwich he would have repelled her and her family to Blackheath; at Deptford he would have driven them to Shooters Hill—and so, finally, into the sea. He thought that act might be indictable. George would "square" everything for him. "Depending on his brother as always," Georgiana might say, but proudly.

She would wish to hear his opinion of the lady her brother Henry had married. He had described her a year or so back as a lath with a bodice, fit for nothing but to cut up into cribbage pins, all muslin, feathers and bone. Henry had been smitten with a staff, he had punned, and she might be useful as his walking-stick, his fishing-rod. . . . Yes, he had married her. They had sent him a piece of cake but it had got

268

lost on the way. The lady was excessively quiet before people. "I hope she is always so."

The Dilkes, who had been always good friends of her husband, had given a "piano-forte hop" for him on Tuesday the eleventh—two days ago. There was very little amusement in the room but a Scotchman to hate. "Some people, you must have observed, have a most unpleasant effect upon you when you see them speaking in profile—this Scotchman is the most accomplished fellow in this way I ever met with." He had been a dose of bitters that Keats hoped would improve his digestion. At the hop he had sat near the Reynolds girls and tried manfully to talk to them; but he was afraid to speak to them these days fearing to hear "some sickly reiteration of phrase or sentiment."

Georgiana had once accused him of writing only about Haydon and Company. Now he never saw them. He would not complain or explain. George would tell her. One of his first monologues to George had been of the loan to Haydon. He would like for her sake to be a better gossip, "But bless me, I never go anywhere—my pen is no more garrulous than my tongue. Any third person would think I was addressing myself to a lover of scandal. But we know we do not love scandal but fun, and if scandal happens to be fun that is no fault of ours."

George had taken her mother to see a play: he hoped she, Georgiana, would soon see his and Brown's at Covent Garden. Oh, to be a worthy successor to Shakespeare! He looked at his favorite picture and thanked her for the tassels supporting it. "William," he said aloud. Would he care to be called William? No. What of Edmund, he asked, Spenser and Kean in mind. Yes, "Edmund Keats. . . ." "If you should have a boy," he warned, "do not christen him John. . . . 'Tis a bad name and goes against a man." He thought if he had been Edmund he would have been more fortunate.

269

George was busy in Pancras Lane and with Dilke, meanwhile, but two days later he sat opposite Keats—both writing. The letter to Georgiana flowed on while George copied the "Ode to a Nightingale." Within was warmth and peace and brotherly love. The sun shone upon the snow—like what? like candy, prettier than they had had on Twelfth Night cakes.

Next day George went again to Haslam, who would not let him off from a promise to return, though at Wentworth Place Keats had collected some of the "old set" to meet him at dinner. That was Sunday, and on Monday Keats returned to the letter. Again looking at the tasseled engraving, he recalled a brief conversation of that morning with the Irish maid.

"What do you think of my Shakespeare?" he asked, seeing her eyes upon it.

"He is much like my fayther, Mr. Keats, sir. Only this gentleman hasn't so much coloring."

"Forsooth!" Keats mentally placed the two side by side. "An Irishman and Shakespeare!"

Too bad George had not been at home for the three witty R's: Rice, Reynolds, Richards: Rice, the wisest; Reynolds, the playfullest; Richards, the out o' the wayest.

He sat back, analyzing the three R's. "Rice makes you laugh and think," he summarized. "Reynolds makes you laugh and not think, while Richards puzzles you." How did he feel about them? "I admire the first, I enjoy the second, I stare at the third." He believed the first inspired by Minerva, the second by Mercury, the third by Harlequin Epigram, Esq$^{re.}$ "The first is claret, the second ginger beer, the third Creme de Bzrapqmdra." Let her make what she could out of that last word: maybe she would unravel it to mean "Brama" or "Brahma." No matter. She knew it stood for something indecipherable, mysterious.

Looking back at last night's dinner, he saw Rice helping himself to fowl from the dish the maid was passing, slow of speech, making the table laugh by sagely humorous remarks; Reynolds, sloven and loose of garment, lively in speech; Richards, uncomfortable in stiff visiting clothes, slow or rapid as he might be at the moment. While they sat and talked and ate, and Brown played the sedulous host, he himself had been comparing them each to this man or that—in literature or out of it.

When he had become too quiet, Brown "drew" him. "Friends," he began too seriously, "what d'you think of Keats's honesty?" They waited, knowing this a mere bit of rhetoric. "I was reading aloud to George yesterday my story of the old woman and the devil when George interrupted, 'But I've heard that before!'"

Eyebrows went up; glances focused on Keats. "It seems," continued Brown, "he had palmed it off as his own, in a letter to America."

"Ah, Keats!" They looked at him as if saying "Tchuh-tchuh!" But Brown had "tipped them the wink," and they knew he jested.

Keats, about to protest, caught the drift of Brown's remark, and quite seriously said he would ask Georgiana to let him know whether he had given it as his own. "I will show Brown wrong, I think, by her evidence." While their wit sparkled, he tried to think of the dullest three men he knew. He captured the foolishest, the sulkiest, and a negative. "A makes you yawn, B makes you hate, as for C you never see him though he is six feet high. The first is gruel, the second is ditchwater, the third is spilt—he ought to be wiped up."

2

Living in America—Keats was considering George, who faced him on the other side of the fireplace, or got up to tread the room restlessly—had surely if subtly changed him. Was it that with a family to support, indebted to friends who had, he said, "staked" him for awhile, he must repay them and was troubled over finances? Had George ever got anything back from that steamboat loss? Pioneering must be difficult; not yet twenty-three, George bore himself like a man of thirty. His hair *was* thinner. Keats thrust long fingers through his own mop, and reported to himself, "Feels like full plumage." George had begun to talk and was wearing his most business-like expression.

"So if you wish to lend me some of your stock, some of your cash—I am forcing Abbey to settle up, you see—and one hundred seventy pounds coming to you from Tom's estate, why, I'll be able, John, to pull through."

"How much stock and cash, George?" At the reply, he refrained from staring like a fish agape. "That seems like a good deal of money, George. Surely, it will set you on your feet?" He could not take in the sums or rather their meaning. He had not thought there was so much left for himself.

"I think so, with my part," George smiled winningly.

"I wrote you, dear George, and told you in the letters you have not received that I wish to do now and always what is possible. Make the arrangements."

George shook his hand warmly before going out to "arrange." Hand on doorknob, he called back, "Your signatures will be necessary. I'll either bring the papers or else have you go down with me."

"I wonder I can possibly have anything left." Keats was thoughtful. "I owe at least eighty pounds, and that's a fact." Remembering his desire to help the young family in

272

America, recalling all that George had done often to shield him, he told himself: "Though there seems so much more for myself than I believed, still there is not enough for—" and thinking hopelessly of Fanny Brawne, he stared hard at the tasseled Shakespeare. Distrait, vaguely uneasy, "More than ever I must write. But—I know not why—I never felt less like work."

George brought all the documents for the signatures. "You, John," he rested his hand a moment on his brother's shoulder, "have so many friends they will be sure to take care of you."

"But I must take care of myself—" Something did not ring just right. He told Brown he had received only sixty pounds. . . . "That was not fair, Brown, was it?"

Brown pursed his lips. After a little he said the best thing he could think of. "George has a great belief in your powers, Keats."

January 28, George left on the six o'clock coach for Liverpool.

"Absent-minded wretch that I am! I've forgotten Georgiana's letter." Keats was saying good-by. "I'll send the sheets on to your ship. They'll get there in ample time by post to cross with you."

He came home, indescribably saddened at the second loss of his brother and still troubled at something he could not or would not put into words. In a whirl of inspired puns, nonetheless, he finished his budget to Georgiana. Some of this fun-making recalled that he was still sometimes addressed as Junkets. Junkets? Never again would he feel like Junkets!

"Good-by, Junkets." The words died on the air and in his heart.

He should make allowance for George's eager haste to get back to the two Georgianas. George could do more with the

money than he could have done. He himself had proved he
was not a man of business, or he would have obviated this
journey to England. It had cost George a hundred and fifty
pounds at least. . . . Well, George would see that he lost
nothing by letting him have all—except sixty pounds—he
had on earth.

The little joy and zest that had remained to him in living
was gone. Forever? Had there been in his mind a deep-
seated hope against hopelessness, that somehow money
would come to him? that he would go with it to Fanny
Brawne, place it in her hands; "All I have is yours"?

3

February 3, he had been visiting friends in town and rode
on top of the stage back to Wentworth Place. "Bitter cold,"
he wished for his greatcoat, but too often it was merely a
burden.

Numb, stiff, miserable, he stumbled into his room.

Brown sat there, dozing by the fire, which he had made up.
It was now eleven. "Why—Keats—Keats, you are not intox-
icated? No, no, it's not that." He took Keats's hand.
"Fevered!"

"I was chilled—but I don't feel it now. Perhaps a little
hot, for reaction."

"Get into bed at once, Keats." Instantly he knew that was
what he most wished to do. Brown hurried out for remedies
possibly on the shelves.

"These sheets are as if wrung out of ice-water," Keats had
crawled under the covers as Brown came back. He coughed,
knew "a violent rush of blood to the lungs," tasted the
sweetish taste of blood, and saw that a drop or two had fallen
to the sheet. "Bring me the candle, Brown, and let me examine this blood." He took the taper, looked steadily at the

274

spot on the linen and then up at Brown. "I know the color of that blood," he said calmly. "It is arterial blood. It is my death-warrant. I must die."

"Lie quite still, dear fellow." Brown ran for the surgeon.

In a few minutes, Keats heard the old familiar, "We must bleed him."

Both Dr. Bree and Dr. Darling declared his lungs uninjured.

"But," insisted Keats, "I know the color of that blood. I'm a doctor of sorts, ain't I?" He tried to smile. He was glad George had got away before seeing him so ill. His brother had been gone exactly one week.

"You must remain in your room some time," the doctors told him. Friday morning he wrote to Fanny Brawne, "The consciousness that you love me will make a pleasant prison of the house next to yours." She must come often to see him and forgive him if he spoke in the low tone prescribed. Brown had told him the Brawnes were all out. "I have been looking for the stage the whole afternoon," he added. Never a wheel rattled over the pavement that he did not turn his eyes to the casement, awaiting its magic.

When she came, all sweet solicitude, he would not permit her to stay long, though his eyes were on her until she had crossed the threshold.

All London had been betrayed into leaving off heavy clothing. George III had died three or four days before his own collapse. He lay, convalescing, he hoped, reading the public prints full of anecdotes of the late king, who had nodded to a coal-heaver, laughed with a Quaker, liked a boiled leg of mutton. Brown was active but also a trifle "wheezy" in this particular brand of bad weather. From his upstairs window, Keats could see the garden and the dingy grass. "There is nothing to enliven one," he wrote, "but a few cabbage stalks that seem fix'd on the superannuated list."

Then the Wylie boys dropped in and Mrs. Reynolds had called.

"Shouldn't you like to move downstairs?" Brown turned from the dreary late-winter aspect of the garden and the half-built houses opposite to the bed where Keats lay, his face hectic above white garments and white sheets. His letter to Fanny Keats lay beside him on the table, folded for sealing.

"On the sofa?" He felt better already.

Brown had that very idea. "We can make you comfortable. I don't need to tell you the parlor window looking onto the grass plot is better than this." He made a gesture that swept the desolate garden.

"I am getting a little tired of the withered grass, and the bed-curtain patterns," he confessed. "And down there I can see what happens on the heath."

"Also, Miss Brawne would find it more convenient," Brown teased sympathetically. She had been to see Keats every day, leaving him little notes which, he could have told nobody, gave him more joy than everything else.

Down on the sofa, he saw coals being brought in, the pot boy with the one o'clock beer. Out there on the heath he saw old women with bobbins and red cloaks and "unpresuming bonnets" creeping about; saw gypsies in red and yellow, looking for whatever they could find. "There's a chap going by with a wooden clock that strikes a hundred and over, while I see and hear." There were passers-by, always. Two old maiden ladies in Well Walk were anxious about their lap-dog, a "corpulent little beast," which they coaxed along with an ivory-tipped cane.

On the fine eleventh of February, he wrote his sister, he walked for a quarter-hour in the garden. Around Valentine's Day he told her he had so many presents of jams and jellies they would reach the length of the sideboard. She must, he told her, wear warm clothing in a thaw. And when Reynolds got off for a holiday in Brussels, some three weeks later, he was cautioned to "have some flannel against the wind. Should it rain do not stop upon deck though the passengers should vomit themselves inside out."

To Fanny Brawne he wrote briefly, passionately, and regularly, looking forward to health, spring, and the routine of their old walks. He was happy now if she but sent him "Good night" to put under his pillow. Dr. Darling cautioned him against writing poetry, even reading it, forbade his seeing "Miss Brawne" often—and counseled patience.

Now unselfishness, of a truth, must conquer desire. He had wished her not to go often to town, not to dance at many balls. Now he must say, "Let me no longer be the cause of your not going." Yet, without fail, send him her good night. "You know our situation," he wrote sadly; "what hope is there if I should be recovered ever so soon? My very health will not suffer me to make any great exertion." Though hopeless, he did not despair. "I cannot say forget me, but I would mention that there are impossibilities. . . ."

Her little note showed she was hurt. He wrote again, "The utmost stretch my mind has been capable of was to endeavor to forget you for your own sake. . . . I should as soon think of choosing to die as to part from you."

She understood. "Then all we have to do is to be patient. . . . I do not think I could bear any approach of a thought of losing you." Undoubtedly, it was better that he see her seldom, though he could not sleep without her usual good night.

Illogically enough, now there was a chance of his leaving the world, he was filled with a sense of its beauties. "Like poor Falstaff, though I do not babble, I think of green fields." He lay there recollecting all the flowers he had known since infancy, their shapes and colors, all seeming as

277

new as if he had created them from a superhuman fancy. He wanted to see again the simple flowers of an English spring. "If you ever catch me," he wrote Rice—who had also suffered a relapse—"on a stage coach in the winter full against the wind, bring me down with a brace of bullets, and I promise not to 'peach.' "

Brown was in and out of his room, all day, bringing with him his work in sepia and copying works of artists more famed than himself. He had bought Hogarth's "Credulity, Superstition, and Fanaticism," a picture that gave Keats a bad dream. He was nervous, too nervous.

"Miss Brawne stays too long with you, Keats," said Brown, "though she comes so seldom for a long visit."

"Perhaps you are right. That medicine makes me nervous." He added, "I will tell her to come tonight for only a few minutes near six." That written good night, however, he must have. He could not explain to himself or others his insistence there. He only knew if he did not get it, he was alone on a wide, wide sea, with never a saint to take pity on his soul.

Outwardly, he became his usual self. One day while sitting in the back room, reading Ben Jonson—Brown's very best book—he was handed a jar of black currant jelly. Between him and Brown they managed to smear the book and the letter he was writing to Fanny Brawne. "I have licked it," he told her, "but it remains very purplue." Interesting word! "I did not know whether to say purple or blue, so in the mixture of the thought wrote 'purplue,' which may be an excellent name for a color made up of those two."

He was greatly improved, he knew, when his old ache for Fanny was stronger than his feeling of illness. In a letter of late February, he told her, "When I send this round I shall be in the front parlor, watching to see you show yourself for a minute in the garden." Many nights he lay awake, thinking sad thoughts; but he comforted himself, he wrote, by saying,

"If I should die, I have left no immortal work behind me—nothing to make my friends proud of my memory—but I have loved the principle of beauty in all things, and if I had had time I would have made myself remembered."

The "weight and tightness" about his chest was still troublesome, preventing his complete belief that, as the doctors said, he was better. "God alone knows," he wrote Fanny, "whether I am destined to taste of happiness with you: at all events . . . I consider it no mean happiness to have loved you thus far—if it is to be no further, I shall not be unthankful—if I am to recover, the day of my recovery shall see me by your side from which nothing shall separate me. If well, you are the only medicine that can keep me so."

His friends came to cheer, new ones with the old: among them Bryan Waller Procter, who looked forward impatiently to Keats's next volume. "Will you write my name in an early copy and send it to me?" he asked, in a letter intended to be sent with his own *Marcian Colonna*. It was Mrs. Procter, Keats recalled, whom Haydon had chosen for the chief woman-figure in the mammoth painting.

Lying there with his books, he hoped he might soon be well enough to get on with his "faeries," "The Cap and Bells." Brown came in to remark silently his feverish countenance, and to say, "Let me put up your pen and paper." Keats drank the medicine, but insisted, "I'll have finished in a moment." Brown went out.

"Thank God," he concluded, "I am born in England with our great men before our eyes. Thank God that you are fair and can love me without being letter-written and sentimentalized into it." Oh, this northeast wind! He tried to sleep, to be patient.

Now another torture superseded some conquered agonies. Was Brown flirting with Fanny? Certainly, he had looked upon her warmly. Could his dear love and his best friend be encouraging one another? "I dare not think of you much or write much to you," he had said to Fanny—and she had looked distressed. He suspected he was difficult!

"But why can't she have another man in the room without showing she is aware of him?" And what must he make of Brown's behavior! He wrote to clear purpose: "My dear Fanny, I think you had better not make any long stay with me when Mr. Brown is at home. Whenever he goes out, you may bring your work." Would she think him petty? He was beyond caring if she did. He simply could not bear that the three of them should be in the room at once and he, prone, unable to feel other than hurt and pain at the conduct of each—as he saw it. He would rather watch Fanny pass the window, see her walking over the heath, than to have her in the room except alone with himself. Would she come toward evening, not before dinner? If before, he had nothing to look forward to after she left. He must see her now, this instant. "Come round to my window," he begged, "for a moment, when you have read this."

To surprise him, Fanny soon brought a ring with her name and his entwined. It made him happy as a little boy, and he kissed the hand that honored his ring—the "engagement ring" gemmed with a purplish-red garnet—she had promised to wear forever. Though a prisoner, he would expect health as his Heaven with her for his houri. He wondered about that word. Singular or plural? Anyway, "if only plural, never mind—you are a thousand of them."

At the end of February he was still in bed.

XVI. *Return to Semi-Health. Relapse*

"WHY don't we hear from George?" Mrs. Wylie was visiting Keats, who sat up against his pillows. "We are well into March and not a word."

"We must wait at least a month after he has landed," he reminded her.

She sighed. "I wish they were in England."

"If Georgiana lived at York, it would be just as far off."

The lady shook her head in denial.

"If George succeeds," Keats reasoned, "it will be better that they stop in America. If not, why not return? But I have good hopes of George. By this time he should be taught alertness and carefulness."

"Come in for a half-minute," he wrote Fanny Brawne. She emphasized the time, in replying, "I fear you do not love me so much as I wish."

To this sad plaint, "My dear Girl, I love you ever and without reserve. The more I have known you the more I have loved. . . . Even my jealousies have been agonies of love. In the hottest fit I ever had I would have died for you." She was always new. When he saw her pass the window yesterday on her way in, he was filled with as much admiration as if seeing her the first time. Was she still half-complaining that he loved only her beauty? Now he saw also a winged heart imprisoning itself with him; no ill prospect had turned her thoughts away. Let him continue to repose in her with undistracted enjoyment: "My mind has been the most

281

discontented and restless one that was ever put into a body too small for it."

Permitted to sit by the fire, he stretched himself to the full five feet to test his strength. He was weak; he was not given enough to eat—he was hungry. "Wrong," said the doctor. He made out with the jellies and jams and toast, and the oranges his dear girl had brought were just *à propos*. Now he hoped to take a walk with her on May Day. Meantime, here was his manuscript of "Lamia, Isabella, and The Eve of St. Agnes." Would she read it all before he finally sent it to the publishers?

Fanny missed not a word of the long, closely written pages, and praised with discrimination. Not for worlds would she have confessed that studying the verses in so brief a time was not so easy for her as the writing had been for him over a longer period.

She showed fatigue. "You must look a little brighter this morning," he commanded. He would not have her obscured like glass breathed upon. For himself, he thought feeding upon sham victuals and sitting before the fire would completely annul him! He was melting away like a wax image.

Shakily up and about, he confessed to himself and Fanny the chance of slipping into the ground instead of into her arms was horrid. Death must come at last but he would try more pleasures she could give. With what appeared the restoration to health, returned also "that last infirmity of noble mind." Give him "another opportunity of years" and he would not die without being remembered. He had no more inflammation, took no more medicine to keep his pulse down. But he still felt heart palpitations, increased by worry over Fanny's going into the wintry weather. "You will be as a topsail in a north latitude—I advise you to furl yourself and come in a doors."

"You are certainly better," said Brown.

Return to Semi-Health. Relapse

"With the thrush outside my window, a man's diet again, and the thought of seeing Miss Brawne's flowers in bloom—" He broke off, to dream of Fanny in the new black dress he liked so much, while envying her brother Sam, who would be walking with her. . . . Before many days, he walked around to her door and surprised her with a knock.

So far recovered, he accepted an invitation from Taylor to dinner, for March 14, and was well enough to be there. He was sorry to miss John Clare, the peasant poet, whose "Solitude" Taylor read aloud.

"What do you think of it?" The publisher laid down the script.

"The description prevails too much over the sentiment," Keats said thoughtfully.

"That's a good fault," and Taylor spoke editorially; "besides, you know I must have something to cut out."

"Pruning would not harm it—"

He suffered a relapse from that outing and a week later wrote his sister, "The Doctor says I must not make the slightest exertion." But when he read an invitation from Haydon to see "Christ's Entry into Jerusalem"—finished after six years—he exerted himself to look his best at Dr. Darling's visit. "You may go," said the physician, "but do not stay long. There will doubtless be a mob."

There was. Slowly walking up to the entrance of Egyptian Hall, the twenty-fifth of March, he looked with astonishment on carriages lining both sides of the street. "Why, Hazlitt!" he exclaimed. The two eagerly shook hands.

Together they studied the giant canvas, much elaborated since the dinner of 1818, and commented on the portraits recognizable. Keats was just above and back of Wordsworth.

In his excitement Keats began to cough; Haydon came across the room. "We are rejoicing with you," said Hazlitt, but at this moment the Persian ambassador, manly, black-bearded and splendidly arrayed, greeted the artist. "I like the elbow of soldier," said he, searching for a compliment, and Keats hurt his lungs, trying not to cough—or laugh.

While the throngs milled about, commenting on the concept, whispering, "The figure of Christ resembles the artist," and observing the portraits of living men and women thrust back eighteen hundred years, a hush descended. Sarah Siddons was entering "with all the dignity of her majestic presence, like a Ceres or a Juno." While she stood before the painting, the spectators continued silent and allowed her to think.

After a few moments, Sir George Beaumont anxiously asked, "How do you like the Christ?"

Again the room was suspended. After a dramatically timed pause, she said, in a deep, loud, tragic tone, "It is completely successful."

Keats and Hazlitt saw Haydon presented to her, and thereafter soon escaped.

After this second venture out, Keats remained in his room, faint and tight of chest. But old interests and loyalties were waking with the spring. His sister's little pet dog was unwelcome at Walthamstow. "What shall I do with him?" she asked. "Send your spaniel to Hampstead," he replied at once. "I think I know where to find a master or mistress." Those Abbeys! though he assured Fanny that if she turned the dog loose in the common road it would find an owner. Abbey was behaving worse than usual, he suspected, because George's bringing him to terms had broken his petrified complacency. Brown had written Abbey, as if from Keats—who sorely needed funds—twice without reply. He could only surrender a correspondence in which "all the letters are on one side."

April first, Keats dated his note to Fanny and in a few days followed it with the assurance that her dog should be taken care of. He, himself, was still "on the mending hand." When she wrote of further troubles, however, he became nervous and wrote that he could enter into no discussion in which his heart was concerned. Unable to come to Walthamstow, he could only advise her to keep from low spirits, "great enemies to health." Mrs. Dilke's brother had the dog, which was "being attended to like a prince."

April 20 Henry Wylie looked in, bearing a letter from George to his mother-in-law. Keats read with relief that George had landed and he immediately wrote his sister. But George had not written to him. . . .

2

Back into a semblance of the old routine, he was lingering one April morning with Brown over the breakfast cups.

"Should you care to try another walking trip into Scotland?"

"Have you spoken to Darling?" Keats felt an instant's surprise.

"He's for it, thinks your health quite returned."

But Keats was uncertain. "What do *you* think?"

"If I could be sure there would be no severe privations and no bad weather—"

"No counting on lack of either. I'll think it over, nonetheless." He needed short thinking to be convinced he could not attempt the tramp. "It might help me to get rid of the nervousness; it might do for me in throat and chest."

"You won't object—can fend without me—if I set off alone?"

"I should not dream of keeping you," he passed an arm about Brown's husky shoulders. "You've been confined here almost as much as if you yourself had been ill. Seven long weeks you were my constant nurse. Good God, get

285

ready!" He knew that Brown still depended upon the summer rent from his house.

"I've another idea," Brown spoke after some days, in which Keats had seemed to him a lost soul. "Why don't we go to Scotland by the smack—you stood the other voyage well—then you might return by stage or water, while I continue as before—walking back."

That might be well, Keats considered. The doctor said, "Yes; change of air and the exercise will be good for you."

But only a day or so of merely meditating upon the plan made him more nervous. "I can't do it," he said. And that Brown might not think he felt deserted, he continued, he feared too transparently, "Kentish Town is a mile nearer my sister than this place, and there I should be near Hunt."

Believing this move best in the circumstances, Brown engaged a room—paying a week's rent in advance—at 2 Wesleyan Place, which his friend would occupy immediately after they surrendered Wentworth Place quarters.

Probably, thought Keats, he might not come back to Wentworth Place. He returned all borrowed books and cleared out his possessions. When able he would try one of two ventures: life in South America, or—the old idea—life on an Indiaman. On the sixth of May he moved; on the seventh he went with Brown as far as Gravesend.

3

Kentish Town would have been unendurable but for Hunt. Fanny Brawne seemed far away. All day he kept his eyes fixed on Hampstead or on his ring finger, or on the vase of flowers she had sent. Dear Fanny! But, he wrote, "I can not see you yet; it would be so much pain to part with you again." Unable to compose verse, daily he read his volume of Spenser, marking for her the most beautiful passages—to give her a pleasure however small. Absence from her was torture. In fancy, she flitted about his room, in her pretty shepherdess dress. How his senses were ravaged! "Were you to loose a favorite bird from the cage, how would your eyes ache after it as long as it was in sight; when out of sight, you would recover a little." Yet if he could not be convinced of her love, he must die in agony. He was raving, he felt, but could do no other than write, "You must be mine to die upon the rack if I want you." Not much longer could he endure the agonies and uncertainties she was so peculiarly made to create. "For God's sake, save me, or tell me my passion is of too awful a nature for you." Would she, reading, be afraid —of *him?*

Brown he also missed horribly, but Brown—thinking to keep him occupied—had insisted on his sending some stanzas on "The Cap and Bells," and he had not felt like working on even that light poem. Anyway, if he wrote, he would not date his letter from such a place as his present number and street!

To save his sanity, here was editorial work in the proofs of his book, part relief for aching loneliness. At least he must see that no foolish alteration intruded, though either Taylor or Woodhouse might propose something better than he had set down.

By the time he arrived at Stanza VII of "The Eve" he was annoyed. He read it again, frowning at the words:

> *—her maiden eyes incline*
> *Still on the floor, while many a sweeping train*
> *Pass by—*

"My meaning is quite destroyed," he wrote, and repeated his original version:

> *—her maiden eyes divine*
> *Fixed on the floor saw many a sweeping train*
> *Pass by—*

The editors had mistaken *train* for *concourse of passers-by;* he had meant "skirts sweeping along the floor."

He reread the proof. Something in the first stanza was wrong: here the typographer had set:

> *St. Agnes Eve—Ah, bitter cold it was!*
> *The owl, for all his feathers, was a-cold.*

He had written ". . . bitter chill it was!" to avoid the echo, he informed the editors, in the next line.

Writing poetry was a poor business. His spirits were high enough, he would tell Brown, but hopes were low. This volume was his last trial; he was about to see what he could do as apothecary. By reverting to his profession, he could at least make a livelihood. Lonely, he was not alone; everybody was kind; but he was solitary in the crowds for lack of Fanny Brawne. How happy he was to have her mother come to see him!

"Will you meet some of our friends at supper?" he was asked in June.

"Who'll be there?" he wanted to know.

"Wordsworth, Southey, Haydon, Talfourd, and Lamb."

The Lake poets would expect tribute; he did not wish to see Haydon; and Lamb, with sallies of wit, would make him cough. "I can't risk going out at night," and felt no regret.

He did go to an exhibition of old English portraits in Pall Mall. Among pleasant countenances by Kneller, Lely, Holbein, and Van Dyck, he stared at the painting of ill-favored James I, who roused his sense of humor: "His appearance would disgrace a Society for the Suppression of Women." Brown would like that comment, also that George II looked like "an unintellectual Voltaire, troubled with the gout and a bad temper." When he wrote in a day or so, he promised to begin soon upon "Lucy Vaughan Lloyd," the name under which he purposed to publish "The Cap and Bells."

Hunt continued kind, but always at his home were too many writers and artists. "Come over on the twenty-second of June," he invited. "The Gisbornes will be here." Keats would like to meet Maria Gisborne.

Hunt, himself ill, grave and serious, saw Keats enter. Pale, unusually silent, speaking if at all in a low tone, he told Hunt he had had only that morning another hemorrhage. "Under sentence of death," Maria Gisborne wrote a fortnight later, "and emaciated."

He looked at Mrs. Gisborne; she recognized him. Nobody spoke of his being the author of *Endymion,* which she liked, but one glance at his eyes persuaded her he was the man. They talked, of music, of Italian and English singers. . . . Even so slight an exertion, he knew that night, had been too much. All alone, he endured another attack of blood-spitting. "My dear Keats," Hunt was the old familiar friend, "you must come to stay with us, at Mortimer Terrace." He moved over on the twenty-third of June.

For two weeks he lay quiet, content in being with friends —better for a line from George in Louisville where he, with his family, was well. Yet without occupation, he could but dwell upon his love and write impassioned letters showing that he suffered in their not being together.

Though he and Brown had parted as best friends, he now convinced himself that he had seen a flirtation practiced before his very eyes by that friend and his love. Now whom had she been smiling with? How had she passed the time since he had seen her? She did not know what it was to love— He wrote frenziedly: "I appeal to you by the blood of that Christ you believe in: do not write to me if you have done anything this month which it would have pained me to have seen." If she was still behaving in dancing rooms and other societies as he had seen her, he did not want to live. "I cannot live without you, and not only you but *chaste you;*

289

virtuous you." He declared he would never see or speak to Brown until they were both old men.

And yet after sending that letter he longed for Brown's steadying presence. What extremes, what madness, would this illness and this love and this jealousy force him to utter. How shocking to write as he had just written! Why, a common streetwalker should not be so insulted.

Brown was now in Dunvegan Castle, Isle of Skye, thinking of Fanny no more than of any other woman. Fanny was hurt and sore at heart, but she knew her lover was a man who had been sick five full months—and longer.

XVII. Preparation for Italy. The Voyage

AT the end of June came copies of *Lamia, Isabella, The Eve of St. Agnes, and Other Poems*. By John Keats, author of *Endymion*. London: Printed for Taylor and Hessey, Fleet Street, 1820. Keats turned to the end fly-leaf: Printed by Thomas Davison, Whitefriars.

The book was a Dead Sea apple. He felt no enthusiasm over the small volume, and held it a moment, listlessly. But opening it at the Advertisement, dated June 26, he read with ever higher indignation: "If any apology be thought necessary for the unfinished poem of HYPERION, the publishers beg to state that they alone are responsible, as it was printed at their particular request, and contrary to the wish of the author. The poem was to have been of equal length with ENDYMION, but the reception given that work discouraged the author from proceeding."

That final sentence drove him to write in the copy, one for presentation, "This is a lie," with a line preceding the "Advertisement": "This is none of my doing. I was ill at the time." On a copy beautifully bound for Fanny Brawne, he inscribed at the top of the title page: "To F.B. from J.K." He gave away a few other copies, including one to Charles Lamb, and another specially bound for his sister.

The tenor of a letter from George alternately strengthened and depressed. "You must go to Italy, John. Be guided by Brown. I will send money when possible and hope to do so before long." Hunt continued agreeably sympathetic and apparently pleased to give him harborage, while Mrs. Hunt

291

was most kind. While he read propped up on two chairs, for instance, she amused him by cutting a silhouette of his bathrobed figure. In a fortnight or so, he was able to walk twice daily a half hour up and down the terrace among street cries, ballad-singers, and organ-grinders.

Kaleidoscopic images of his lost Fanny persisted. Broodingly he lived over the recent past, seeing her at the window, in his room, on the heath, dashing out to the coach for London. When strong enough to walk from Mortimer Terrace to Wentworth Place he dared not. "I cannot bear to see her. . . . I am not strong enough for that kind of pain." He would write a poem, he told her in August, if his health would bear it. "I would show some one in love as I am, with a person living in such liberty as you do."

Go to Italy and leave her behind? Impossible! "I should like to give up the matter at once—I should like to die." Nerves, temper could stand no more. "I am glad there is such a thing as the grave—I am sure I shall never have any rest until I get there." Death: the only end, even a desired end, to all agony, all uncertainty.

One morning at Hunt's while he looked out of the window, eying the landscape, Hunt saw him change countenance in a manner more alarming than usual.

"I beg you, Keats," his host said gently, "to let me know how you feel, that I may do what I can for you."

Turning an awful look upon his friend, "My feelings, Hunt," he said, "are almost more than I can bear. I fear for my senses."

They paced the room together a few moments. "How would you like us to take a coach and ride about the country together?"

"*Cui bono?*" Keats looked at him.

"To vary the immediate impression—sometimes all that is formidable—which may come to nothing."

292

At that, Keats looked happier and Hunt ordered the carriage.

Though restored by the ride, while they were sitting on the bench against the wall, in Well Walk, he said, explaining the too-ready tears, "My heart is breaking."

Again Hunt was all sympathy. "Can you not tell me—in expression lose some of your pain?"

"I have a doubt," he told Hunt. "It may be groundless. I prefer telling you when I know it is so." Afterward, he told Hunt the doubt was without foundation.

The inexcusably unkind letter he had written in July. Fanny did not reply at once. How could she? Though almost instantly forgiving, she wished to find the right words. When she did write, she said, "You do me wrong in word, thought, and deed." While she and her mother debated what was best to do, he suffered further indignities or fancied indignities. Thursday evening, August 10, he left the living room at Hunt's for his own chamber. A note from Fanny came, and Mrs. Hunt—busy with the baby—asked the servant to deliver it to Keats. Friday, the servant left and before going handed ten-year old Thornton Hunt the note, which had been opened, asking him not to show it to his mother until Saturday.

When Keats heard the story he could not credit that anybody would treat him so inconsiderately. That the communication was not, in itself, important made no difference: it was from *her*. So secretly he had guarded their love—that it might have become known to a meddling servant racked him. For several hours he wept and, worse for the indulgence, packed up despite Hunt's entreaties to remain, thinking he would go back to kind Mrs. Bentley. He left without his individual cup and saucer; nobody remembered it.

First he would see Fanny or her mother or both and explain so far as he could the outrage. He appeared at their door so emaciated, so hectic, Mrs. Brawne took him in as if he were her own son, put him to bed, and sent for Dr. Darling. For days he lay quietly with a book, giving as little trouble as possible, his fevered face and gold-tangled hair vivid against the white pillows. At first he received supinely or indifferently all visitors from outside; to men such as Haydon he showed a contempt of the world and hopelessness for any other. In circumstances than which none, he well knew, could have been happier in his present state, he improved again. To feel so much better was to stir hopelessness into hope for restoration in Italy.

"Generous Shelley!" he read a letter from Pisa, dated July 27, and lingered over the lines, "Mrs. Shelley unites with myself in urging the request that you would take up your residence with us. You might come by sea to Leghorn," and for a few minutes he lived in the prospect of being in Shelley's home. Another brief space reversed that possible felicity; he knew that even at the Shelleys' he would soon weary of the bedposts—he could not remain in one place long enough for that. Was he afraid, he wondered, of literary patronage? He did not think so; that did not matter now. But he had had enough of such patronage to last his life through.

He went on with the letter: "I have lately read your *Endymion* again & ever with a new sense of the treasures of poetry it contains, though treasures poured forth with indistinct profusion. This, people in general will not endure, & that is the cause of the comparatively few copies which have been sold.—I feel persuaded that you are capable of the greatest things, so you but will."

"Well said, Shelley!" But he had a Roland for that Oliver. "I am glad you take any pleasure in my poor poem, which I would willingly take the trouble to unwrite, if possible, did I care so much as I have done about reputation.

294

. . . You, I am sure, will forgive me for sincerely remarking that you might curb your magnanimity, and be more of an artist and load every rift of your subject with ore." The thought of discipline must fall like cold chains upon Shelley, who had perhaps never sat with wings furled for six months together. For himself, his mind like a pack of playing cards was picked up and sorted to a pip. "My imagination is a monastery and I am its monk." He looked forward to the promised copy of *Prometheus Unbound*.

2

"I will go to Italy," he told himself, "as soon as I can arrange to leave England." Not so simple as it seemed. He must meet the expense of the voyage, the cost of a year's residence in Rome. "I wish Brown were here." Who of his friends was the best man to consult? Woodhouse, Taylor, Haslam, Reynolds, Rice?

Haslam was most concerned about a companion. "If he dies out there alone," he insisted to any and all of the friends he saw, "we shall never know what became of him." They must never let him make that voyage without somebody. "You know Keats cannot live alone."

Of the invalid he inquired casually, "Will Brown be back in time to go along?"

"I think not." Keats paused. "I wrote him the other day, telling him I had resolved upon Italy and begging him not to tease himself about me."

"But wouldn't he wish to be with you, if at all possible? At least give him the opportunity."

Toward the end of August, then, Keats wrote again to Brown, "I ought to be off at the end of this week as the cold winds begin to blow toward evening—but I will wait till I have your answer to this."

He could not know that Brown, stopping at every post office on his tramp in the North was disappointed until September 9, at Dunkeld, he received the two letters from Keats and at once "undeviatingly" turned homewards.

Haslam was cudgeling his brains. Keats was happy. Mrs. Brawne had urged, "Do not hurry away. Feel that this is your home, where you must stay as long as you will."

Tardily ashamed of his childish outburst at Hunt's, he apologized as well as he could. "I am really attached to you for your many sympathies with me and patience at my lunes." Meaning to continue "The Cap and Bells," he asked Hunt to send it back by the bearess. He faltered somewhat, but finally wrote, "My best remembrances to Mrs. Hunt." He was pleased that Hunt thought him wise to put up at the Brawnes, "instead of that solitary place . . . if wisdom loves to live with children round her knees, sick wisdom, I think, should love to live with arms about its waist." That was kindly thought! "Thank God, I have had uplifting arms," but he was not saying so to Hunt. "She has been with me more than any other."

No word from Brown in the flying days. No success on Haslam's part until, capturing an idea, his feet turned toward Joseph Severn. Severn was eager for an artist's chance in Rome. September 11, Haslam called upon Severn, who lived in the home of his musician father. "The voyage to Italy is no longer a vague suggestion—"

Severn was delighted.

"We cannot hear from Charles Brown," Haslam went on. "He would gladly go with Keats, we believe, but delay is too hazardous. Even now the ship may face equinoctial gales."

Severn had not yet got the drift of Haslam's talk.

"Invalid as he is, he must go alone," he waited for Severn

296

to get the full import, "unless you will venture with him for friendship's sake."

After his surprise, Severn hesitated. He thought of his poverty.

"If he goes alone, he will drop out of sight in a strange land. Nobody would ever know what became of him."

"I'll go," said Severn.

Haslam spoke of the need for haste. "Keats is occupied with final arrangements. When can you be ready?"

"In three or four days, and I will begin to prepare this very minute." He would go first, last, always for John Keats —whom he had loved, admired, since first they met; but he had leaped also to the possibility Haslam had foreseen —the study of art in Rome.

Haslam hurried back to Wentworth Place.

Severn called upon Sir Thomas Lawrence, who wrote a letter of introduction to Canova. He was ready by the sixteenth.

Keats had been busy over ways and means. Accustomed to rely in other years on George and latterly upon Brown, he was nonetheless sure of one thing in his exhausted physical being: He had some knowledge of business so far as his world understood the word.

He asked Taylor to ascertain the expenses of the voyage and a year in Rome, and proposed the sale of certain copyrights of his books. The publishers accepted his suggestions. He awaited results.

As early as August 14 he enclosed to Taylor a testamentary paper he thought might be serviceable. In this "Will" he desired that Brown and Taylor be the first paid creditors. With matter-of-factness he stated what he believed true: "All my estate real and personal consists in the hopes of the sale of books publish'd or unpublish'd." After holding his pen poised a moment over the scrap of paper, he wrote a final line: "My chest of books divide among my friends."

One self was saying, "I shall never return." In another self, still lived his peculiarly hopeless hope.

In that mid-August letter he confided, "Somehow a copy of Chapman's *Homer* lent to me by Haydon, has disappeared from my lodgings . . . and Haydon urges the return of it." Would Mistessey get a copy and send it along to Lisson Grove? Taylor himself was commissioned to take a peep at the berth if the ship was yet in the river.

"Damn all thieves!" he ended the note. "Tell Woodhouse I have not lost his *Blackwood*."

His new book, selling slowly, gave no cause for rapture over a better income but it had been highly rated and that was comforting. In his endeavor to make up a purse "as long as possible," he tried Abbey again. That tea-and-coffee gentleman agreed to nothing except maintenance for the day. He was grumpier than ever. For one thing, John had lent his money to George much against Abbey's will; and to add to that cause for grudge, George had somehow got through the settlement of moneys due him fifty pounds over and above what Abbey knew about! Whereat John frowned in some perplexity. This letter did not chime with Abbey's accustomed speeches about himself and George. Had George "got the best" of Abbey? But why bother to think of him.

September 11 Taylor wrote they were paying £100 for the copyright of *Endymion*, reminding Keats they had paid £200 for the three volumes. They were now £135 out of pocket on *Endymion*. "You shall have £50 more to take you to Italy, and from thence you must draw for what you want, but I think you will not wish us to pay these bills without placing some money in our hands for that purpose."

Fifty pounds would be enough. . . .

Fanny Brawne came in. What could she do? "If you would let me dictate to you a letter for my sister—" She hurried to get paper and her own pen. He was not too ill to write, he explained, but had been advised to avoid every sort of fatigue. He would not be able to see her before leaving for Naples and Rome. "I have received your parcel and intend to take it with me."

Fanny, writing, wondered what present she might offer. He had the ring with their names. She had given him a carnelian or sard, her birthstone, a little white oval ball, as a luckpiece, or to play with when nervous. He needed a knife. She would buy him one of silver. When his traveling cap came and she saw the inside was unbeautiful, she lined it with silk.

Woodhouse, aware of the arrangement with Taylor and Hessey, wrote offering assistance some six months hence. "What is the value of pelf after the supply of one's wants? Of none to me," and nobody would be more welcome to his little superfluities—he had none just now—than Keats.

3

Brown was speeding home from Dundee. Three days after Keats left Hampstead and Fanny, to stay from the night of September 13 through the night of the sixteenth at Taylor's home in Bond Street, where all the transactions were completed—beautifully engrossed contracts, which pleased everybody—the smack with Brown aboard turned into the mouth of the Thames. Keats could not know.

Nor, fortunately for his peace, was he aware that Severn's father had worked up a passion over Joseph's persistence in going to Italy. When the young man needed help in moving a trunk, the musician declared that if without his touching it the trunk was never to be lifted at all, it would never be touched by him. Worse, when Joseph started upstairs to say good-by to his brother Tom, his father struck him down.

Tom rushed to hold the older man against the door but had to have assistance against his rage. "I'll go with you," and Tom drew on his blue coat—Joseph would remember that coat a long time—while they got away. It was the early morning of Sunday, the seventeenth of September, when they left, "in the glow that slowly became the chill morning twilight." The *Maria Crowther*, brig of 130 tonnage, was to sail at seven o'clock.

Keats journeyed to the docks with Haslam, Woodhouse, and Taylor—who presented him with a New Testament in Greek and Latin—and William Smith Williams, twenty-year-old apprentice of the publishers. Of the two voyagers, Severn looked more wan and drawn: his had been a harrowing experience for a young man leaving home. After a little, Taylor and Williams said good-by, with much outward good cheer. Haslam and Woodhouse would go as far as Gravesend.

They looked about the cabin. Six beds. A Mrs. Pidgeon who had come aboard in London was disposing her possessions needed on the voyage. All would sleep in that one room, a curtained partition shutting off the ladies.

"May I, Keats, take a lock of your hair?" They were moving slowly down the river. John bowed his head to the shears Woodhouse had brought along.

When Severn saw Keats studying a passport he was dismayed. He had come without one. "Never worry," said Haslam. "I'll see that you have it before the ship sails from Gravesend." And when they tied up for the night he hurried back to town.

At last, all slept, and near enough for hailing was the smack from Dundee, Brown hoping he would see Keats next day.

At the request, "Will you go ashore and get some apples, biscuits and medicine for me?" Severn took a number of prescriptions—some, he saw, made up in Keats's hand—to

300

be filled at a chemist's. "A bottle of laudanum," Keats casually concluded the list, and Severn wondered whether his friend took opiates for sleeping.

When he returned he was considerably relieved at the arrival of his passport on the six o'clock post. "Most unfortunate," he thought on meeting Miss Cotterell, a consumptive come aboard, also bound for Naples to see her brother Charles, a banker. But soon he was helping Keats make the girl "laugh and be herself."

The two invalids were already comparing notes. While they talked, up strolled Mrs. Pidgeon and, looking from Keats to Severn, asked, "Which is the dying man?" Besides his unhappy leave-taking, Severn had a liver complaint that added to his haggard paleness. On the whole, he thought, the stupid remark could not harm Keats if there was a doubt over the indentity of the one about to die. Later, he pronounced the woman a most consummate brute, "who would see Miss Cotterell stiffened like a corpse without lending aid"; he put her to bed a dozen times, while Keats from his berth issued orders for her treatment, "like Esculapius of old in basso-relievo."

4

Wednesday, September 20, the first equinoctial storm lashed the Channel. Water poured from the skylight of the rolling vessel into the cabin, where all had taken refuge in bed. Severn tried to get to Keats's berth but fell to the floor, though later managing to crawl to a hatchway where he watched mountainous waves sweeping across the deck. Later, still, water rushed into the cabin by the bucketful; and once more Severn gingerly got out of his berth.

"Pretty sea-music, Keats?" he was afraid the sick man might be suffering without chance of assistance.

"Yes," in a cheerful voice. " 'Water parted from the sea.' "

"If he can quote the first words of the popular Vauxhall song—" and Severn rested.

At breakfast, the coffee pot shot into Mrs. Pidgeon's lap, a ham into Severn's and, although the cabin boy was detailed to hold the table fast, he was thrown and lay upon it. Keats, a good sailor, remained placid and undisturbed.

They had been blown off their course, here at the outset, as far as Dungeness, where they lay in a dead calm for several days in the Dundee Ness Roads. Severn went ashore with the captain, crossing a wide expanse of shingle over which still dashed waves ten feet high.

In the Solent they were delayed by strong winds and, September 28, put in at Portsmouth. "Can you say how long we shall be here?" Keats asked Captain Walsh. "No getting away for twenty-four hours at best," and Keats landed. He took a coach to Bedhampton, only seven miles distant, to visit the Snook family. What a long time it seemed since he and Brown had walked across the fields from Chichester—only last year!

"Is Brown about?" he wished to know as soon as he and Severn had greeted the family.

"Over at Chichester," Mrs. Snook regretted.

Two days later, the thirtieth, Keats wrote Brown how they had been at sea a fortnight without making headway and were now lying up at the Isle of Wight, off Yarmouth. He was "very provoked" that Brown had been at Chichester. Not wishing to write on subjects that would agitate him, he must mention one. "The very thing I want to live most for will be a great occasion of my death." He would have Charles be a friend to Miss Brawne, the thought of leaving whom was beyond everything horrible. "Is there another life? Shall I awake and find all this a dream?" "There must be," he answered himself. "We cannot be created for this sort of suffer-

302

ing." He wished every day and night for death, to deliver him from the pain of loving, and then he wished death away for it would destroy those pains, which were better than nothing.

Once more, finally, he landed at Lulworth Cove, Dorset. "I know this place well, Severn. You must see the grotto," and while they walked toward the cavern on the shore, he told with a sort of ownership of the time he had first seen the spot.

After they returned to the *Maria Crowther*, he wrote on the blank leaf of the folio Shakespeare, which Fanny Brawne had given him, a copy of his sonnet, "Bright Star." As he copied, even then making subtle, small changes for the better, he thought, "If I die, I shall leave this book to Severn in memory of our voyage."

"I like this best of all your poems," said Joseph on reading the sonnet. Not knowing the verses were composed some time before, he was thinking, "His writing it inspires me with the hope he will recover." He did not dream that Keats had already given himself up for lost.

After a little, they left Land's End astern, hoping for fair or milder weather. But in the Bay of Biscay another night storm threatened to engulf them in water rushing up and down the cabin and roaring Deucalion-like in the darkness.

When favorable weather set in, Severn sketched Keats reading in his berth. Later the two read aloud *Don Juan* to each other until they came to the "mocking cynicism" of the shipwreck canto. Keats was "so wrought upon that at last he flung the volume aside in contemptuous anger."

Off Cape St. Vincent ensued a calm. If Severn had loved the ocean in storm, though it made him ill, Keats—the good sailor—preferred it serene. "Smooth as oil," said Severn. He looked at the "undulating motion, with the bright sun-shine upon it."

Suddenly they were too near for comfort to a Portuguese man-of-war, the large four-decker *San Josef*. Captain Walsh paid no attention to their signals until receiving a shot across the *Maria Crowther's* bows, whereupon the two vessels drifted toward each other and soon were speaking each other through trumpets. "Have you seen any ships that look like privateers?" the Portuguese captain wished to know. Captain Walsh had not, and while the conversation went on, Keats and Severn kept their eyes on the savage, dirty sailors "who showed themselves at every point."

"See those chaps high in the rigging?" Keats pointed them out, swaying with the masts.

They sailed on slowly, the captain mistrusting the Portuguese and fearing for the *Maria's* safety. Before night, they met an English sloop-of-war, "Clean and brilliant after that dirty *San Josef,*" Severn remarked.

"Hear," said Keats, "another speaking-trumpet talk is on." Informed of the Portuguese vessel, the sloop "promptly turned about in pursuit in gallant style."

Passing Gibraltar before dawn, they could but just see through the cabin ports the enormous outline. A trifle later, the big headland "glowing like a topaz," fell astern, and the Barbary Coast lighted up by the sun stretched away, "blue as a sapphire, into the pearly sea." Or so Severn's eye saw it. Keats lay entranced, "a look of serene abstraction upon his worn face." Glad of the easy motion and "genial warmth," Severn sat near and made a sketch in watercolors.

Four weeks and three days after sailing from London, October 21, the *Maria Crowther* entered the Bay of Naples.

"A paradise!" Severn exclaimed over the green islands and the white houses of Naples, rising tier upon tier above the blue bay. Keats delighted in the olive trees and vineyards about the houses, and then "Vesuvius!" The volcano, slowly approaching, had built up "an immense line of smoke-clouds, which every now and then opened and changed with the sun's golden light. . . ." To the right, the mountains of Sorrento and the Isle of Capri were all blue and gold under a purple haze.

"Beautiful," murmured Keats. *"Bella Napoli,"* chanted the sailors, who had been there before.

5

They anchored near the Castel di Nuovo and now the government officials came aboard with an order. "No passengers to debark for ten days." An epidemic of typhus in London had inspired the Neapolitans to this precaution. After the initial disappointment, "This is far less evil than it might have been," thought Severn. But Keats suffered at night in the stifling cabin.

By day, fortunately, the views were unrestricted: they saw far off the long range of the Apennines; and, near at hand, the white-sailed numerous craft in the bay.

"What a relief he is so taken out of himself!" Severn's watchful eye traced Keats's endless interest in activities aboard the small vessels. "He has been so often distraught— so sad an abstracted gaze—"

Keats divined he had perplexed Severn but as yet was unable to confide the reason for his peculiarly unhappy state. His grief was still too great for words . . . and when on the twenty-fourth of October he wrote Mrs. Brawne, he closed the letter, "Good bye, Fanny. God bless you." He could say no more. But he told those on the ship all the classic stories he could remember of this enchanted land, "and he made it all live again, that old antique world when the Greek galleys and Tyrrhenian sloops brought northward strange tales of what was happening in Hellas and the mysterious East."

Entranced by the environment, he was outwardly gay—punning, he said, more than he had done in a year.

The Italian small boats were colorful with vintage clusters and other fruits, merry with happy laughter and tinkle of guitars sounding from near or far—all deepening for Severn the illusion the *Maria Crowther* had touched the shore of Paradise.

Unexpectedly, they had an addition to their numbers. From the English fleet, lying in harbor, the Admiral sent an officer with a boat's crew to ask the *Maria,* "who and what are you?" Instead of remaining outside to make inquiry, the deputed Lieutenant came aboard with six of his men, unwittingly transgressing the law of quarantine. Annoyingly without accommodation, they spread out on deck and in chance niches for the full ten days.

Apparently much better, Keats matched Lieutenant Sullivan's stories and jests. Miss Cotterell's brother Charles afforded welcome diversion with great baskets of fruit for her and her fellow-passengers. Cotterell was most grateful to Keats for looking after his sister and to Severn for his humbler labors. Keats admired and ate the grapes, thinking, "I'd like to throw Toots a bunch!"

Such flowers he had never seen, though declaring to Severn, "I'd give them all for one wayside dog-rose covered with pink blooms," and he looked westward.

Cotterell's devotion to his sister and gratitude to Keats brought him aboard to share their enforced stay on the *Maria.* He could keep the company supplied with fruit, fish, fowl, and do so by talking in the lazzaroni-patois nobody on the ship could manage. The little boats were jocular over the blunder that had captured a Lieutenant and six men, saying things which—on Cotterell's translation—drew "roars of laughter."

"Not one whit behind the Lieutenant and Mr. Cotterell," Keats joined in the fun.

Yet even then he was writing to Mrs. Brawne and telling Fanny good-by. The only comfort he had had, he told Mrs. Brawne, was thinking for hours together, "of having the knife she gave me put in a silver case—the hair in a locket—and the pocket book in a gold net. Show her this." To Brown a week later, he was writing: "The silk lining . . . in my traveling cap scalds my head. I see her, I hear her. There is nothing in the world of sufficient interest to divert me from her a moment."

He did not wish Mrs. Brawne to think him so ill as his letter might suggest, "for if ever there was a person born without the faculty of hoping, I am he." He remembered the children: Sam would be interested to know the fishermen here caught with a line a little fish much like an anchovy.

Severn was regretful when quarantine ended. They had been warned by Cotterell that on landing they would see the beauty disappear in the dirt and filth of Naples. And Severn declared the ten days had covered a scene of splendor and gayety such as he had never imagined—never expected to realize again—and of that gayety Keats's wit and brilliance would be forever a part.

The last day of October they were permitted to land. Meaning to be their guide and friend so long as they remained in the city, Cotterell conducted them to the Villa da Londra. Keats was depressed. Next morning his misery was so great, Severn—who wrote Haslam he had stood it firmly till that morning—gave way to "a plentiful shower of tears," unseen by Keats and somewhat assuaging to Severn. At length, Keats confided all the reasons for his misery and utter wretchedness without hope. "He told me much—very much," wrote Severn.

Later on, that first day of November, 1820, Keats wrote

307

a letter overbrimming with despair. "My dear Brown," he said, "the persuasion that I shall see her no more will kill me . . . I should have had her when I was in health, and I should have remained well. I can bear to die—I cannot bear to leave her . . . My dear Brown, for my sake, be her advocate forever."

XVIII. Rome, Death, and Immortality.

WARNED of disappointment in Naples at closer acquaintance, they were nonetheless amazingly offended by dirt,
smells, and clamor, finding compensation as they drove afield
in the autumn atmosphere and gayety of the vintage season.
The city seemed one big kitchen, with cooking in progress at
almost every house, either out of doors or on the thresholds.
Near the Capuan gate, returning from a drive with Charles
Cotterell, they watched a group of laborers devour macaroni,
using their hands to convey the long strings into their big
mouths. "I like this," and a look of interest crossed Keats's
wan face; "these hearty fellows scorn knives and forks. Fingers were invented first. . . . Glorious sight! How they
take it in!"

At night he was kept awake by beggars, however musically
they sang or strummed guitars, and the red-capped fishermen
still hawking at the tops of their voices the odoriferous catch
of the day. Besides, the populace was in fiesta mood, intoxicated with what they believed to be liberty: a constitutional
government had just been declared. On the very afternoon
they landed, Keats and Severn saw a review of troops.

"What a fine martial appearance!" exclaimed Severn.

"No backbone in them," returned Keats. A day or two
later he might have said, "I told you so," when King Ferdinand escaped to Vienna, having got absolution from the Pope
even while conspiring with Austria.

After the first day, which tired Keats out, he roused himself to costumes, customs, scenery when Cotterell drove them

309

to the Museums, or up Posolipo way or toward Pompeii and Vesuvius.

"Let's see what they have in opera," he proposed. "We should visit San Carlo." There Severn condemned both acting and singing but praised the scene painting: the portrayal of two sentinels, one at each side of the stage, was unusually clever. To the surprise and indignation of Keats, the sentries moved off at the end of the act. "And this outrage is permitted to pass without challenge!" exclaimed Severn. This instance of tyrannical despotism was more than either could stand. In controlled frenzy Keats got up, "Severn, we leave at once for Rome."

"I know that I shall not last long," he explained, after they were outside, "and it would make me die in anguish if I thought I was to be buried amid a people with such miserable political debasement."

Already he had informed Dr. Clark of landing at Naples, and now wrote that he and his friend were setting out at once. Would the doctor find rooms for them? He had no sooner posted the letter than one came from Shelley. "The second he has sent," Keats remarked gratefully, on reading a renewed invitation to Pisa. But he would not consider it. "Our plans are made," he told Severn, "and I must refuse." Even had he wished to change his mind, he knew the artist's eagerness for Rome.

On the sixth of November they had their passports viséd by the British Legation; next day, by the Consul General for admission to the Papal States. Severn arranged for a sort of light carriage (*vettura*) and driver, making it clear they must progress slowly and yet arrive in Rome before the nineteenth. While he saw to details of traveling, Keats read *Clarissa Harlowe*.

"You will surely give me the pleasure of a farewell dinner

in my home," urged Cotterell when he saw they were about to set out.

"He's been such a good fellow, Severn, we must accept," Keats made a special effort—though he felt not at all like doing so—and Severn thought him "very entertaining" that last evening.

Before sleeping, Keats remarked, "I think I'll finish *Clarissa*," and got through the ninth volume before they left for Rome.

2

Roads were bad. Accommodation at inns along the 139-mile route was, in this second week of November, "villainously coarse and unpalatable." Against these discomforts, the weather was delightful, and Severn—able to walk much while the horses plodded on slowly—gathered many wild flowers to place beside Keats. The scenery was exhilarating, the air sparkling. The walker was strengthened but the rider became more apathetic, remembering how he had preceded Brown in their scrambles only two years ago, except when the view was unusually fine or the breeze brought fragrance or his slow-crawling vehicle was heaped with autumnal reds and yellows. Of these things, Severn saw that he never tired; they gave him a singular and almost fantastic pleasure akin to a strange joy.

The journey was without incident—except for a final visé at Terracina—until they reached the Roman Campagna. "These billowy wastes are like an inland ocean," said Keats, "only more monotonous than the one we have lately left." And his thoughts turned to the play of breezes over English fields. Caen Wood, Well Walk— No, no! That way lay despair. He forced himself back to the present to hear, "What under the sun is that?"

Severn had caught sight of a crimson cloak toward which they were moving and, as they drew nearer, they recognized the wearer as a Cardinal and saw he was shooting birds. He had an owl loosely tied to a stick, from which depended a mirror. Sunlight striking the glass attracted the quarry. Keats and Severn watched while they approached and passed the party—for two liveried footmen were kept loading guns for the Cardinal, who killed an astonishing number of birds. "The whole merit of the sport," remarked Severn, "seems to be in not shooting the owl."

A few moments later they were in sight of Rome, exclaiming over the uniqueness of the city, which they entered through the Lateran Gate. Almost immediately they passed the Colosseum which, for its rugged, broken circle and noble proportions, struck admiration in both. They lost no time in observation; Keats was eager to see his new physician, and they headed for his address in the Piazza di Spagna.

The thirty-two-year-old doctor welcomed them genially. "I have your letters," he told Keats, "and have been expecting you." He asked about their journey and presented them to Mrs. Clark.

"Have you found a home for us?" Keats was worn from the tedious trip and the excitement of entering Rome.

Dr. Clark drew them to a window. "Over there," he indicated. "The first floor of the house on the right-hand side of the steps leading up from the Piazza to the Church of Santa Trinita dei Monti at the top." They followed his gestures. "It is, you see, just opposite my own house."

Keats felt a rush of gratitude. Dr. Clark had planned to be near him at all times; his room was the one overlooking the steps. . . .

Severn's heart was beating high for Keats: surely, he would be restored in so famed a place. For himself, only to

312

be with this friend was in itself an event. In Rome how much an event!

Dr. Clark, after questioning the invalid while he and Mrs. Clark chatted, now turned to him, "And what will you do, Severn?"

He heard about the letter to Canova and remarked that he could add something to that chance. "I will speak of you to John Gibson, the sculptor."

Fully aware of his great need for Severn, Keats had determined to be as unselfish as possible. "You must go," he urged, "straight to Gibson's studio." Severn soon went, to return praising Gibson, who had shown him the same consideration as that bestowed on another visitor, an eminent connoisseur. "If Gibson can afford to do such a thing as this," he said, "then Rome is the place for me."

Delighted, Keats discussed plans. "You must begin a picture at once," he said, "or at least make a sketch." He knew Severn hoped the Royal Academy, which had granted him the Gold Medal, might award to him also the three-year pension of traveling student. This prize carried with it payment of expenses to and from Rome and the annual sum of £130.

Despite his hopes, Severn knew the Council would hear of his having got to Rome on his own account and so think he was above needing a pension. This fact he thought might be counterbalanced by the Gold Medal award and their desire to subsidize him further. Keats believed his chances were slim, and reported what he had heard at the dinner with Hilton's brother-in-law.

"So I'm an old fellow and the Council gave me the Medal because I'd tried so many times. Out of pity!" But the artist felt now so remote from jealous rivals he was not distressed.

"I hadn't told you before," Keats explained, "for the fear it might disturb you. But now it is best that you lose no time

313

in contending with your artistic enemies before they try to harm you further." He ended in agitation, for he was placing himself in Severn's position. As he rose, eyes shining, Severn saw "How he towers in stature! What a contrast between this indignation and his charming manner in tranquillity."

"Always ready to speak of my small worries, yet never saying much of his own," Severn was appreciating Keats as never before, and he had never lacked appreciation for both the man and the genius. "Yet he cannot refrain from signifying his engulfing trouble in a hundred ways, though he shrinks from speaking about it directly."

"I will paint, then," Severn agreed at Keats's urgency, "in what leisure I can find." Knowing the invalid's sensitiveness, he would not declare, "My first consideration is yourself." Very soon he began a sketch of his "Death of Alcibiades," though his anxiety over Keats, he felt, would render impossible his painting anything worthy enough to compete for the pension. He rejoiced to see the invalid so greatly consoled by his trying.

They sat together one day in the apartment. "Could we not have a pianoforte?" Keats asked. "You understand it, Severn, and you know I'm fond of music. It would soothe my nerves."

Severn rented a piano from Anna Angeletti, and Dr. Clark helped him to get many volumes and pieces of sheet music, all of which Severn saw were a "welcome solace." Haydn's Symphonies pleased Keats most. "This Haydn is like a child," he exclaimed after hearing a number of pieces; "there is no knowing what he will do next."

At first they had difficulty in getting good food, having it sent from a restaurant and paying a large price. Every day it got worse but they stood it for a week, when Keats said he had a simple idea for insuring improvement.

When the porter entered and began unpacking dishes from

314

the basket and setting them upon the table, Keats sat up alertly and smiled at his friend. "Now, Severn, you will see it!" whereupon he opened the window over the front steps and taking each dish quietly emptied it out of the window, returning the plate to the basket. So went a fowl, a rice pudding, cauliflower, macaroni, while the porter and the padrona stood by astonished. He then asked the man to take away the basket. The porter took it and went.

"Now, Severn, you'll see. We shall have a decent dinner."

He was right. In a half hour or so the basket-bearer returned with an excellent meal; and every day they were treated to one over which they had no complaint. Nor were they charged, reported Severn, for the one thrown from the window.

3

Keats seemed stronger, though he had written Brown in late August, "I think there is a core of disease in me not easy to pull out"—thinking of "boils" he had dressed in hospital days. Was hope kindling again from embers he thought dead? He took no long sight-seeing expeditions but sauntered in the November sun along the Corso to the Porto del Popolo or slowly climbed the "Spanish Stairs," upon which his door opened, and rested at the top while he studied the changing scenes and tried to forget his lost love. Or he sat among ilexes and olives on the Pincian Hill, often his goal. Sheltered from the north wind, warm as summer, it was a favored spot for walking or sitting while he gazed toward St. Peter's on the hill opposite. Here young Lieutenant Elton, tall, handsome, cheerful, though also doomed by consumption, was an ideal companion. Regularly he had strolled at first with both Keats and Severn.

"See the celebrated beauty," someone pointed out the sister of Napoleon, the Princess Borghese. Handsome in face and figure, proud of bearing, she did not disdain coquettish glances. "Quite an Armida," remarked Severn, who had been reading with Keats the *Jerusalem Delivered*, and recalling the enchantress.

"You've seen Canova's statue of the lady?" asked Elton.

They had not and soon afterward went to look at it. Keats said, "The Aeolian Harp," and so named it enduringly, at the same time he condemned the figure as being in "beautiful bad taste."

Before long, the Princess, who had an eye for a finely setup man, began to "cast languishing glances" at the young Lieutenant. Keats's "I'm thankful I'm not the attraction" gave place to a jarring of his nerves. Henceforth they walked elsewhere. Elton was glad to go along with them, and for a time Severn accommodated his buoyant stride to their snail's pace.

It occurred to him they might try horseback riding, and soon they were walking their mounts—as slowly as they themselves had walked but able to travel farther. Severn, meantime, roamed about alone, strengthening himself for what might come . . . One day at the Colosseum he smelled a delightful fragrance and at last discovered the source—a flower high up in the ledges of the structure. At the risk of his life, he climbed up and brought it down—for Keats. Dr. Clark would not let his patient ride to see "stupendous and world-famous sights," fearing excitement might start anew the bleeding. Keats and Elton met on one of their easy walks or rides a Spanish Señor, Valentine Mario Llanos y Gutierrez, "everything that a Spanish cavalier ought to be." Casually meeting a few persons was about his only excitement.

Yet, if he was not better he was pretending to be—for Severn's sake—and the artist wrote home they might expect further encouraging news. While he worked in the Vatican or followed from afar Michelangelo, Keats read English books or continued to study Italian, soon reading with fair enjoyment the poets. Charles Brown had given him a pleasing initiation to the original of Ariosto.

He did not write but contemplated the prospect and surprised Severn happily by asking, "What do you think of a long poem on the subject of Sabrina?"

"As you might treat it, worthy to rank with your 'Lamia,'" Severn told him.

And, as always, dejection succeeded gleams of false hope, and ever the lower state was lower. Reading one day in Alfieri he came upon the passage beginning:

> *Misera me! Sollievo a me non resta*
> *Altro che'l pianto,* ed il pianto e delitto—

and threw the book away.

The next collapse was worse. The hemorrhages came back, preceding a fever that led to increased wasting and weakness. Severn was with him constantly, and Dr. Clark came day or night when a serious change seemed imminent. Keats was too wretched to see anyone else. For these he never quite lost the play of his "cheerful and elastic mind," said Severn, however great his misery. Severn concluded from the apparent spirits, "I suspect these bursts . . . are called up by a great effort—on my account."

"I must not show him," thought Keats, "that I am too painfully alive to his situation—knowing he must support himself by his art. I cannot hurt so kind a fellow." He tried to command his wit to call up only pleasant things.

While in his utter wretchedness he was so determining, Severn was writing, December 14, to Mrs. Brawne: "I fear poor Keats is at his worst." After a few lines he was unable to go on with the letter before the seventeenth. "Not a moment can I be from him," he told her; but now Keats lay asleep, the first sleep in eight nights and that from exhaus-

317

tion. He told her, too, how suddenly in a merry mood his poor friend had been stricken with a gush of blood from the lungs. Bleeding and being bled and unable to take food yet starving for lack of food, he had come to a pitiful pass, and Severn made no effort to conceal the fact.

"His imagination and memory present every thought to him in horror; the recollection of his good friend Brown, of his four happy weeks spent under *her* care, of his sister and brother. Oh! he must mourn over all to me whilst I cool his burning forehead. . . ."

Mrs. Clark now prepared his food—nobody else could do so—and had only just sent in a carefully dressed special kind of fish the doctor had scoured all Rome to find, when Keats was seized with a hemorrhage.

The melancholy days wore on to Christmas, "the strangest and saddest yet not altogether the least happy" Severn had ever spent, he wrote his sister Maria. Now after three weeks, Keats showed no signs of recovery, but wished night after night for death. Christmas Eve he was much worse: "The continued stretch of his imagination has already killed him," wrote Severn, who knew he needed some kind of hope to feed his "voracious imagination."

Out of all impossibility, he grew better once more. The day after Christmas he was considerably improved, and by New Year's Day the fever had left him. Severn was one in whose breast hope sprang eternal. He wrote Mrs. Brawne, January 11, 1821, "I most certainly think I shall bring him back to England. Half the cause of his danger has risen from the loss of England, from the dread of never seeing it more." But slowly, gradually, Keats's mind grew quiescent: he had surrendered and resurrendered himself finally, completely, to the idea of extinction. Severn, not knowing, believed recovery possible from the very tranquillity he did not fathom as numbness of despair. Even Dr. Clark was deceived into seeing reason for hope.

In the small room that Keats now called home, Severn had his own trials. The landlady reported to the police that she had a lodger dying of consumption. She well knew the Roman law that everything, even to the paper on the walls in each room the patient had been in, must be destroyed by fire. She knew as well the loss must be made more than good by the dead man's friend or friends. Severn looked about their sitting room appalled: here was at least £150 worth of furniture besides the piano, their own books and private possessions—all of them—invaluable. And he a man who would be rich on a pension of £130!

Wishing to dress Keats and to put clean things on him in the sitting room, he had the problem first of getting the invalid into it without anybody's knowing. The landlady's apartment was on the second—or same—floor; her servant waited on them—when it pleased her—and usually entered by the door into the adjoining room.

But Keats needed to be shifted while his room was cleaned and aired, and Severn set his jaw. He blocked up the door so nobody could enter, then made up a bed on the sitting-room sofa, gathered Keats up gently and laid him down there. Now a new difficulty arose—to allay possible suspicions of Keats himself. Pretending he was at his own dinner—Severn went dinnerless that day—he swept the room, made the bed, and later told Keats the servant had cleared up while he was eating. Keats had a suspicious look on his face, but saw no reason for making accusations and said nothing. He was put back in his bed, and only Dr. Clark was told the truth—later narrated to Mrs. Brawne.

"What enrages me most," Severn wrote her, "is making a fire. I blow, blow, for an hour—the smoke comes fuming out—my kettle boils over on the burning sticks—no stove—

319

Keats calling me to be with him—the fire catching my hands, and the door-bell ringing—all this to one quite unused and not at all capable—"

He had been also harassed by financial troubles, chiefly from a technicality over cashing the money Taylor was advancing, and nervous until a letter from the publishers removed the difficulty.

One thing Severn regretfully told Mrs. Brawne. Keats could not see letters: "They affect him so much and increase his danger. The two last I repented giving; he made me put them back in his box—unread." But he had much happiness hearing from Severn—who by and by thought it mentionable —of a sentence in Mrs. Brawne's reply to Severn's earlier letter: "Tell him," she bade, "that all desire to be kindly remembered to him, and shall feel happy to pay his sister every attention. Fanny and she have constantly corresponded since he left England." His eyes lighted at that. . . . A letter from Brown, dated December 21, also kept him smiling, when he was so much improved in January, the rest of the day.

4

At the end of January, he relapsed—finally. Extreme hemorrhages he declared the forerunner of the end. "I know the signs," he told Severn. "I saw them die at Guy's. I nursed poor Tom."

Late that month, when Severn dared not sleep, so sorely he might be needed, he sat looking at the wasted face on the pillow and was moved to tears. Quietly he brought his drawing-board and made a sketch of his friend yet living, but the fine eyes were closed, the once luxuriant hair thin and unkempt, the handsome face wasted beyond the semblance of its former self. Yet, even so—Severn held up the sketch—something marvelously fine and lovely there . . .

320

Despair reached a climax when the sufferer, fearing he might linger through the spring, tormented by hunger—he was reduced to one anchovy a day, with a morsel of bread—asked for the laudanum Severn had bought at Gravesend. Severn refused.

"It is mine. I claim it as my right," Keats begged. "My death is certain. I only wish to save you from the miseries of attending and beholding it. It may yet be deferred. . . . You will ruin all your prospects."

Severn protested against such thought, tried to soothe him, but Keats went on, "I am keeping you from your painting. I am sure to die. Why not let me—now? I have determined to take the laudanum and anticipate a lingering death, while emancipating you."

"You are mad, my friend," Severn told him firmly. "Think of your friends—their efforts for you. I am the chief of these, now, and assure you I shall never be tired of you or my ministrations." For his own prospects, he now confidently expected the Student's Pension of the Royal Academy.

This encouragement calmed Keats but as Severn still refused the laudanum he lashed himself into a fury, which passed to piteous supplication, and at last to the hope of shaking Severn by describing the horrid manner of his death. Again he became violent and Severn feared he might die from despair. There was no fear of death, no lack of courage; there was only, Severn knew, the desire to save him trouble; dying was quite secondary. "So for long we contended; he for his bottle, I for his life."

When Dr. Clark came, he took the bottle away with him. Keats, resigned to the truth, sank into "solemn seriousness." The doctor came now several times daily, "and it was an awful sound and sight to see Keats look round upon the doctor, with his large increasingly hazel eyes (for as his face decreased his eyes seemed to enlarge and shine with un-

321

earthly brightness) and ask in a deep pathetic tone, 'How long is this posthumous life of mine to last?'" The doctor, unable to answer, assured Severn he could not stand the intense look of his patient's eyes. At times, Severn thought they had the expression of a supernatural being who knew all that was passing in Dr. Clark's mind, though the doctor spoke no word.

Daily for a week he asked the same question and finally becoming more calm, harrowed Severn by recounting the minutest details of his last moments. Severn knew that sore weakness and desperation so provoked him, and never lost temper or patience.

All but *in extremis,* Keats became convinced he was not behaving as he should or as he would wish to behave. Severn made his coffee. He threw it away. "Then I made some more, and he threw that away also." But when Severn made it the third time, he was deeply affected and said in effect: "I have no agony so great as that I feel for you, and your endurance of my savageness arises from your prayers and patient devotion."

"Severn, I now understand how you can bear all this," he said late in January. "It is your Christian faith, and here I am with desperation in death that would disgrace the commonest fellow. How I should like it if it were possible to get some of Jeremy Taylor's works for you to read to me. I should gain consolation, for I have always been a devoted admirer of this devout author." He remembered the picture that hung over Bailey's desk . . . the Jeremy Taylor courtship . . . long, long ago.

Severn found a copy of *Holy Living and Holy Dying,* and read until Keats went to sleep, lulled by comforting passages.

And now he spoke of the quiet grave as the first rest he would ever have, though in the final fortnight he asked for books, amusing himself with them for all of three days. "He kept continually in his hand a polished, oval white carnelian, the gift of his widowing love, and at times it seemed his only consolation, the only thing left him in this world, clearly tangible."

On Valentine's Day, Severn wrote that little change had taken place, "except this beautiful one, that his mind is growing to great quietness and peace," and though this change was partly from bodily exhaustion, it seemed to him like a delightful sleep, so long he had been beating in the tempest of Keats's mind. This very night he talked much but afterward easily fell into seemingly "comfortable dreams without nightmare."

"Many, many things," said Severn, "he has requested of me tonight. This is the principal, that on his grave shall be:

Here lies one whose name was writ in water."

A letter came from Fanny Brawne. Severn thought it from Mrs. Brawne and let him see the superscription. "It tore him to pieces," and the effects were with him for several days. He did not, could not, read it but asked Severn to place it in his coffin, together with a purse and letter unopened of his sister's. For some reason he later requested that *that* letter be not placed in his coffin but only his sister's letter with the purse and some hair.

Worn out, frayed, Severn got an English nurse, whom fortunately Keats seemed to like, for two hours every day. The third day she was taken ill and came no more, but so brief a respite gave Severn a chance to regain his own sorely tried health. Keats was now living on milk, "delicious to all the senses," sometimes taking a pint and a half every day.

Dr. Clark said the expectoration was the most dreadful he ever saw, and he never knew an instance where a patient was so quickly pulled down after seeming recovery.

Toward the end, when Severn fearing he would fall asleep

323

and the wax taper would wear out, leaving Keats to the horror of darkness, attached a string between the stub and an unlighted candle. He did not tell the sick man, who woke to find the first candle flickering and Severn asleep. Reluctant to wake the exhausted companion, he watched—sweetly surprised by the light traveling along the line. "Severn! Severn!" he called. "Here's a little fairy lamp-lighter—"

In mid-February he asked Severn to visit the place where he was to be buried. ". . . By the pyramid of Caius Cestius, in the Protestant Cemetery, in that peaceful valley. . . ." Severn was not able to begin or to end. But Keats expressed pleasure and Severn, controlling himself, spoke of the grass and many flowers, particularly the innumerable violets this month had brought.

"I saw a young shepherd with his flock," Severn went on.

The fine eyes showed no morbidity, only an envisioning of beauty. Presently he said, "Already I feel the flowers growing over me."

Shortly before the end he was often in danger of suffocation and always called Severn to lift him up. "He has sunk in the last three days," Severn wrote Haslam, "to the most ghastly look." And still he lived. Four nights Severn watched, expecting each night to be the last. On the fifth, Dr. Clark prepared him.

At the last, Keats warned Severn to take care of himself, not to look at him in his dying gasp nor breathe his passing breath. Quietly he gave directions for carrying out his last wishes. Thereafter, he was calm to the end, which began about half past four in the afternoon of Friday, February 23.

While yet he could speak, he said, "Severn—I—lift me up, for I am dying. I shall die easy. Don't be frightened. Thank God, it has come." Severn lifted him "and the phlegm seemed boiling in his throat. This increased until eleven at

324

night." Holding Severn's hand, he looked up until his eyes "lost their speculation and dimmed in death."

Saturday, casts were made of face, hands, and feet. Sunday, the body was opened: the lungs were completely destroyed. The three doctors of the post-mortem findings could not understand how he had lived for the past two months.

Severn held up until with Dr. Clark, the English Chaplain, William Ewing, Ambrose Poynter, and one or two others, he followed the body to the grave one morning before daybreak. For nine days afterward he could not sleep. He began a letter to Brown describing the death but after some words dropped his pen.

May 23, writing to Fanny Keats, Fanny Brawne said of her lover's death, "I have not got over it and never shall." In that same month, Severn went again to the spot, where he would rejoin his friend more than half a century later. Daisies covered the grave. The only sounds in that quiet vale were the tinkling bells of a few goats and sheep.

"In water writ: 'Twas well, for all the sea-washed lands have heard Keats' name. . . ."—PAULINE V. ORR.

Notes

II

Page 33. Mrs. Dilke. Charles W. Dilke and Charles Brown, who owned Wentworth Place in common, had been living in the house, consisting of two semidetached parts, about a year.

III

Page 45. Jack Randall's in Chancery Lane, was the scene of professional sparring. Keats's "set" sometimes went there not only as onlookers but to take part.

This Randall is the same who fought a famous prizefight with Ned Turner, December 5, 1818. At that date Tom Keats lay unburied but John's friends prevailed upon him to go to Crawleyhurst, where Randall won in the thirty-fourth round. For obvious reasons, I have not included the excursion in the text of this work, though Reynolds and others were right in drawing Keats out of his misery and away from the painful scenes of recent weeks.

IV

Page 69. Not then but later Keats might have credited the following words and behavior of Bailey. July 7, 1820, Bailey stated of Keats that he had not kept the best society for one of his character and condition; many of his moral principles were loose; he had substituted the phantom of honor for the truth and substance of religion. Further, when Taylor thought of writing a biography of Keats, the Reverend Benjamin Bailey wrote, from Dallington, asking what was happening to Keats's papers. He, Bailey, had written the poet free and confidential letters, which he hoped had been burned before Keats left England. He sent some letters from Keats, thinking they might be of service to a biographer. Then he added, "If you notice his visit to Oxford, I should wish it to be done anonymously—that he visited a friend who was graduating at Oxford and who staid there during the long vacation." He hedged a little by saying, "My memory often reverts with melancholy pleasure to the time he spent with me," and so on. But, obviously, he was protecting himself. He had written rather freely about the Bishop of Lincoln (to Keats) and had enjoyed at least one very unorthodox party with Keats, to mention two instances recorded in this volume. I am indebted to Mr. Edmund C. Blunden, author of *Keats's Publisher, a Memoir of John Taylor*, 1936, for most of the other information of this paragraph. Page 87, *op. cit.* and ff.

By the time Monckton Milnes had finished his biography *(Life and Letters)* of Keats, a quarter-century or so later, Bailey had more to say, in a somewhat nostalgic vein, of the time he and the poet were together. In the beginning he valued highly this friend, writing for the Oxford *Herald*, May 30 and June 6, 1818, eulogistic if amateurish expressions of appreciation. The letters, signed, "N.Y." are now in the Harvard Keats Memorial Collection, where I read them in the original script.

Pages 70, 71. Long before Haydon killed himself by a gash in the throat and a bullet through his head, he wrote in his diary, November 14, 1831:

"I dreamt last night of dear Keats. I thought he appeared to me and said, 'Haydon, you promised to make a drawing of my head before I died, and you did not do it. Paint me now.' I awoke and saw him as distinctly as if it was his spirit. I am convinced such an impression on common minds would have been mistaken for a ghost. I lay awake for hours, dwelling on the remembrance of him. Dear Keats, I will paint thee worthily, poetically." *Op. cit.* See bibliography, Penrose ed. of *Autobiography*, Page 409.

VI

Page 94. "He has repaid me," etc. Letter from Brown to Dilke, September 6, 1824. In Memorial Library at Hampstead. Courtesy of Miss Naomi Kirk (see Preface).

Page 96. The apothecary's sign. Not, I think, to be translated "ounce," as it has been. Keats made in the air the sign for "drachm" not "ounce" and made it later in writing. He would not have lost that chance to pun. On the scenery Brown wrote then, drawing upon his notes and memory for the *Plymouth and Devonport Weekly Journal*, October 1, 1840.

Page 97. The White Lion was afterwards the Royal.

Page 102. "Enitials verse-wise," etc. Before Keats sent the acrostic to America, September, 1819, he had discovered his wrong spelling of "initials," and changed the line to: "Exact in capitals your golden name."

Page 102. "Fledged with ash," etc. See the "Ode to Psyche":

"Far, far around shall those dark cluster'd trees
Fledge the wild-ridged mountains steep by steep."

Notes

Page 103. The Druid Temple, now better known as Castlerigg Stone Circle.

VIII

Page 132. I have taken some liberty with facts, not truth, in this conversation. When Keats wrote George and Georgiana, October 16, 1818, "I have not seen Taylor," he probably meant he had not seen Taylor since the return from Scotland. Yet he must have called at 93 Fleet Street and *if* he did *not* see Taylor, he probably saw Woodhouse or Hessey, either of whom would have known about Gifford's article. In any event, I am convinced he had an interview similar to the one I have written. If not with Taylor or Hessey or Woodhouse, then with somebody who had been told the facts mentioned on Page 132.

Pages 133, 134. Where did the reviewer get his information? From Bailey. August 29, 1818, Bailey wrote Taylor: "I fear Endymion will be dreadfully cut up in the *Edinburgh Magazine.*" He tells of meeting "a man"—Lockhart, of course—at Bishop Gleig's home, and says, "I could hardly keep my tongue." At this remote date, it seems clear enough that he made no effort to hold it but wagged it, either to show he knew about a poet he believed was of importance, or with intentions to help Keats. He could not but have succeeded in making matters worse, though he appears not to have seen this truth in all the long years following. Thirty-one years later (May 7, 1849) he wrote Milnes: "I took occasion seriously to expostulate with this gentleman regarding Keats. . . . I gave him an outline of Keats's history, that he had been brought up as a surgeon and apothecary ["What grist to my mill!" the "man" must have chortled to himself] and though not highly, that he was respectably educated. I insisted, if I rightly remember, on the injustice and cruelty of thus condemning and crushing a young man, who from feelings most honorable to human nature adhered personally to the man [Hunt] who had befriended him when he was friendless, and needed a kindly eye and a helping hand."

Lockhart must have been avid for more, and lured the patronizing Bailey on. "But I distinctly remember saying something to this effect: 'Now, do not avail yourself of my information [Then why does he tell me? that "principal contributor" to *Blackwood's* must have asked himself] which I give you in this friendly manner, to attack him in your next-number of *Blackwood.*' His answer, too, I well remember, was to the effect that he certainly should not do so." A reader today must ask himself, "Could stupidity ever have done more than willful malice to damn a poet as Bailey damned Keats?"

This conversation took place at the latter end of July, 1818, says Bailey,

329

Notes

and in the following month of August "came out that infamous article, ending with 'Go back to your gallipots, Johnny.' " Lockhart must have seized hat and coat and rushed off immediately after dinner.

If a coincidence, Bailey heavily comments, it was so extraordinary, until cleared up—"and it never has been cleared up to this day, now nearly thirty-one years agone—my inevitable conclusion was that my communication had been taken advantage of." He was pained to think his confidence had been abused! He did not know the person, he says gravely [so making his conduct the more reprehensible]. Such breach of friendship, or such fatuity, illumines the character of Benjamin Bailey more brightly than anything Keats said of the "parson" to close friends after Bailey proclaimed himself "a ploughman in need of a wife." Keats was easily deceived in character, at the beginning. Inclined to pedestalize, he suffered when clay ankles broke and images tumbled headlong.

I am indebted to the Harvard Keats Memorial Collection for the privilege of reading this letter of Bailey's (in his daughter's script), though much if not all of it has been published.

Page 143, line 1. "speculation." See John Middleton Murry's "Keats's Use of Speculation," Page 93, *Studies in Keats, op. cit.*

IX

Page 158. "She manages to make her hair look well." She curled it herself, see *Letters from Fanny Brawne to Fanny Keats*, Page 53, *op. cit.* But doubtfully Keats knew that.

Page 158. "she is not seventeen." She was past eighteen, born August 9, 1800. "monstrous in her behavior." Fanny Brawne conveys a fair picture of herself—"not at all bashful and hardly modest." "Plague take it!" she writes of an annoying circumstance. Mrs. Abbey she dubbed "a worthless old woman." *Op. cit*, Pages 53, 54, 74.

X

Page 169. "A handsome Mrs. Jones," etc. Though she existed, Amy Lowell would have nothing of her, believing "Jones" stood for "Brawne."

Page 171. "St. Agnes Eve" was first used as title.

Page 182. Brown's anagram on Keats's name is mentioned in his letter of December 21, 1820—the last Keats received from this friend: "Do you recollect my anagram on your name?—how pat it comes now to Severn! My love to him and the said anagram.—*'Thanks, Joe!'* "

Brown liked to play with curiosities of language. The palindrome here

330

Notes

given occurs, with others, in a letter from him to Richards, April 2, 1822. *(Some Letters,* etc. p. 12, *op. cit.)*

XI

Page 185. "like the picture of somebody reading." The lines that inspired Severn to paint a portrait of the reading Keats.

Page 185. "Your affectionate Parson John." This letter alone goes far to deny Bailey's statement made some thirty years afterward that Keats had no religious instruction. If he had not, he got it for himself—even the Catechism formulas.

Page 199. Compare E. M. Forster's "Mr. and Mrs. Abbey's Difficulties" (in *Abinger Harvest*) for a similar point of view—that the Abbeys read letters to Fanny Keats.

Page 200. Keats's notice of Reynolds' "Peter Bell, A Lyrical Ballad" has been reprinted. A convenient place for reading it is in H. Buxton Forman's five-volume *Keats* (Glasgow, 1901). *Op. cit.*

XII

Page 209. N.B. April 3, 1819, Mrs. Brawne came to C. W. Dilke's part of Wentworth Place, Brown and Keats occupying the other part of the semidetached house.

Page 220. I am indebted to Mr. Douglas Bush, whose comparison between "Lamia" and the story in John Potter's *Archaeologia Graeca,* or *The Antiquities of Greece,* first appeared in *Publications of the Modern Language Association,* Sept. 1935 (L, No. 3, 785-806). With most of the comparison I am in agreement, but (page 793), Mr. Bush quotes L. 195:

"And after lifting up his aged hands,"

following it with the excerpt from Potter, i, 286: "It was also an usual gesture in praying to lift up their hands toward heaven."

Keats's familiarity with the *Aeneid,* which he translated at least in part, would have made him recall: "Ingemit, et duplicis tendens ad sidera palmas," etc. *(Aeneid,* Bk. I, 1. 93, etc.), rather than Potter's words.

Pages 220, 221. I have taken Keats's marginalia from the copy made by H. B. Forman. I used his Glasgow edition of the *Complete Works of John Keats,* III, 268.

Page 225. "Cold pig" is, according to M. B. Forman, page 327, *op. cit.* "a wetting with cold water to awaken him."

331

Notes

XIII

Page 233. Of these sixty lines from "Lamia," eighteen were omitted in the published version.

XIV

Page 250. Many details point to Brown's absence in Ireland in the three weeks away from Winchester. It is possible that his son Carlo was born at this time think some students who believe Brown fabricated the story for his son Carlino that he went to marry Abbie this August, 1819. Despite the arguments brought to bear by Dorothy Hyde Bodurtha and Willard Bissell Pope, *op. cit.* p. 108, the details may be turned equally well to point to the conclusions I make—which are by no means novel, nor taken without due consideration from all contributory evidence.

It is quite possible that Keats knew of Brown's relations with Abbie, even without the statements made in his letter of Dec. 21, 1820. The doubt lies in answer to the question, "*When* did Brown tell Keats of the boy Carlino and the reason for the absence from Winchester?"

"Brown had four letters from me all in a lump," quoted by Bodurtha and Pope, *op. cit.*, p. 108, may be countered by M. B. Forman's note on Keats's statement to Dilke in the letter of Sept. 22, 1819. He speaks of an extraordinary mischance having befallen two of the letters, and M. B. F. comments, "Neither of them extant so far as I am aware." Note, p. 394, *op. cit.*

There is one other point of view, whatever may be thought of Brown's acts, so far. If Keats *knew* he was lending himself to cover his friend in a way so pointed, he was not Keats. That sort of deception was not in him. He would have said nothing or said, "That is Mr. Brown's affair."

For the right to reprint the letter on pages 256 and 257, I am indebted to the Library of Haverford University, which owns the script and kindly gave me permission to include it in this volume.

XV

Page 269. George and Georgiana christened their fifth child John Henry. Born 1827, he lived to 1917. His daughter, Miss Juanita, is living, also her cousin Alice (Clarence George Keats's daughter). With their passing, the name of the George Keats family (as a surname) will be extinct. There are many descendants by other names, as Miss Naomi Joy Kirk's "Life of George Keats" fully shows. (See Preface.)

Notes

Page 271. The story is embodied in Keats's letter of Feb. 14–May 3, 1819, to George and Georgiana. Page 299, M. B. Forman, *op. cit.*

Pages 272, 273. According to Amy Lowell (II, 382, ff.) George found on his return to England that Tom's estate, which had amounted to 1100 pounds, was reduced to 900 pounds, by John's drawing 100 pounds for himself, and 100 pounds for George. Another 100 pounds George now drew for Fanny, equating the parts each had now received. Of the remaining 800 pounds, each would receive some 266 pounds, but George asked John for all but 100 pounds to take home for investing in America. [But John told Brown he had received only sixty pounds. As for George, counting all he got together he had something like 700 pounds, which he took back home with him, and it was this sum at which John stared.]

John told Fanny Brawne, "George ought not to have done this. He should have recollected that I wish to marry, myself—but I suppose having a family to provide for makes a man selfish." See *Fanny Brawne to Fanny Keats, op. cit.*, p. 34.

George later stated in effect that he let John believe he was helping more than was actually the fact, not wishing to depress further his brother's lowered and perturbed spirits. The record however, is that he left 60, pounds, or 70 or 80, to John, who owed it all, or more. George, further, was unable to pay John anything before John's death but later settled all his debts. There was still a residue for John from the estate, which covered the expenses to which George had been put and, if they desired it, enough to pay the friends who had relieved John with gifts of money.

Fanny Brawne thought George "might be a cause of the dreadful consequences, but only a very indirect and accidental one." *Op. cit.*, p. 33. Brown, who nursed John for seven weeks, was not inclined then or ever to think George had acted well or wisely. George himself confessed that he was wrong in leaving John with the idea he was helping more than he really was. C. W. Dilke always upheld George completely after hearing George's side of the transaction.

Page 280. Fanny Brawne wore the ring with the almandine, a finest variety of garnet, until her death (1865).

XVII

Page 291. "This is a lie," etc. written in the copy for B. Dav⟨ This copy and the one for Fanny Brawne are in the Harvard K⟨ morial Collection. See facsimiles in Lowell, *op. cit.*, opp. pp. 424,

Page 292. Silhouette. See "Within the Compass of a Print⟨

Notes

cit. also Lowell, *op. cit.* opp. p. 436. Now in Harvard Keats Memorial Collection.

Pages 292, 293. "One morning at Hunt's," See Leigh Hunt's *Lord Byron*, etc. *op. cit.* pp. 408-450.

Page 293. Cup and saucer. When the Hunts went to Italy some time later, Mrs. Hunt gave them to Charles Cowden Clarke. See E. C. Blunden, *Shelley and Keats*, etc. *op. cit.* p. 94.

Page 296. Throughout the remainder of this volume, I rely much upon William Sharp's *Life and Letters of Joseph Severn, op. cit.* Unfortunately, Severn's letters at the time do not always square with the reminiscences, written many years later, to which Sharp had access. This is particularly true of the period in quarantine and in Naples.

Pages 295, 299, and other brief references elsewhere, from *Life of John Keats* by Charles Armitage Brown, *op. cit. passim.*

Page 300. *The New Testament*, now in the Harvard Keats Memorial Collection, was published at Amsterdam, 1717. Taylor probably thought Keats would study Greek, aided by the medium of Latin with which he was familiar. The book, which appears hardly to have been opened, is inscribed: John Keats from his/ friend John Taylor/ Sept. 1820.

XVIII

Page 314. Severn's painting, "The Death of Alcibiades," won the three-year pension.

Anna Angeletti. Receipt for rental of the piano from Nov. 29–Dec. 28, 1820, was found, 1911, by Severn's daughter (Mrs. Eleanor Furneaux) and presented to the Keats-Shelley Memorial, Rome. The price was about thirty shillings for the month. See p. 95, No. 2, of the *Bulletin and Review of the Keats-Shelley Memorial*, Rome.

Severn doubtless gave up the piano when he recognized that it might be burned and charged to him.

Page 316. Spanish Señor. Keats would have been glad to know that the engaging cavalier would marry his sister Fanny. For the line describing him, see *Fanny Brawne to Fanny Keats, op. cit.*, p. 47.

Page 321, and ff. The speeches of Keats, as Severn remembered them after long years, smack more of Severn's manner than Keats's. The death speech is more like what one would expect. It was in the bit of a letter begun to Charles Brown and found long years afterward. See *Bulletin and Review, op. cit.*, pp. 42, 43.

Notes

Page 325. Accounts of the few who followed Keats's body on that early February morning are not the same. At most, there were:

Severn, the Chaplain, Seymour Kirkup, Dr. Clark, William Ewing, Henry Parke and Ambrose Poynter,—seven altogether. Hewlett, *op. cit.*, p. 388, quotes a memorandum in the Keats Memorial House, in which Ambrose Poynter mentions Severn, Henry Parke (architect), the English Chaplain and himself, architect. But others are not of necessity barred.

Page 325. Keats was the fifty-first person buried in the Protestant cemetery.

Bibliography

I, 1

A selected list of works consulted. (See Bibliography II for the several chapters.)

ADAMI, MARIE. *Fanny Keats.* New Haven, 1938.

ASKWITH, HON. BETTY. *Keats.* London, 1941.

BALDWIN, DANE LEWIS. *A Concordance to the Poems of John Keats.* Compiled by D. L. Baldwin and others, 1917.

BARRATT, THOMAS JAMES. *The Annals of Hampstead.* London, 1912.

BATE, WALTER J. *Negative Capability, The Intuitive Approach to Keats.* Harvard University Press, 1939.

BLUNDEN, EDMUND C. *Leigh Hunt's Examiner Examined.* London, 1928.

────── *Leigh Hunt.* London, 1930.

────── *Keats's Publisher: A Memoir of John Taylor.* London, 1936.

────── *Shelley and Keats as They Struck Their Contemporaries.* London, 1925.

BRAWNE, FANNY. *Letters of Fanny Brawne to Fanny Keats, 1820-1824.* Ed. with a Biographical Introduction by Fred Edgcumbe, Resident Curator of the Keats Memorial House, Hampstead. Preface by M. B. Forman. New York, 1937.

BROWN, CHARLES ARMITAGE. *Life of John Keats.* Ed. with an Introduction and Notes, by Dorothy Hyde Bodurtha and Willard Bissell Pope. London, 1937.

────── *Some Letters and Miscellanea of Charles Armitage Brown.* Ed. by M. B. Forman. London, 1937.

BUSHNELL, NELSON S. *A Walk after John Keats.* New York, 1936.

CLARKE, C. C. and M. C. *Recollections of Writers.* New York, 1878.

COLVIN, SIR SIDNEY. *John Keats, His Life and Poetry, His Friends, etc.* New York, 1917.

DILKE, C. W. *Papers of a Critic.* 2 vols. London, 1875.

ERLANDE, ALBERT (pseudonym for Albert Jacques Brandenburg). *The*

Life of John Keats. Tr. from the French by Marion Robinson. Pref. by J. M. Murry. New York, 1929.

Fausset, Hugh L'Anson. *Keats, A Study in Development.* Natl. Bibliophile Service, 1922.

Finney, Claude Lee. *The Evolution of Keats's Poetry.* 2 vols. Cambridge, Mass., 1936.

Forster, E. M. *Abinger Harvest.* New York, 1936. See pages 232-241 for "Mr. and Mrs. Abbey's Difficulties."

Garrod, H. W. *Keats.* New York, 1926.

Hale-White, Sir William, K. B. E. *Keats as Doctor and Patient.* London, 1938.

Hancock, Albert Elmer. *John Keats, A Literary Biography.* Boston, New York, 1908.

Haydon, Benjamin Robert. *The Autobiography and Memoirs of.* Compiled from his *Autobiography and Journals* and *Correspondence and Table-Talk.* Ed. by Alexander P. D. Penrose, M.A. London, 1927.

———— *Autobiography and Journals.* Ed. by Tom Taylor.

———— *The Autobiography and Memoirs of* (Ed. from his *Journals* by Tom Taylor). Ed. by Aldous Huxley, 2 vols. New York.

———— *Correspondence and Table-Talk.* Ed. by Frederick Wordsworth Haydon, 2 vols. London, 1876.

Hewlett, Dorothy. *Adonais.* London, 1937; Indianapolis, New York, 1938.

Houghton, Lord (Richard Monckton Milnes). *Life and Letters of John Keats.* London, 1867. First time pub. in one volume ("World's Classics Series"). London, 1931.

Hunt, Leigh. *The Autobiography of, etc.,* 3 vols. New York, 1850. Rev. ed., 1860.

———— *Lord Byron and Some of His Contemporaries.* London, 1828. 2nd. ed. 2 vols., 1828.

Keats, John. *Anatomical and Physiological Note Book,* Reprinted from the Holograph in the Keats Museum, Hampstead. Ed. by Maurice Buxton Forman, Oxford University Press, 1934.

———— (Volumes published in his lifetime): *Poems.* London: C. and J. Ollier, 1817. This book of 120 pages may be found in the Noel Douglas Replica, 1927. *Endymion.* London: Taylor and Hessey, 1818. *Lamia,* etc. London: Taylor and Hessey, 1820. To be found in Margaret Robertson's Facsimile Reprint, Oxford, 1909. I consulted copies of first editions in the Morgan Library (New York City) and in the Harvard Keats Memorial Collection, as well as a number of the scripts.

Bibliography

———— Letters. Those extant, or known, range from 1815 to 1820, the larger number falling in 1818 and 1819 and a smaller proportion for 1820. Since Monckton Milnes's work (*q.v. infra*) these letters have been published in whole or in part as discovered and brought to light. Sir Sidney Colvin, published (New York, 1891) *Letters of John Keats to His Family*. With *Papers and Other Relics*, G. C. Williamson published (London, 1914) a number. H. B. Forman became the leader in this interesting phase of Keats's activity, as he was a leader in all that revealed the poet, and after his death his son Maurice Buxton Forman took up the heritage. In 1931 he published 2 vols. of *The Letters of John Keats* (London). In 1935: *The Letters of John Keats*, edited by Maurice Buxton Forman, appeared. My copy is of the second edition with revisions and additional letters, Oxford University Press, 1935.

———— *The Complete Poetic Works and Letters of John Keats*. Ed. by Horace E. Scudder. Boston and New York, 1899.

———— *The Complete Works of John Keats*, in 5 vols. Ed. by H. Buxton Forman. Glasgow, 1900 and 1901; 1924.

———— *Poems*, with notes by Lord Houghton (Monckton Milnes), Memoir by John G. Speed. 2 vols. New York, 1883.

———— *Poems*. Ed. by E. de Sélincourt. New York, 1905; London, 1912, 1920; 5th ed. 1926.

———— *Poems of Keats. Endymion, etc.* Ed. by W. T. Young. Cambridge University Press, 1917.

———— *Poetical Works*, Globe Edition. Edited by William T. Arnold. London, 1908.

———— *Poetical Works*, with a Life by James Russell Lowell. Boston, 1854.

———— *Poetical Works*. Ed. with a memoir by W. M. Rossetti. London, 1872, 1880.

———— *The Poetical Works of John Keats*. Two parts in one volume. New York: Wiley and Putnam, 161 Broadway, 1846.

———— *The Poetical Works of John Keats*. Ed. by H. W. Garrod. Oxford, 1939.

———— *The Poetical Works of John Keats*, reprinted from the original ed. with notes by Francis T. Palgrave, 1922.

———— *The Poetical Works and Other Writings of John Keats*. Ed. with notes and appendices by H. Buxton Forman. Revised with additions by Maurice Buxton Forman, with an introduction by John Masefield. New York, 1938 (Morgan Library Copy, Number 611) Limited ed. of 1025. Type destroyed. This is The Hampstead Edition.

The Keats House, Hampstead, England, Public Libraries Committee, 1925.

John Keats Memorial Volume. Issued by Keats House Committee, London, 1921.

John Keats—Selections from:

——— *Keats.* Ed. by Alfred Noyes, with notes, etc. London, 1925.

——— *Odes, Lyrics, and Sonnets.* Ed. by M. Hillis, New York, 1916.

——— *Poems,* with intro. by Walter Raleigh. London and New York, 1898.

——— *Poems.* Ed. by Lawrence Binyon. London, 1903 (with notes by John Masefield).

——— *Poems,* with intro. by Alice Meynell. London, 1903.

KIRK, NAOMI. "George Keats." Unpublished script, cited by recent Keats scholars. I register special thanks for the privilege of reading this work (see Preface).

See also The Hampstead Edition, *op. cit.* for her "Memoir of George Keats," I, lxxiii-xcviii; and listing of "The Girl Who Shared Keats's Fate," in the *American Scholar*, VI, No. 1, Winter 1937.

LOFTIE, W. J. "Keats at Enfield." (In Andrew Lang's *Poet's Country,* 1907.)

LOWELL, AMY. *John Keats*, 2 vols. Boston, 1925; 1 vol. ed., 1929.

MILNES, RICHARD MONCKTON. *Life, Letters, and Literary Remains of John Keats.* Edited by R. M. M. in 2 vols. London, 1848.

MURRY, JOHN MIDDLETON. *Keats and Shakespeare.* New York, 1925.

——— *Studies in Keats.* New York, 1930.

——— *Studies in Keats New and Old.* New York, 1939.

O'NEIL, GEORGE. *Special Hunger.* New York, 1931.

OSLER, SIR WILLIAM. *John Keats, The Apothecary Poet.* Baltimore, 1896.

OWEN, F. M. *John Keats, A Study.* London, 1880.

PROCTER, BRYAN W. *Autobiographical Fragment,* etc. London, 1877.

RIDLEY, MAURICE ROY. *Keats' Craftsmanship.* 1933.

ROSSETTI, W. M. *Life of John Keats.* London, 1887.

SHARP, WILLIAM. *The Life and Letters of Joseph Severn.* London, 1892.

SPURGEON, CAROLINE F. E. *Keats's Shakespeare,* etc. London, 1928.

THORPE, CLARENCE DEWITT. *The Mind of Keats.* New York, 1926.

WELLER, EARLE VONARD. *Autobiography* (of Keats), Compiled by E. V. W. Stanford University Press, 1933.

——— *Keats and Mary Tighe.* New York, 1928.

WILLIAMS, BRISTOL. *Orion and Other Anonymous Poems, etc.* attr. to

Bibliography

John Keats. Transcribed and prepared by B. W. (Not by Keats but showing a pale kinship.)

Winwar, Frances (pseudonym for Mrs. Grebanier). *The Romantic Rebels.* Boston, 1935.

I, 2

Periodicals and pamphlets.

Beach, J. W. "Keats's Realms of Gold," *Pub. Modern Lang. Assn.* (PMLA), March, 1934, XLIX, No. 1, 246-57.

Blackwood's Edinburgh Magazine, III, April-Sept., 1818, August No. (No. xvii) 519-24. "The Cockney School of Poetry," No. IV, signed "Z"; and other numbers of this periodical.

Blunden, Edmund C. "New Sidelights on Keats, Lamb, and Others," London *Mercury*, IV, 141-49, 1921.

Bookman (London), Keats Double Number. Oct., 1906. See article by H. B. Forman.

Briggs, H. E. "The Birth and Death of John Keats, A Reply to Mr. Pershing" *(q.v. infra)*, PMLA, LVI, No. 2, June, 1941, 592-96.

Bush, Douglas. "Notes on Keats's Reading," PMLA, L, No. 3, Sept. 1935, 785-806.

Catalogue of a Loan Exhibition Commemorating the Anniversary of the Death of John Keats 1821-1921, Held at the Public Library of the City of Boston, February 21 to March 14, 1921.

Clarke, Charles C. "Recollections of Keats," *Atlantic Monthly*, January, 1861, pp. 86-100 (Unsigned. Cf. *Recollections of Writers, supra*).

Cornelius, Roberta D. "Two Early Reviews of Keats's First Volume," PMLA, XL, 1925, 193-210 (Reviews by Haydon and G. F. Mathew). The *Athenaeum*, Boston, reprinted part of G. F. M.'s review, the first criticism of Keats to appear in America.

Elliott, G. R. "The Real Tragedy of Keats," PMLA, XXXVI, Sept. 1921, 315-31.

Evans, B. I. "Keats's Approach to the Chapman Sonnet," *Eng. Assn. Essays and Studies*, XVI, 26-52 (Cf. article by J. W. Beach, *supra*).

Forman, W. C. "John Keats and Winchester," *Cornhill Magazine*, London, 1921, n.s. L, 144-46 (with diagram).

Jones, Sir Robert Armstrong. "Some Remarks on Keats," *Annals of Medical History*, New York, 1938, n.s., X, 433-44.

Kirk, Naomi J. *The Filson Club Historical Quarterly*, Louisville, Kentucky, 1934. See article pp. 86-96, with much information included in the (script) "George Keats."

341

Forever Young

LANDRUM, GRACE WARREN. "More Concerning Chapman's Homer and Keats," PMLA, XLII, 1927, 986-1009.

OLNEY, CLARKE. "John Keats and Benjamin Robert Haydon," PMLA, XLIX, No. 1, 258-75.

PERSHING, JAMES H. "John Keats: When Was He Born and When Did He Die?" PMLA, LV, No. 3, Sept. 1940, 802-14.

Quarterly Review. "Endymion: A Poetic Romance by John Keats," London, 1818. XIX, April and December, Article vii, Anonymous [William Gifford].

SHACKFORD, MARTHA H. "Eve of St. Agnes and the Mysteries of Udolpho," PMLA, XXXVI, March, 1921, 104-18.

THORPE, CLARENCE DEWITT. "Keats's Interest in Politics and World Affairs," PMLA, XLVI, No. 4, Dec. 1931, 1228-45.

II

Chief references, chapter by chapter of this work.

I

Introductory quotation, page 1, from Keats to Bailey, Jan. 23, 1818.

Keats to George and Thomas Keats, letter from Southampton, April 16, 1817.

The brief description of Keats's watch, page 1 (and *infra*, p. 164) is made from the original, Harvard Keats Memorial Collection (HKMC). It is attached to a curiously wrought-gold fob, ending in a red carnelian seal, J. K.

For Keats's reflections on his "Chapman Sonnet," I am indebted to B. Ifor Evans, *op. cit. supra,* and J. W. Beach, *op. cit. supra.* Keats's copy of Robertson's *History* was of the Dublin edition, 1777. Mine is of the eleventh edition, London, 1808, 4 vols.

For my conclusion of Chapter I, see Keats's letter to Leigh Hunt, May 10, 1817.

Champion, March 9, 1817.

Examiner, December, 1816.

C. C. Clarke. *Recollections of Writers, op. cit. supra.*

Charles G. Harper. *Stage Coach and Mail in Days of Yore,* 2 vols. London, 1903. *Passim.*

W. Outram Tristram. *Coaching Days and Coaching Ways.* London, 1914.

H. W. Garrod, Ed. *Poetical Works of John Keats, op. cit. supra.*

Bibliography

II

Keats to Leigh Hunt, May 10, 1817; to B. R. Haydon, May 13, 1817; to Taylor and Hessey, May 16, 1817; to Fanny Keats, Sept. 10, 1817; to Jane Reynolds, Sept. 1817 (2 letters); to J. H. Reynolds, Sept. 21, 1817; to Haydon, Sept. 28, 1817.

Haydon to Keats, May 11, 1817.

Benjamin Bailey to Monckton Milnes, May 7, 1849. Script—in the hand of Bailey's daughter, HKMC.

C. F. E. Spurgeon, *Keats's Shakespeare, op. cit. supra,* for Keats's underlined *Tempest* passages, pp. 70, 79.

C. C. Clarke, *op. cit.*

Garrod, *op. cit.*

III

Keats to Fanny Keats, Sept. 10, 1817; to Bailey, Oct. 8, Nov. 3, 22, 1817; to George and Thomas Keats, Dec. 21, 1817; to Jane Reynolds, Oct. 31, 1817; to J. H. Reynolds, Nov. 22, 1817.

Eclectic Review, September, 1817.

Constable's Scots and Edinburgh Magazine, October, 1817.

H. B. Forman. *The Complete Works of John Keats, op. cit. supra,* Vol. III, Essays and Notes.

For the dinner at Haydon's, see Haydon, *Autobiography and Memoirs,* Ed. Penrose, *op. cit.,* which I have used largely with two notes from letters of Keats.

IV

Keats to George and Thomas Keats, Jan. 5, 13, 23, Feb. 14, 1818; to Haydon, Jan. 10, 1818; to John Taylor, Jan. 10, 23, 30, Feb. 27, 1818; to Bailey, Jan. 23, 1818; to John Reynolds, Jan. 31, Feb. 3, 19, 1818.

Catalogue of a Loan Exhibition, *op. cit. supra,* for the binding of Keats's *Poems* by the Wordsworths.

H. B. Forman, *op. cit.*

IV (and Notes on IV)

Edmund C. Blunden. *Keats's Publisher, op. cit. supra.*

Letters of Benjamin Bailey to the Oxford *Herald,* May 30 and June 6, 1818. Scripts in HKMC.

V

Taylor to Hessey, March 6, 1818, for Keats's going off in the storm, on top of the coach. Script in Morgan collection (The Pierpont Morgan Library, New York City).

Keats to Bailey, March 13, May 21 to 25, June 10, 1818; to J. H. Reynolds, March 14, Apr. 9, 10, 27, May 3, 1818; to J. Rice, March 24, 1818; to Haydon, Apr. 8, 1818; to J. Taylor, Apr. 24, June 21, 1818; to Mrs. Jeffrey, May, 1818.

Thomas Keats to Mary Ann Jeffrey, May 17, 1818. In this letter, T. K. quotes the Chaucerian passage and remarks, in effect, that if lisping was objectionable in a monk, how much more so in a young lady. Script in HKMC.

Garrod, *op. cit.*

VI

For the travels in North England and Scotland, I have relied upon my own travels, on many occasions, to that region, and upon:

Nelson S. Bushnell. *A Walk after John Keats, op. cit. supra.*

Prints in HKMC.

Keats to Thomas Keats, June 25-27, 1818; to George Keats, June 27-28, 1818; to Fanny Keats, July 2, 1818; to Thomas Keats, July 3-9, 1818; to J. H. Reynolds, July 11-13, 1818; to Thomas Keats, July 10-14, 17-21, 31, 1818; to Bailey, July 18-22, 1818; to Mrs. Wylie, Aug. 6, 1818.

Charles Brown to C. W. Dilke, Aug. 7, 1818.

Garrod, *op. cit.*

See also Notes for this chapter.

VII

See bibliography for preceding chapters.

VIII

See bibliography for preceding chapters, and:

Keats to Fanny Keats, Aug. 18, 25, Oct. 9, 1818; to C. W. Dilke, Sept. 21, 1818; to Reynolds, Sept. 22, 1818; to T. Richards, Oct. 9, 1818; to J. A. Hessey, Oct. 9, 1818; to George and Georgiana Keats, Oct. 14-31, 1818; to R. Woodhouse, Oct. 27, 1818.

Bibliography

Charles Brown to C. W. Dilke, Aug. 7, 1818.
R. Woodhouse to Keats, Oct. 21, 1818.
Blackwood's Edinburgh Magazine, op. cit. supra.
Quarterly Review, op. cit. supra.
Garrod, *op. cit.*

IX

Keats to George and Georgiana Keats, Oct. 14-31, 1818, Dec. 16, 1818–
Jan. 4, 1819; to Fanny Keats, Nov. 5, Dec. 1, 1818.
W. Haslam to R. M. Milnes, May 8, 1847 (for place and date of Tom's
funeral). Script in HKMC.

X

Keats to George and Georgiana Keats, Dec. 16, 1818–Jan. 4, 1819; to
R. Woodhouse, Dec. 18, 1818; to Haydon, Dec. 22, 1818, March 9,
1819; to J. Taylor, Dec. 24, 1818.
B. R. Haydon to Keats, Jan. 7, Apr. 12, 1819.
Keats and Charles Brown to Charles W. and Maria Dilke, Jan. 24, 1819.
Keats to George and Georgiana Keats, Feb. 14–May 3, 1819.
Garrod, *op. cit.*

XI

Keats to George and Georgiana Keats, Feb. 14–May 3, 1819; to Fanny
Keats, March 13, May 26, 1819; to Haydon, Apr. 13, 1819; to W.
Haslam, May 13, 1819; to Miss Jeffrey, May 31, June 9, 1819.
B. R. Haydon to Keats, Apr. 12, 1819.
Garrod, *op. cit.*

XII

Keats to Fanny Keats, June 9, 16, July 6, 1819; to Haydon, June 17,
1819; to Fanny Brawne, July 1, 8, 15, 25, Aug. 5, 6, 1819; to
Reynolds, July 11, 1819; to C. W. Dilke, July 31, 1819.
Douglas Bush, see *op. cit.* and notes for this chapter.
H. B. Forman, for his marginalia, see notes for this chapter.
M. B. Forman, for his note, see notes on this chapter.
Garrod, *op. cit.*

XIII

Keats to Bailey, Aug. 14, 1819; to Fanny Brawne, Aug. 17, Sept. 13,
1819; to J. Taylor, Aug. 24, 31, Sept. 5, 1819; to Fanny Keats, Aug.

Forever Young

28, 1819; to Hessey, Sept. 5, 1819; to Reynolds, Sept. 21, 1819; to Woodhouse, Sept. 21, 1819; to George and Georgiana Keats, Sept. 17-27, 1819.
Charles Brown to John Taylor, Aug. 24, 1819.
Richard Woodhouse to John Taylor, Sept. 20, 1819 (Morgan Collection).
John Taylor to Richard Woodhouse, Sept. 25, 1819 (HKMC).
M. B. Forman. *The Letters of John Keats, op. cit. supra,* particularly a note, p. 364, itself a quotation. Also, a note, p. 377, quoting the pertinent passage from *Mandeville.*
Garrod, *op. cit.* "Otho the Great," in particular.

XIV

Keats to Taylor and Woodhouse, Sept. 21, 1819; to Dilke, Sept. 22, Oct. 1, 1819; to George and Georgiana Keats, Sept. 17-27, 1819; to C. Brown, Sept. 23, 1819 (2 letters); to Haydon, Oct. 3, 1819; to Fanny Brawne, Oct. 11, 13, 19, 1819; to Fanny Keats, Oct. 16, Dec. 20, 1819; to Joseph Severn, Oct. 1819; to J. Taylor, Nov. 17, 1819; to George Keats, Nov. 19, 1819; to J. Rice, Dec. 1819.
Garrod, *op. cit.*

XV

Keats to Georgiana Augusta Keats, Jan. 13-28, 1820; to Fanny Brawne, Feb. 4, 10, 1820, and ten undated letters, probably of Feb. 1820; Feb. 24, 28, 1820; to Fanny Keats, Feb. 6, 9, 11, 14, 19, 1820; to J. Rice, Feb. 14, 1820; to Reynolds, Feb. 28, 1820.
B. W. Procter to Keats, Feb. (?) 1820.
Fanny Brawne. *Letters of Fanny Brawne to Fanny Keats, op. cit. supra.*
C. A. Brown. *Life of John Keats, op. cit. supra,* pp. 25, 112, 113.

XVI

Keats to Mrs. Wylie, March (?) 1820; to Fanny Brawne, nine letters (March) 1820, three letters, May, 1820, July 5, 1820; to Fanny Keats, three letters, Apr., 1820; to C. W. Dilke, May, 1820; to C. Brown, May 15, 1820, June, 1820.
Blunden, E. C. *Shelley and Keats as They Struck Their Contemporaries, op. cit. supra,* p. 72.
Haydon, B. R. *Autobiography* (Penrose, *op. cit. supra*) pp. 241, 242.

Bibliography

Quotation from Maria Gisborne's *Journal*, cited by M. B. Forman, *op. cit.*,
   p. 498.
Garrod, *op. cit.*

XVII

Keats to Fanny Brawne, July, Aug. 1820; to Fanny Keats, Aug. 14, 1820,
   to Fanny Keats (dictated to F. B.), Sept. 11, 1820; to P. B. Shelley,
   Aug. 14, 1820; to Haydon, Aug. 14, 1820; to Taylor, Aug. 14,
   1820; to Hunt, Aug. 1820; to Brown, Aug. 20, Aug. ?, Sept. 30,
   1820; to Brown, Nov. 1, 1820; to Mrs. Brawne, Oct. 24, 1820.
C. C. Clarke to L. Hunt, Sept. 20, 1823.
P. B. Shelley to Keats, July 27, 1820.
Haydon to Keats, July 14, 1820.
Hunt to Keats, Aug., 1820.
R. Abbey to Keats, Aug. 23, 1820.
R. Woodhouse to Keats, Sept. 16, 1820.
J. Severn to Haslam, Nov. 1, 1820.
Garrod, *op. cit.*
HKMC

XVIII

William Sharp. *The Life and Letters of Joseph Severn (op. cit. supra)*.
Charles Macfarlane. *Reminiscences of a Literary Life*. London, 1917, cited
   by Colvin, *op. cit. supra*.
Bulletin and Review of the Keats-Shelley Memorial, Rome, *passim*.
Keats to C. Brown, Nov. 1, 30, 1820 (the last letter).
C. Brown to Keats, Dec. 21, 1820.
Dr. J. Clark to J. Taylor, Apr. 16, 1821.
Amy Lowell. *John Keats, op. cit. supra, passim*.
Most of this chapter rests on Severn's letters at the time and upon his later
   reminiscences, cited by Sharp, *op. cit.*

Index

349

Index

Index

Index

Index

Index

Hair: Fanny Brawne's, 151, 330; Keats's, 151, 272, 294, 300; Milton's, 71

Hammond, Dr. (Thomas), 9, 42, 50, 262

Hampstead, 4, 70, 77, 99, 135, 242, 253, 284, 286, 299; Heath, 6, 47, 59, 107, 162; Weald, 91

Harvard Keats Memorial Collection, xix, xxii, xxiv, 328, 330, 334

Haslam, William, xix, xxii, 67, 85, 147, 156, 160, 171, 185, 206, 242, 268, 270, 295, 296, 297, 300, 307, 324

Hastings, 20, 28

Hastings, Lady met at, 28, 147, 178

Haverford College Library, xxiv, 332

Haydn, 314

Haydon, Benjamin Robert, xvii, 4-6, 14, 16, 22, 23, 25, 32, 43, 47, 51, 58, 68, 77, 83, 85, 90, 136, 160, 170, 172, 181, 182, 192, 216, 217, 254, 269, 279, 283, 284, 294, 298, 328

Hazlitt, William, xv, 51, 68, 71, 76, 83, 89, 91, 113, 134, 156, 159, 162, 184, 193, 259, 283, 284

"He is to weet," 197

"Hearken, thou craggy," 112

Heart of Midlothian (opera), 192

Helvellyn, 101, 102, 104

"Hence, burgundy, claret, and port," 74

Henrietta Street, 240, 252

Henry IV, 52

Henry VI, 55, 57

"Hercules, Methodist A," 244

"Here lies one," 323

Hessey, James Augustus ("Mistessey"), xxiii, 25, 79, 92, 143, 232, 237, 240, 298, 329

Hilton (William), 185, 259, 313

History of America, 11

(History of) Greece, 3

Hodgkinson, Mr., 29

Hogarth (William), 278

Holbein (Hans), 288

Holborn, 3, 66

Holinshed (Raphael), 261

Holmes, Edward, xv, 266

Holy Living and Holy Dying, 32, 322

Homer, 13, 59

Hone, William, 58

Honiton, 90

Hood, Thomas, xix

Houghton, Lord (Richard Monckton Milnes), xi, xii, xiii, xix, xxiii, xxv, 328, 329

Houses of Parliament, 255

"Human Seasons, The," 80

Humphry Clinker, 251

Hunt, Henry, 249

Hunt, J. H. Leigh, xv, 5, 6, 21, 22, 47-50, 69-72, 75, 92, 134, 137, 140, 147, 156, 159, 167, 172, 191, 262, 286, 289, 291-293, 296, 329, 334

Hunt, Mrs. J. H. Leigh, 69, 291, 296, 334

Hunt, Thornton, 293

Hunter College Library, xxiv

"Hymn to Apollo," 48

"Hymn to Pan," 18, 89

"Hyperion," 70, 157, 160, 165, 167, 247, 291; *see also* "Vision of Hyperion"

355

Index

Index

Index

Index

363

Index